C000220899

WRITING ANTHRO

WRITING ANTHROPOLOGY

CAROLE MCGRANAHAN, EDITOR

ESSAYS ON CRAFT & COMMITMENT

DUKE UNIVERSITY PRESS
Durham and London
2020

© 2020 DUKE UNIVERSITY PRESS. All rights reserved
Printed and bound by CPI Group (UK) Ltd, Croydon, CR0 4YY
Designed by Courtney Leigh Baker
Typeset in Minion pro and Trade Gothic by
Westchester Publishing Services

Library of Congress Cataloging-in-Publication Data
Names: McGranahan, Carole, editor.
Title: Writing anthropology : essays on craft and commitment /
Carole McGranahan, editor.
Description: Durham : Duke University Press, 2020. | Includes
bibliographical references and index.
Identifiers: LCCN 2019042306 (print) | LCCN 2019042307 (ebook)
ISBN 9781478006848 (hardcover)
ISBN 9781478008125 (paperback)
ISBN 9781478009160 (ebook)
Subjects: LCSH: Anthropologists' writings. | Anthropology—Authorship.
Classification: LCC GN307.7.W73 2020 (print) | LCC GN307.7 (ebook) |
DDC 301—dc23
LC record available at https://lccn.loc.gov/2019042306
LC ebook record available at https://lccn.loc.gov/2019042307

Cover art: *Morning Light*, © Laura E. Watt. Courtesy Moment Open/
Getty Images.

ACKNOWLEDGMENTS

Writing is one of the most solitary things we do, yet it requires community. I am grateful to all who have taught, inspired, and supported me over the years. Ann Armbrecht was the first to show me how anthropologists could be writers. Mary Moran, Michael Peletz, Sal Cucciari, and Ann Gold introduced me to ethnography and to the range, the wonderful range, of possibilities for ethnographic writing. Ann Stoler taught me to pay attention to words and sentences, reading her own drafts aloud to me, constantly working on substance, feel, and precision in relation to concepts, stories, and moods. Gina Athena Ulysse modeled writing and speaking with presence. Donna Goldstein shared the value of an editor and care for the individuals about whom one is writing. Lobsang Tinley taught me about trust.

Teaching provides important insights about writing. It is one thing to read a book for one's own research and interests, and another to read a book to teach it. Teaching anthropology is stories all the way down: our telling of another anthropologist's telling of stories told to them. A book that works well in the classroom is almost always a well-written one. But bad books can be pedagogically useful too in helping to articulate what it is that makes both research and writing successful. For discussing books both good and bad with me over the last two decades, I thank the thousand-plus undergraduate and graduate students who have taken my classes. Together we have roamed the world without leaving the classroom, and their collective appreciation for good ethnography—smart, meaningful, compelling, well written—drives me in my own writing.

I am lucky to be able to work with Ken Wissoker and the talented editorial and design team at Duke University Press, including Joshua Tranen, Susan

Albury, Donald Pharr, and a group of sharp, thoughtful reviewers. I first pitched this book to Ken on an impromptu phone call. He didn't flinch but instead immediately shared his thoughts on what such a book could and should do. This gift of editorial creativity and support is one I truly appreciate. Before the idea of a book, however, there was the series of essays. Many of the essays in this book started life as posts on the *Savage Minds* anthropology blog (now retitled *Anthrodendum*). I am grateful to my colleagues on the *Savage Minds* editorial collective for the freedom to write, create, and invite so many new voices to our online world. The contributors to this volume include some of the original online authors and some new ones. All have been a pleasure with whom to work, learn, and think out loud about writing.

For your words and insights, thank you to Whitney Battle-Baptiste, Jane Baxter, Ruth Behar, Adia Benton, Lauren Berlant, Robin Bernstein, Sarah Besky, Catherine Besteman, Yarimar Bonilla, Kevin Carrico, C. Anne Claus, Sienna Craig, Zoë Crossland, Lara Deeb, Kristen Drybread, Jessica Falcone, Kim Fortun, Kristen Ghodsee, Daniel Goldstein, Donna Goldstein, Sara Gonzalez, Ghassan Hage, Carla Jones, Ieva Jusionyte, Alan Kaiser, Barak Kalir, Michael Lambek, Stuart McLean, Lisa Sang-Mi Min, Mary Murrell, Kirin Narayan, Chelsi West Ohueri, Anand Pandian, Uzma Rizvi, Noel Salazar, Bhrigupati Singh, Matt Sponheimer, Kathleen Stewart, Ann Laura Stoler, Paul Stoller, Nomi Stone, Paul Tapsell, Katerina Teaiwa, Marnie Thomson, Gina Athena Ulysse, Roxanne Varzi, Sita Venkateswar, Maria Vesperi, Sasha Su-Ling Welland, Bianca Williams, and Jessica Winegar. Donna Goldstein, Carla Jones, and John Quintero gave me much-appreciated suggestions for the Introduction. At the University of Colorado, Ariela Rotenburg helped me imagine this project into being, and Anden Drolet helped make it a reality. Thank you, both, for your work and ideas.

Finally, I thank my family, who make so much possible. My parents and siblings for their unflagging support of my lifelong reading habit. My husband, who loves books possibly even more than I do. And my son and daughter, who are not only voracious readers but who as "the Story Kids" also wrote and sold short stories for a school fund-raiser. It is with family that so many of our stories start, in family that many of them are told, and it is a joy for our stories to continue to unfold together.

ON WRITING AND WRITING WELL

Ethics, Practice, Story

Carole McGranahan

Scholars have always been writers. Anthropologists are no exception. We research. We teach. We write. We figure things out in part by writing about them. Writing is thus not merely the reporting of our results but is as much process as product. However, we have not always paid attention to writing as craft or practice, rather than thinking of it as a (formulaic) vehicle for communicating knowledge. In many disciplines, thinking of writing as a core part of scholarship is a relatively new development. Historically, some anthropologists wrote well or wrote across genres or broke conventions, but such writing was not expected. This has now changed. A narrative turn in the 1970s and the literary turn in the 1980s brought new collective energy and attention to writing, and to writing well. Writing takes time. Writing well takes time and practice. This book is about both.

What counts as good writing changes over the years. In some periods, cultural anthropologists favored a detached social scientific voice. In others, we valued a more conversational, narrative style. Currently, we've moved to a more humanistic style of writing. Yet such a style can also be found throughout the discipline, going back to the nineteenth century. We need to be careful not to homogenize writing in the past as opposed to writing now. A twenty-first-century publication date is no guarantee that a text will be livelier or more compelling than something written in the early or mid-twentieth century. Individual style and skill are involved, as is a willingness to meet or exceed current expectations. Developing one's own style as a scholar is not a project with an end. Writing styles evolve in relation to research foci, methodological sensibilities, theoretical affinities, and, of course, the times. Over the course of a career, the aesthetics of our writing—voice, language, and imagery—may shift as much as the content, both with and against disciplinary norms.

Putting pen to paper, or fingers to keyboard, is often an exercise in both joy and pain. We delight in having time to write but can be quickly frustrated by the realities of thinking through arguments, deliberating over words, and crafting and then editing sentences, paragraphs, and chapters in an effort to get them right. In this, there is a lot of history: our writing is situated in the discipline, in the community, and in our own experiences. We write for, we write with, and we write against. A lifelong love of books often prepares scholars for this. In an essay on reading and writing like a Black girl, anthropologist Signithia Fordham reflects on her efforts to write to transform the world: "The pen is the most powerful weapon of human civilization, the instrument that can be used to enslave, emancipate and everything in between."[1] As scholars, we can use our knowledge in ways that affect people's lives, and there is thus great responsibility in writing this knowledge to be both useful and efficacious. It is our job to conduct ethical, rigorous research and to present it through clear, compelling writing.

We write as experts, experts who are perpetual students perhaps, but experts nonetheless. Expert knowledge requires a convincing demonstration of authority and thus credibility. Different audiences have their own ways to recognize and measure authority. Writing for a judge in a political asylum case is different than writing for a peer-reviewed journal, and both are different than writing an online essay for the public. Across these audiences, authority is recognized differently. Within cultural anthropology our case for ethnographic authority and knowledge involves showing the immediacy of "being there": showing that you the researcher, the author, were in the field long enough to produce professional research. Good research might not always lead to good writing, but it is surely a precondition.

I once asked Lily King about this. She is the author of *Euphoria*, a novel about the research connections and love triangle between anthropologists Margaret Mead, Gregory Bateson, and Reo Fortune in 1930s Papua New Guinea. In 2016 King was a special guest at the American Ethnological Society annual meeting, where she spoke to an anthropological audience about her book for the first time. "For anthropologists," I said to her, "the notion of 'being there' is crucial, showing that you've spent enough time in the field to have gained deep knowledge. When writing *Euphoria*, what were your strategies for convincing readers that you had been there in this way?" Her facial expression revealed that this was not something she had considered, and after a pause she replied: "I didn't want the reader to feel that I as author was there but that they were there. The goal was for the reader to feel they were there. That is what fiction does." The need to generate this sense for the reader was as obvious to her as showing skill in being there as scholar was to me. Establishing credentials as a scholar differs from demonstrating skill as a writer of fiction. There is something to be learned here about being both a writer and a reader.

What fiction does is not necessarily the same as what anthropology does. Yet writing well matters to both. Writing amplifies what anthropology and other forms of scholarship can and should do. Writing well is also part of the desire for our reading to be enjoyable: enjoyable not solely in the sense of theoretical argument matching empirical data but also in the sense of giving pleasure in itself. If we write to be read, and not just to be counted, then how we write matters as much as what we write.

An Ethics of Writing

Anthropological writing is a form of accountability and an ethical practice. We write to share scientific findings, to tell stories that matter, and to share new insights about the human world that might change it for the better. In anthropology there is an idea that, at a minimum, a fuller, deeper understanding of the breadth of human life is useful knowledge. At a maximum, we believe this knowledge can be transformative. As an anthropologist and historian, I think of myself as a guardian of other people's stories. The responsibility to tell the stories trusted to us is substantial. Many scholars share a sense of writing as commitment to the communities in which and with whom we do our research. Politically engaged, public scholarship requires this. It requires a commitment beyond funders or evaluators to the people whose stories we are telling, or, as my colleague Jason De León succinctly put it in a conversation we had about writing, "Writing is a commitment to people." Yes. In my research experience, people who have taken the time to share their stories with me have done so in part because they wanted them to be known by others. Tibetan resistance army veterans told me again and again they wanted their stories to be told, to be in a book so that people around the world would read and learn their stories and, hopefully, act upon them.[2] My responsibility is thus to collect stories and then to tell them, to think with them, and to do so in ways that honor the commitments I made during my fieldwork.

To do anthropological research is to learn and then tell people's stories. However, although many anthropologists currently practice anthropology this way, such has not always been the case. In earlier decades, social scientific styles of writing were more detached and were often about structures and practices rather than about the people who lived the very structures and practices the anthropologist was describing or explaining. People were part of the research but not always part of the story. I like to think that this is a past-tense thing, the sort of practice that anthropologists no longer conduct. But that is not true, as some still do. This volume is composed of scholars from across the subdisciplines who write on a wide range of topics and for whom telling people's stories matters. Telling people's stories is what we do. Who we tell them to is another important part of our scholarship.

Who makes up anthropological audiences? What audiences do we imagine, and how do they access our writing? For decades, anthropologists have fretted over how to get nonacademics to read what we write, to take anthropological knowledge and put it to use in effective and needed ways. We may agree that it is a scholarly responsibility to share "anthropological knowledge in straightforward, powerful ways," but it is not always easy to do so.[3] For example, Helena Wulff writes of publishing in newspapers and magazines where her fieldwork community would actually be able to read her writing.[4] From 1962 through 1978, Margaret Mead famously wrote a monthly column in the women's magazine *Redbook*, writing anthropology for a broad audience.[5] Two twenty-first-century examples of anthropologists writing regularly in mainstream media are Thorgeir Kolshus's column in *Aftenposten*, the largest Norwegian newspaper, and Gina Athena Ulysse's essays in the iconic *Ms.* magazine, now collected in her book *Why Haiti Needs New Narratives*.[6]

Potential nonacademic audiences vary depending on one's research topic, but often include policy makers, journalists, politicians, one's relatives and friends, and, of course, the "general public." I always envision my students and academic colleagues as audiences, but my primary audience and first readers are from the Tibetan community with whom I do my research. Social media makes this possible, as does widespread community fluency in English, the language in which I teach and publish. Getting one's writing to dispersed and diverse communities is easier now than ever before. Yet this still requires initiative. Often it is not only about postpublication reading. It is about sharing drafts and writing together. It is getting feedback on one's writing while it is still in progress. After writing sketches of people, I often read those passages aloud to their family members. Over the phone, sometimes across countries, I ask if this sounds like their loved one. Laughing, one woman says to me after I read some draft text aloud, "Oh yes, that's her."

Writing for nonacademic audiences and thinking of research as collaborative are not new to anthropology. The writings of Zora Neale Hurston and Laura Bohannan and Ella Cara Deloria alone make these points. However, the mid-twentieth-century adoption of a new social scientific writing style changed anthropological writing—think of the detached observer, claims to objectivity, and a mostly dry, affectless, and thus "authoritative" writing voice. Jonathan Spencer described this as "ethnographic naturalism," in which peoples are homogenized, singular claims to truth cancel out other possibilities for interpretation (anthropological or local), conditions and procedures of actual research are obscured, and an invisible, omniscient narrator speaks from a generalized point of view.[7] As a result, instead of us writing for multiple audiences, our presumed audience shrunk as did ideas about who scholars were and how they should write. Some communities were to be researchers, and some were to be researched. Ethical standards at the time did not necessarily include communities of research as scholars or as readers.

Ethnographic writing clearly demonstrates changes in ethics over the decades. The best way to see this is by reading. One course I teach for undergraduate anthropology students is Reading Ethnography. A main course goal is to determine what makes something sufficiently ethnographic in contemporary anthropology. To assess this, we read ethnographies from the 1980s to the present, along with a series of essays about ethnography and ethnographic genres. We compare ethnographies from the 1980s and 1990s with ones from the 2000s and 2010s, consider the experimental and *Writing Culture* moment, discuss the simultaneous omission and contributions of feminist ethnography, and compare aspects of "realism" in ethnographic fiction and nonfiction. The first time I taught this course in 2012, my students and I made a list of what made something ethnographic then (as opposed to earlier decades). Our list for what ethnography needs in the present was this: anthropological purpose established via research question and argument; a direct address of issues of local concern; the articulation of insider/native points of view; a focus on ethnographic realities, on life as lived, on everyday life and ordinary time; showing people as named individuals rather than only as belonging to descriptive categories (e.g., kin or occupation); a clear demonstration of the production of ethnographic knowledge (i.e., of how the anthropologist knows what he or she knows); the provision of sufficient context and background in terms of the literature, history, theory, etc.; a clear explanation of the ethnographer's relationship with the community about which they are writing (e.g., how trust was gained, how relationships of care were forged); and the author's scholarly credibility established such that the reader trusts their credentials.[8] This list has held its form in my classes ever since, although I can see changes taking place in the discipline and world right now that a future list will need to name.

A shift in ethics is the most prominent difference between the 1980s and the current moment. Ethics is no longer reckoned only in an academic scientific sense. Research is expected to be collaborative, worked out in part with the community with which a scholar works. In ethnographic writing now, community is present. When we read an ethnography, we expect to meet people, not just categories of them. And we expect that some of the people we meet are those to whom the scholar is accountable, by whom the research will be assessed as it unfolds. This accountability is part of research design. We are accountable to the discipline, to our funders, and to the community in which we conduct research. Anthropological research needs to matter to each of these groups, but more so than ever before, perhaps, it needs to be considered valuable and necessary by members of the community.

Transparency and trust are also important in new ways. As readers, we expect to learn clearly the scholar's relationship to the community. How were they positioned by the community, and how did they develop relationships that led to the production of this knowledge? Ethnography as method is experiential, and this aspect is newly foregrounded in our contemporary writing. The rigor and challenge of using oneself as the instrument of knowing continue in the writing process, as some authors explore in this volume.[9] This is unique to ethnography but also true to what we know of cultural life as systems of lived contradiction. One result is that good ethnographic writing acknowledges not only hierarchy but also discomfort. Tracking both is a job for the reader. Learning how to read ethnographies is something I teach my students, starting with the cover of a book. We discuss both the title and cover image, then turn to the back cover to consider the summary, as well as the "blurbs," as part of an academic economy of authority. We then open the book and move through the front matter to the acknowledgments. How, I ask the students, do you decide if the research is valid? Ethnographic research cannot be replicated in a laboratory sense. Instead, we have different markers of credibility such as correspondence with related scholarship.

Other classic markers of validity are thick ethnography, rigorous theory, and excellent writing. All of these can be persuasive.

A sometimes overlooked source of insight for assessing credibility is the acknowledgments section. It is in the acknowledgments that thanks are given, intellectual networks sketched out, and fieldwork communities honored. Acknowledgments reveal the heart of a book's production: who enabled this research and participated in it, gave their trust and their stories to the scholar. This is one place where authors move beyond a sense of "being there" to a sense of trusting and being trusted, and thus toward establishing integrity. This is part of the commitment we make to people to tell their stories, and to tell them well.

A Writing Practice

Anthropology is a writing discipline. In the field, we write constantly. We write down results and observations, interview and survey data, questions and concerns. We write field notes. We write grant proposals to get funding for research. We write seminar papers to advance us to the grant-writing stage. All of these are important, and each represents a different genre of writing. Of them all, field notes are perhaps most unique to anthropology. "Write your field notes every night," I was told by multiple professors before going to the field for my first summer of research as a graduate student. Don't sleep on it, I now tell my own students: write your field notes every night. If you wait until the next day, you will lose things. The stories you want to write down will turn to fragments or, worse, to information. You will end up with staccato notes that will not make sense to you a few months from now. Things you think you could never possibly forget will slip away with time. This daily research method of ours, to capture all that happened in a day, all we learned, the questions we still have, the confusions that persist, is a crucial part of anthropology as both a scientific and humanistic investigation.

What is your writing practice? There is no right way to write, no magic formula for how many minutes or words or pages you should write each day. Some days the writing will flow. Other days it won't. Not all you write will be usable, but save the text you cut rather than deleting it. I call this rejected text my "outtakes," files of text that didn't make the final cut for one project but that might work elsewhere; in some cases, upon revisiting files you might find yourself glad you deleted them in the first place. However, either way—whether you are writing good text or bad text—writing as practice is good. Writing moves your thinking forward, and writing improves your writing. The more you do it, the more you think about it; the more you seek out guidance, the better your writing gets.

Location, materials, sounds, time of day—all of these things matter. I wrote this in my home at a table my friend made, looking out at the national forest. But sometimes I like to write outdoors or away from home. Think about where and how you write best. On a computer or by hand? And in what font or with what sort of paper or pen? Attention to such details can shape your writing and ground it in productive ways. Rituals might also be part of your practice. Making coffee or tea first. Making offerings. Music might be playing, or you could be surrounded by white noise from a café or by silence. So many things can affect what is right in any given moment: the quality of light, your mood, what it is you are writing about.

Know your writing needs, and meet them. Change them as needed. Some writers like to make outlines. I play endlessly with titles and subtitles, collecting long lists of titles for articles and books I'd like to write one day. Recognize when you need to stop writing to think or to read more or to exercise or talk with a friend. Sometimes what I need is to go back to my field notes. Rereading these, thinking again of different moments and lessons from fieldwork, of conversations and dialogue recorded, and of questions along the way is one of the best writing prompts we have. Good field notes are a gift we give to ourselves whose value is rarely expended. Then, after stepping away, you can get back to the writing, refreshed and ready.

Surround yourself with good writing. Read broadly. Read your own writing out loud. Don't start in the beginning. When I was a graduate student, I asked several of my professors for writing advice. Twenty years later, I still use the tips they shared with me. One professor advised me to always read outside of anthropology—fiction, poetry, nonfiction—and to read things that were well written. Another professor advised writing at the same time each day and to count editing time as writing time. Have a handful of good ethnographies nearby as you write, suggested another. But the piece of advice I share most frequently with my own students is this: read your words aloud as you edit. Hearing your language and arguments enables a different sort of editing than does seeing them on paper or a screen. Along with having a set of trusted readers (what I call "internal peer review"), reading my own writing out loud is my single most effective writing strategy. Finally, if you're sitting down to write and don't quite know where to start, one piece of wise advice I received is to not start in the beginning but somewhere else, in a place where a story needs to be told.

Writerly Confessionals, or Introducing Ruth

One genre of writing in anthropology is biography, including stories of the anthropologist becoming a writer. Some individuals arrive in graduate school as already accomplished writers, but others do not become writers until further along in their careers, in grad school or even later. For me, it was later. One issue for many scholars is that writing is not taught; one is expected to know how to write; one is expected to be a good writer. Right now, writing matters, and this is reflected in much of contemporary ethnographic writing. Of course, beautiful writing is not enough, but in the hands of a skilled ethnographer and thoughtful theorist, good writing honors the people whose stories are being shared.

How do you learn to write? Again: by reading good writing and through the practice of writing over the years, but also increasingly through courses and writing workshops offered at universities and conferences. Discussing writing, not just theoretical arguments or disciplinary history, is a part of all the graduate seminars I teach. In 2016 the anthropologist and writer Ruth Behar came to our campus to give a talk and lead a writing workshop. Her tips from the workshop are included in this volume ("Read More, Write Less"). As a graduate of the University of Michigan, where Ruth has long taught, including a course on ethnographic writing, I was asked to introduce her when she came to the University of Colorado. Here is some of what I said about Ruth, her writing, its mark on the discipline, and its influence on me as a writer:

"What people remember is Ruth's reflexive writing, such as her story in *Translated Woman* of receiving the MacArthur Fellowship (popularly known as the Genius Grant) and then tenure. They remember passages from *The Vulnerable Observer* that are intimate and conflicted, and that others read as sensational and scandalous. Ruth has indeed embodied certain aspects of the reflexive turn, including, in her own words, the "emotional hemophilia" involved in the telling of stories. But her oeuvre goes well beyond this. Her scholarship consists also of deep genealogies and tributes to those writers and scholars who came before. There was a moment in the 1990s when she and many other anthropologists thought that attentiveness to writing as craft was going to be run out of the discipline, that a dry, utilitarian way of writing would win, that we would lose the beauty of language in favor of the function of it. They were wrong, and happily so. In thinking of a writer like Ruth, this is best explained in a way inspired by her writing style. It is best explained with a personal story. So here is a story that is mine to tell, but one I have never written about before, although I think of it frequently.

"The summer before I started graduate school, I was out at a bar with a group of friends, and I overheard two of them, both aspiring novelists (and one my then-boyfriend), talking about writing. I'll call them Brian and Susan because those were their names. Susan said to Brian, "Carole is a writer too." And he said back to her: "Carole is not a writer. She's an anthropologist." I got to Michigan, and those words haunted me. "Carole is not a writer." Anthropologists aren't writers. Or at least not *real* writers."

I publicly told this story to Ruth on that day in Boulder to explain, twenty years later, why I never took her seminar on ethnographic writing, my one real regret from grad school. But I got the syllabus for the course and read everything on it, talked with friends about writing, and even secretly wrote poetry (none of which appears in this or any other book, and thus fits into an anthropological tradition of writing outside of conventional genres and then publishing those writings under pseudonyms or not publishing them at all). Simply being in that space she created where anthropology was writing, and where writing was about craft, had a deep impact on me. It took getting through grad school, getting to the point where I was writing about research I had done with people about whom I cared deeply, for me to consider myself a writer.

There is no single way to write anthropology; I am indebted to Ruth for insisting on this. Instead, styles and genres and voices are particular to scholars and to projects. Variation enlivens our writing, yet consistency is also important. Whether I am writing an online essay, a conference paper, a peer-reviewed journal article, or a book, my voice should be consistent; a reader should recognize an author's voice as she moves through different genres. My scholarship takes place in all of these forms. However, for a long time not all forms have counted or have counted in the same way. Alma Gottlieb writes poignantly of not putting her coauthored 1994 memoir *Parallel Worlds* into her tenure file although it was published by a top anthropology press.[10] Although such writings were once excluded from tenure files, there are now formal AAA guidelines for how to count such public scholarship at tenure and promotion.[11] Sometimes anthropology is written as literature, and sometimes it is written as science, and each of these has its place in forming and sustaining the discipline.

A Note on This Volume

Most of the essays in this volume were part of a series on writing I edited on the group anthropology blog *Savage Minds: Notes and Queries in Anthropology* from 2014 to 2016. Although writing had become an open topic of concern in anthropology, I was hungry for more conversation about it. I wanted to think out loud about writing, but I mostly wanted to hear and learn from others. Knowing that colleagues craved the same, I created a weekly space for anthropologists to write about writing, and I invited scholars from across subfields, generations, and countries to contribute essays to the series. Some are known for being leaders in, and even pioneers of, ethnographic writing. Others were scholars I knew who were good writers or who I thought had something valuable to say. These were not necessarily the "go-to" scholars for a conversation on writing. This volume puts together new essays with many of the original and revised essays from the series. All are short, roughly 1,000–1,500 words, and are examples that showcase the possibilities of the (then new) online essay genre. My instructions to the authors were simple: write something on writing. All of the authors responded to that request in their own creative, inspired way.

The book you hold in your hands, or read on your screen, compiles these essays in one neat but untidy package. Here are fifty-three essays, spilling over into one another, some contained within their own narrative, others deep in conversation with what came before, yet each offering us new thoughts, prompts, and agitations for writing. The essays are organized in ten sections: Ruminations; Writing Ideas; Telling Stories; On Responsibility; The Urgency of Now; Writing With, Writing Against; Academic Authors; Ethnographic Genres; Becoming and Belonging; and Writing and Knowing.

Section 1, "Ruminations," sets the tone for this wide-ranging volume. Ieva Jusionyte reflects on the varied shapes and realities of writing during fieldwork, especially the shared experience many of us have, often again and again, of trying to figure out what and how to write in the field. We move next to questions of ethnographic possibility in an essay from Sasha Su-Ling Welland on lists as types of anthropological writing. Lists as cultural forms, writes Welland, "can distill a life in a few short lines." How to tell the story of someone's life is a lesson Paul Stoller learns in the field from Adamu Jenitongo, including how his own story must also be considered in the process. There is the process of writing, and then there is the experience of it. In "The Ecology of What We Write," Anand Pandian contemplates the circumstances of our writing in relation to the company we keep. Even though our writing is most often done alone, scholars find ways to socially measure and share it. Kirin Narayan explores word count as the most recent way to do this, reminding us that not all words are equally measurable.

Read more, write less—this is the message (and title) of Ruth Behar's essay that opens section 2, "Writing Ideas." Her advice on reading in a writerly way is followed by her workshop tips for ethnographic writing. This gift is followed by another: C. Anne Claus's reflections on taking a writing course with a professional writer while writing her dissertation. Such training is often missing from our graduate training, so we often craft our own writing strategies, sometimes more successfully than others. In the next essay, Kristen Ghodsee shares her ten-step process for writing a book, distilling this intimidating and sometimes debilitating process into a manageable list of tasks (in which Stephen Hawking even makes an appearance). Teaching others how to write involves the somewhat lost art of quiet, slow reading, contends Michael Lambek. One cannot be a good writer if not first a good reader. Reading as an art of writing is also part of the Writing Archaeology course that Zoë Crossland teaches. Course readings address relations of form, intimacy, and narrative, whereas assignments build community as a way of addressing the vulnerability of writing through the generosity of reading for others.

Storytelling is the focus of section 3. In the opening essay I argue that we write and teach anthropology as a form of theoretical storytelling but that this narrative, storied component of our practice is underappreciated. Ethnographic writing requires narrative, argument, and context, and thus, Donna Goldstein contends, is a uniquely powerful genre for biography, for bringing people to life through writing. Along with people, places are central to ethnography, both of which the reader wants to know. Sarah Besky suggests that in order to flow, our stories need to be grounded in place, somewhere they too can live. One writing mentor for many anthropologists is Kirin Narayan, who when I asked her in an interview "Why ethnography?" answered this way: "For the discipline of paying attention; for learning from others; for becoming more responsibly aware of inequalities; for better understanding the social forces causing suffering and how people might somehow find hope; and most generally, for being perpetually pulled beyond the horizons of one's own taken-for-granted world." The specific truths and possibilities of ethnography are a shared theme of this section, including in Sienna Craig's closing essay "On Unreliable Narrators." What, she asks, are our strategies for trustworthy storytelling in a world that is often anything but reliable?

What are the responsibilities of the scholar as writer? In her opening essay of section 4, "On Responsibility," Marnie Jane Thomson argues that being a good listener is one requirement. Listening enables dialogue in the writing such that ideas and theories are situated in their moment of generation by those peoples in the field with and from whom we learn. Writing with community is one way that archaeologist Sara Gonzalez works to restore justice to history, connecting past stories to peoples in the present. Writing during fieldwork often extends well beyond field notes. In the context of Bhopal, Kim Fortun reflects on disaster and the necessity of writing alongside colleagues in the field, as well as against and past "the formative conditions of our times." Alongside the conditions are the technologies. In "Quick, Quick, Slow: Ethnography in the Digital Age," Yarimar Bonilla suggests that recognizing digital platforms as socially complex enables responses to fast-moving stories that preserve the depth of slow, contextualized ethnography. Context and complexity are part of Maria Vesperi's deliberations of whether a difficult story should be written as ethnography or journalism. She chooses ethnography, explaining that it will help her readers "to share the tools to see and interpret, to spot fire and give it a name."

Writing in a moment of crisis or distress is not classic anthropological writing. Instead, the essays in section 5, "The Urgency of Now," consider the need to speak to unfolding or troubling events. Kristen Drybread takes us through dilemmas of style and voice in writing about violence, and of discerning and analyzing differences between the emotional and the visceral. Distance and time can often help with writing on difficult topics, but this combination is not always possible. In "Writing about Bad, Sad, Hard Things," I share experiences of writing political asylum reports and the difficult responsibility of witnessing through writing another person's gruesome suffering. Sometimes we write about crises, and other times we write during them. Watching the events of Ferguson, Missouri, unfold and trying to write in a period of "injustice, racism, and death" felt paralyzing to Whitney Battle-Baptiste. Her essay "Writing to Live" is a poignant and intimate look at how family stories of race and trauma helped bring her back to words once again. After her father's death, Chelsi West Ohueri found it difficult to write. In "Finding My Muse While Mourning," she shares her ideas for writing with grief rather than through it. Learning how to do this is not a process with a definitive end, as Adia Benton's essay on being a survivor also reveals. Making use of anger and grief is sometimes exactly what our writing can best do.

Affect and emotion are a bigger part of our writing than we often realize. Section 6, "Writing With, Writing Against," opens with Carla Jones's essay on agitation. Being annoyed, especially by mistruths across cultural and political divides, drives her to write in an effort to bridge gaps and to bring shared sensibilities to light. In his essay "Antiracist Writing," Ghassan Hage speaks of a similar desire to write against, specifically against racism. As a form of antiracist writing, he contends, anthropology has a responsibility to write "to address, understand, and struggle to transform." How might those things we hate inform our writing? In his praise of the sentence, Bhrigupati Singh writes against writing that is overdone, that is too writerly, and he instead pulls us back to the humble possibility of a single sentence conveying ethnographic insight in the form of "love for this world." Singh's challenge to not inflate ourselves and our findings has its pair in the disciplinary gatekeeping criticized in Alan Kaiser's essay "Peer Review: What Doesn't Kill You Makes You Stronger." Taking on issues of justice and gender in a long-accepted plagiarism case, Kaiser encounters strong opposition to righting the record. Similar forms of disciplinary resistance to criticism underlie a joint essay from Lara Deeb and Jessica Winegar. What internal but not necessarily visible structures of power, they ask, shape and constrain our writing in ways that we need to challenge?

Academics are a certain sort of author. This premise grounds section 7, "Academic Authors," which opens with Jane Eva Baxter's eulogy for her coauthor. How does one approach writing "alone" after doing it together for years? In anthropology, coauthorship is an underconsidered type of writing. Unsatisfied with formulaic expectations for multiauthorship, biological anthropologist Matt Sponheimer reflects on strategies to make such writing truly collaborative in practice. Aspects of authorship evident to academics are not necessarily so to nonacademic authors. In her essay "What Is an (Academic) Author?" Mary Murrell presents the legal controversy over Google's mass book digitization, arguing that academic authors' concerns with sharing knowledge directly contradicted trade author and publishers' concerns with profits. As the next two essays concur, this is "just one possible figuration of the academic author." Noel Salazar challenges anthropologists to think more seriously about genre and audience in relation to what anthropology has to offer the world, and Daniel Goldstein ponders the sort of writing we do. Emails, memos, lectures, comments on student work, reviews, reports, and more are things that academics write all day, but are these sorts of writing "real" writing? Grants are another sort of writing that academics frequently do and with which some have a love/hate relationship. With this in mind, Robin Bernstein offers tips for grant writing that capture the excitement of research and thus, she suggests, perhaps even enjoyment in the writing.

What genres best suit anthropology? Certainly not only "scientific" writing, as contributors explore in section 8, "Ethnographic Genres." In the opening essay, Nomi Stone suggests that poetry offers specific and even secret tools for helping anthropology "make a lived world" beyond our usual prose writing. Poetry speaks to materiality and the thresholds of the human in resonant ways, concurs Stuart McLean in his essay exploring the particularity of the language of poetry. In their essay "Dilations," Kathleen Stewart and Lauren Berlant consider resonance—that is, when something registers in and about the world that suggests something new about it. Their experimental writing continues a tradition in anthropology of play with form and genre. Fiction is perhaps the genre with which anthropologists have experimented the longest. In sharing her love and practice of ethnographic fiction, Jessica Marie Falcone explores "genre bending" in the discipline, asking and assessing how fiction in our scholarly writing can serve as a marker of value and integrity. Roxanne Varzi argues for the value of the "space between"—that is, writing fiction into our ethnography rather than having it be separate from it. Fiction, she argues, can give ethnography needed "space to breathe and to change." This might be because fiction is magic. Or, as Ruth Behar explains, fiction possesses an inventive magic not possible in ethnography. Fiction, she learns, has lessons to teach us about meaning, the real, and temporality.

Section 9, "Becoming and Belonging," takes us deeper into lessons of (and for) writing and anthropology. What does it mean to belong not somewhere, but somewhere else, and to write from this position? Uzma Rizvi asks just this in her essay on personal and professional issues of trust and privilege in the way that we live "cartographies of elsewhere." Sita Venkateswar similarly seeks a way to bridge the personal and academic, turning to "memory-work" with family alongside, or even instead of, fieldwork. Katerina Teaiwa's memorywork (and her elsewhere) are on her bookshelf. Confessing that scholarly and literary tomes are not always her reading material of choice, she shares how a life of expansive, eclectic reading grounds her being in the world. Such honesty in our academic persona centers Bianca Williams's "Guard Your Heart and Your Purpose: Faithfully Writing Anthropology." As she shares, bringing heartwork and academic writing together rather than keeping them separate can be an exercise in vulnerability. The work we do, and an awareness of why we do it, is at the heart of Gina Athena Ulysse's written portrait of her journey as a scholar. Knowing oneself, and knowing the gendered, racialized obstacles of academia, are a key and ongoing part of her process. "The Anthropology of Being (Me)," as Paul Tapsell titles his essay that closes this section, is not necessarily a project of reflexivity. Instead, as Tapsell writes, it might be to rethink accountability, genealogy, and the idea that anthropology might be of use in a moment of crisis, only if we are willing to challenge and be challenged.

When do we know what we will write (versus knowing what we want to write)? Barak Kalir's essay on writing and cognition opens the final section of the volume, "Writing and Knowing." Writing, he claims, transforms our thoughts beyond just putting them into words and is a lesson not as easily learned as it should be. Translation offers a poignant example of the relationship between writing and thinking. Reflecting on the difficulty of translating acts of self-immolation, Kevin Carrico returns us to contemplation as a critical component both of and beyond writing. Our writings for even a single project exist in many forms, often without easy transitions between them. In "Freeze-Dried Memory Crumbs: Field Notes from North Korea," Lisa Sang-Mi Min reflects on the energy and labor needed to resuscitate field notes that one was not really allowed to write in the first place. Form may be fleeting and shape-shifting, but content preserves depth and clarity. Ann Laura Stoler next takes us to the "disquiets" of her fieldwork in colonial writing, asking how we account for uncertainty and uneasiness in others' writing when we try to write about this subject ourselves. What we don't know is not what we are supposed to write about, or are we? In the closing essay, "On Ethnographic Unknowability," Catherine Besteman explores the tension between writing and knowing. As she asks, what is it that we, scholars, have a right to know, and what does it actually mean to know through writing?

Read, pause, write. Then read some more. Find the essays you need. Read to help learn where you are and where you want to go. Welcome. Come on in. Get comfortable or get disturbed, or both. Get writing. May your writing be good, clear, and satisfying. May it flow in all the right ways, including pausing from time to time so that you may tend to other things and then return to where you need to be in the writing.

Notes

1. Signithia Fordham, "Write-ous Indignation: Black Girls, Dilemmas of Cultural Domination and the Struggle to Speak the Skin We Are In," in *Anthropology off the Shelf: Anthropologists on Writing*, ed. Alisse Waterston and Maria D. Vesperi (Malden, MA: Wiley-Blackwell, 2011), 91.

2. Carole McGranahan, *Arrested Histories: Tibet, the CIA, and Memories of a Forgotten War* (Durham, NC: Duke University Press, 2010).

3. Maria D. Vesperi and Alisse Waterston, "Introduction: The Writer in the Anthropologist," in *Anthropology off the Shelf: Anthropologists on Writing*, ed. Alisse Waterston and Maria D. Vesperi (Malden, MA: Wiley-Blackwell, 2011), 1.

4. Helena Wulff, "Introducing the Anthropologist as Writer: Across and within Genres," in *The Anthropologist as Writer: Genres and Contexts in the Twenty-First Century*, ed. Helena Wulff (New York: Berghahn, 2016).

5. For a discussion of these columns, see Paul Shankman's "The Public Anthropology of Margaret Mead: *Redbook*, Women's Issues, and the 1960s," *Current Anthropology* 59, no. 1 (2018): 55–73.

6. Thorgeir Kolshus, "The Power of Ethnography in the Public Sphere," *HAU: Journal of Ethnographic Theory* 7, no. 1 (2017): 61–69; Gina Athena Ulysse, *Why Haiti Needs New Narratives: A Post Quake Chronicle* (Middletown, CT: Wesleyan University Press, 2015).

7. Jonathan Spencer, "Anthropology as a Kind of Writing," *Man* 24, no. 1 (1989): 152–54.

8. For a fuller discussion of ethnography as a way of knowing, see Carole McGranahan, "What Is Ethnography? Teaching Ethnographic Sensibilities without Fieldwork," *Teaching Anthropology* 4 (2014): 22-36; Carole McGranahan, "Ethnography beyond Method: The Importance of an Ethnographic Sensibility," *Sites: A Journal of Social Anthropology and Cultural Studies* 15, no. 1 (2018): 1-10.

9. On self as ethnographic method, see Sherry Ortner, *Anthropology and Social Theory: Culture, Power, and the Acting Subject* (Durham, NC: Duke University Press, 2006).

10. Alma Gottlieb, "The Anthropologist as Storyteller," in *The Anthropologist as Writer: Genres and Contexts in the Twenty-First Century*, ed. Helena Wulff (New York: Berghahn, 2016), 93-117.

11. See "AAA Guidelines for Tenure and Promotion Review: Communicating Public Scholarship in Anthropology," accessed November 8, 2018, https://www.americananthro.org/AdvanceYourCareer/Content.aspx?ItemNumber=21713.

For Further Reading

Written guides to writing can also be useful. There are many: some for anthropology, more for academic writing, and a seemingly unending list of general writing books, including on narrative nonfiction. My favorite book on ethnographic writing is Kirin Narayan's *Alive in the Writing: Crafting Ethnography in the Company of Chekhov*. This gem of a book provides guidance, motivation, and encouragement. Five sections deal with critical parts of current ethnography: story and theory, place, person, voice, and self. The book concludes with concrete, thoughtful, usable suggestions for the writing process—getting started, moving forward, dealing with writer's block, revising, and finishing—all designed to cultivate an active, alive writing practice. It is also an excellent book to teach.

Below is an abridged list of articles and books I find useful on writing. In addition to this list, a good print thesaurus is a must, one that you can page through to encounter words for your writing. *The Chicago Manual of Style* is also on my shelf as the often final word on grammar and formatting. Explore and find the writing guides that provide you practical information, delightful inspiration, or both. Find your writing muses. Embrace those whose voice speaks to you; reshelve those who don't. Trust that there is no "right" way, just writing and commitment.

(Sociocultural) Anthropological Writing

Behar, Ruth, and Deborah Gordon, eds. *Women Writing Culture*. Berkeley: University of California Press, 1996.

Besnier, Niko, and Pablo Morales. "Tell the Story: How to Write for *American Ethnologist*." *American Ethnologist* 45, no. 2 (2018): 163–72.

Clifford, James, and George Marcus, eds. *Writing Culture: The Poetics and Politics of Ethnography*. Berkeley: University of California Press, 1986.

Geertz, Clifford. *Works and Lives: The Anthropologist as Author*. Stanford, CA: Stanford University Press, 1988.

Ghodsee, Kristen. *From Notes to Narrative: Writing Ethnographies That Everyone Can Read*. Chicago: University of Chicago Press.

Narayan, Kirin. *Alive in the Writing: Crafting Ethnography in the Company of Chekhov*. Chicago: University of Chicago Press, 2012.

Pandian, Anand, and Stuart McLean, eds. *Crumpled Paper Boat: Experiments in Ethnographic Writing*. Durham, NC: Duke University Press, 2017.

Stankiewicz, Damien. "Anthropology and Fiction: An Interview with Amitav Ghosh." *Cultural Anthropology* 27, no. 3 (2012): 535–41.

Starn, Orin, ed. *Writing Culture and the Life of Anthropology*. Durham, NC: Duke University Press, 2015.

Stoller, Paul. "Ethnography/Memoir/Imagination/Story." *Anthropology and Humanism* 32, no. 2 (2007): 178–91.

Waterston, Alisse, and Maria D. Vesperi, eds. *Anthropology off the Shelf: Anthropologists on Writing*. Malden, MA: Wiley-Blackwell, 2011.

Wulff, Helena, ed. 2016. *The Anthropologist as Writer: Genres and Contexts in the Twenty-First Century*. New York: Berghahn.

Academic Writing

Bammer, Angelika, and Ruth-Ellen Boetcher Joeres, eds. *The Future of Scholarly Writing: Critical Interventions*. New York: Palgrave Macmillan, 2015.

Germano, William. *From Dissertation to Book*, 2nd ed. Chicago: University of Chicago Press, 2013.

Graff, Gerald, and Cathy Birkenstein. *They Say/I Say: The Moves That Matter in Academic Writing*. New York: W. W. Norton, 2016.

Hayot, Eric. *The Elements of Academic Style: Writing for the Humanities*. New York: Columbia University Press, 2014.

Jensen, Joli. *Write No Matter What: Advice for Academics*. Chicago: University of Chicago Press, 2017.

Nelson, Priya. "How to Build a Book: Notes from an Editorial *Bricoleuse*." HAU: *Journal of Ethnographic Theory* 7, no. 3 (2017): 363–72.

Sword, Helen. *Stylish Academic Writing*. Cambridge, MA: Harvard University Press, 2012.

Sword, Helen. *Air & Light & Time & Space: How Successful Academics Write*. Cambridge, MA: Harvard University Press, 2017.

Good Writing in General

Klinkenborg, Verlyn. *Several Short Sentences about Writing*. New York: Vintage, 2012.

Kramer, Mark, and Wendy Call, eds. *Telling True Stories: A Nonfiction Writers' Guide*. New York: Plume, 2007.

LeGuin, Ursula. *Steering the Craft: A 21st-Century Guide to Sailing the Sea of Story*. New York: Mariner, 2015.

Prose, Francine. *Reading Like a Writer: A Guide for People Who Love Books and for Those Who Want to Write Them*. New York: HarperCollins, 2006.

Rabiner, Susan, and Alfred Fortunato. *Thinking Like Your Editor: How to Write Great Serious Nonfiction—and Get It Published*. New York: W. W. Norton, 2002.

SECTION I

RUMINATIONS

1

WRITING IN AND FROM THE FIELD

Ieva Jusionyte

This morning, as I am sitting down to write this blog entry in my rental apartment in Nogales, I peer through the window: the sun has illuminated the dark-brown border wall that coils over the hilly landscape and reminds me of the spiked back of a stegosaurus. Six months ago I arrived in Southern Arizona to begin fieldwork with firefighters and paramedics for a new ethnographic project about emergency responders on both sides of the line, as the international boundary that abruptly separates Mexico and the United States is locally called. Although ethnographic fieldwork takes many forms—I am conducting interviews, participating in the daily activities at the firehouse, volunteering at a first-aid station for migrants, teaching prehospital emergency care at a local fire district, and engaging with the first-responder communities in Arizona and Sonora in multiple other ways—my primary activity continues to be writing.

I have always been a morning writer. When I was working on the manuscript of my first book, I would shut the doors of my childhood bedroom at my parents' house in the forested suburbs of Vilnius, Lithuania, where I was fortunate to spend my research leave, and would sit at my large desk, facing the barren trees outside, until noon. I did it every day of the week for several months during a long and cold winter. The manuscript was complete and sent off to my editor on the eve of spring.

But during fieldwork, keeping a regular writing routine has been difficult. The topic of our research inevitably shapes how, where, and what we write, and my study of fire and rescue services under heightened border security is no exception. Often I spend the entire day on shift with the crew at the fire station, riding along with them to the scenes of emergencies. Other days include training, community events, and long drives to do interviews at more-remote fire districts. Having a background in both journalism and in anthropology affects how I go about conducting research. Instead of dividing my time into chunks for doing fieldwork and writing up field notes, I tend to pursue the story as far as it takes me before I finally sit down to reflect on the new material. I think of it as combining the in-depth view of an anthropologist with the fervor of an investigative journalist. It can be exhausting.

Because of this, I write anywhere and everywhere, whenever I have a minute to jot down my thoughts and observations. I scribble names, places, and dates in my pocket notebook, in a handwriting that has become illegible, especially when the entries are made while riding in the back of a fire engine or on a 4×4 truck plowing through the dirt roads to where the fence between the US and Mexico is nothing more than a four-strand barbed wire. I type abbreviated notes on my cell phone during stops at gas stations along I-19, which connects Tucson with Nogales, and whenever pulling out my phone to quickly enter some text seems more polite—and less intrusive—than opening my notebook. When I am driving and I can't pull over to jot down a thought that I want to keep, I record voice memos; I have done so passing through Border Patrol checkpoints on Arivaca Road and on Sasabe Highway, back when I used to count the times I was stopped and to document what the agents were saying.

I also take pictures. Many pictures. On my cell phone or using one of the two digital cameras that I carry around. I take pictures of dumpster fires and vehicle accidents, of picturesque sunsets over the Tumacácori and the Baboquivori Peaks, of hazardous materials equipment and of *tacos al pastor* being prepared for dinner at the firehouse. In fact, photography has been a particularly important ethnographic tool. I am frequently asked to take pictures of official community events, binational meetings, and training exercises, and to later share them with the participating agencies and the media. As a designated photographer, however, I may not have time to take notes, so the pictures later become cues for the activities that took place and help me write about what happened. Writing from photographs changes the way we convert experiences and events into prose, suggests Casey N. Cep.[1] They serve as powerful tools to enhance memories about the encounter that begin to twist immediately after it is over. When I finally open my laptop and begin writing, I draw on all of these cues: notes on my cell phone, handwritten memos, voice messages, photos. They neatly fall into places and begin to form a story. I may not have a well-structured writing routine, but this haphazard creation of field notes has been surprisingly productive.

Fieldwork also precipitates other genres of writing, such as writing for the public. There used to be a delay, a long pause, between ethnographic research often conducted in remote locations and anthropological publications carefully crafted at academic institutions and perfected through cycles of rigorous revision. It could take years of going back and forth to the field site before scholars would decide to share their findings with the public. Even now, many monographs and research articles do not see the light of day until long after the events they depict have transpired. But this has been changing. Ethnographic fieldwork and public writing now happen simultaneously. Federal funding agencies that use taxpayer money are pressured to demonstrate the relevance of the research that they support to the society at large. Meanwhile, technological innovation and easy access to the internet allow us to share photos and news about our fieldwork instantaneously via email, blogging, or social media. These developments, among others, have led anthropologists to more openly talk about our work in progress. More of us now report preliminary findings from the front lines of ethnographic research.

While conducting ethnographic fieldwork in northern Sonora and southern Arizona, I wrote across different genres of public writing. I created a public website, http://www.borderrescueproject.com, that I update with news, excerpts from my field notes and interviews, reflections written by my research assistants, and numerous photographs. The website is also linked to the project's Twitter account (@borderEMS) and displays a feed of the most recent events linked to my work. At the request of my contacts in the fire service and emergency management, who invite me to participate in their trainings and meetings, on a couple of occasions I wrote brief news pieces and sent photographs to the local newspaper in Nogales, Arizona. I have also given interviews to several Mexican newspapers and broadcasters in Sonora. As a former journalist, I am familiar with the practice of deploying information to promote activities in the community, and I eagerly engage with the media in ways that benefit the people with whom I work. News media provide a powerful and readily available channel to communicate the significance of the research project to the broader public. With that in mind, I wrote an op-ed for the *Guardian* that was a critical commentary on existing federal policies that blend emergency health care with immigration policing: the riskiest form of public writing I have done.[2] This article likely had more readers than any of my scholarly publications ever will. It was shared instantaneously via social networks and thus was immediately available to the firefighters and paramedics who have been participating in my research project. I had reasons to fear their reaction. Politics are generally seen as a threat to camaraderie and thus are a taboo topic in the firehouse, where people of different political leanings have to rely on one another in life-and-death situations. Had they found my op-ed to be politically aggressive or provocative, my fieldwork relationships could have ended there and then and the future of my research would be uncertain. To my relief, they liked it. A couple of months later I published two op-eds in local press outlets—*Arizona Daily Star* and *Nogales International*—in which I argued that instead of talking about how to reinforce the border wall, we should make it more permeable for firefighters, hazardous-materials specialists, and paramedics who are ready to cross the line to help in emergency situations on either side, as this will ensure the safety and security of people who call borderlands their home.[3]

Messages to the media are different than other narrative genres more familiar to anthropologists. In "Why Ethnography Matters: On Anthropology and Its Publics," Didier Fassin writes about the challenges that scholars face when their research goes public.[4] The shift from the academic realm to the world of news journalism, which substitutes nuanced accounts of complex social reality with flashy, explicit headlines, is often frustrating to those who invest years to understand a multifaceted problem with no easy solutions, such as the political, legal, and economic conundrum on the US-Mexico border. Talking to the press and writing for the public before the research is over can be even more problematic. Preliminary findings can be inconclusive or contradictory. What if, once you are back at your desk, going through your field notes with analytical focus, you regret what you said or wrote while your experiences were still as fresh as wet paint? It seems safer to create a distance between the messy stage of ethnographic research—the fieldwork—and the structured phase of reflection and scholarly production that comes afterward. It may be wise to wait before you reach out to the public. But such caution has its cost: the lost opportunity to build and maintain bridges between the scientific community and the multiple publics that we want and need to address.

Writing in the field and writing from the field are forms of ethnographic writing that, because of their unpretentious character and temporary relevance, are overshadowed by academia's focus on full-length monographs and peer-reviewed scholarly articles. Field notes posted on the blog may be unpolished and haphazardly put together, news articles too narrow and shallow, editorials and commentaries for the press candid and biased ("wrinkles" that anthropologists as authors soften out after long hours spent on drafting and then revising our CV-worthy manuscripts), but they also come with the immediate reward of sharing knowledge in the making.

Writing is not the aftermath of fieldwork. Fieldwork is writing.

Notes

An earlier version of this essay appeared online in *Savage Minds: Notes and Queries in Anthropology,* November 16, 2015.

1. Casey N. Cep, "A Thousand Words: Writing from Photographs," *New Yorker,* February 26, 2014, http://www.newyorker.com/books/page-turner/a-thousand-words -writing-from-photographs.

2. Ieva Jusionyte, "First Responders Want to Help Migrants—but Immigration Policy Gets in the Way," *Guardian,* September 21, 2015, https://www.theguardian.com /commentisfree/2015/sep/21/first-responders-migrants-immigration-policy.

3. Ieva Jusionyte, "US, Mexico Depend on Each Other in Emergencies," *Arizona Daily Star,* December 10, 2015, and Ieva Jusionyte, "When Aid, Not Crime, Crosses the Border," *Nogales International,* December 11, 2015.

4. Didier Fassin, "Why Ethnography Matters: On Anthropology and Its Publics," *Cultural Anthropology* 28, no. 4 (2013): 621–46.

2

LIST AS FORM

Literary, Ethnographic, Long,

Short, Heavy, Light

Sasha Su-Ling Welland

Lists can be tyrannical. They tell us what we are supposed to do and what we have failed to do. They purport to keep us on task. They lead us to derive pleasure from crossing things out. Done! Eliminated! Lists enlist us to worry about rank and order, to aspire to the top ten, top twenty, top one hundred. Lists compel us to click and consume. If you like that, you might also like this. Click through to learn about "13 Animals Who Are Way More Gangster Than You."[1]

These characterizations and their assumption of shared experience speak to cultural patterns of a particular time and place. Lists reveal systems of thought and organization, as Foucault notes in the preface to *The Order of Things*, which opens with his reading of Borges quoting a "certain Chinese encyclopedia." The specious tome's categorical division of animals into an alphabetical series—"(i) frenzied, (j) innumerable, (k) drawn with a very fine camelhair brush, (l) others"—strikes the French philosopher as hilariously distant.[2] As he writes, "In the wonderment of this taxonomy, the thing we apprehend in one great leap, the thing that, by means of the fable, is demonstrated as the exotic charm of another system of thought, is the limitation of our own, the stark impossibility of thinking *that*."[3]

Lists, recorded by the ethnographer, related to the ethnographer, can serve as a form of cultural communication, with the order, logic, and habitus of one way of being weighed against another. Lists demonstrate shared sensibilities. Lists also divulge idiosyncrasies, of personal association, of deviation from the norm, of heterogeneous juxtaposition. They can distill a life in a few short lines. Here is an abbreviated list, one of many, I found amid my father's jumbled papers after his death:

Read Fuster and write regarding hypotheses
Call Sasha
Clean tripod
Get milk

Thinking about lists as a form of ethnographic rumination—list as cultural artifact or writing prompt—led me to think about lists as literary form, about the relation between form and content, and about what formal restriction gives rise to. Vietnam vet Tim O'Brien's short story "The Things They Carried," required reading for the generation of U.S. youth that followed his, rose to the top of my mental list. His evocation of the vulnerability, brutality, fear, loss, and longing humped through the fields of war by American GIs unfolds through list after list: of what they carried in common, of the distinctions between what they carried, of what they discarded, of what they dreaded, of what they dreamed, of what they joked their way into denying. Lists of standard-issue equipment are shot through with lists of individual particularity. After "P-38 can openers, pocket knives, heat tabs, wristwatches, dog tags, mosquito repellent, chewing gum, candy, cigarettes, salt tablets, packets of Kool-Aid, lighters, matches, sewing kits, Military Payment Certificates, C rations, and two or three canteens of water" comes this: "Until he was shot, Ted Lavender carried six or seven ounces of premium dope, which for him was a necessity. Mitchell Sanders, the RTO, carried condoms. Norman Bowker carried a diary. Rat Kiley carried comic books. Kiowa, a devout Baptist, carried an illustrated New Testament that had been presented to him by his father, who taught Sunday school in Oklahoma City, Oklahoma. As a hedge against bad times, however, Kiowa also carried his grandmother's distrust of the white man, his grandfather's old hunting hatchet."[4] O'Brien's lists pile up and push against the silent rows of white tombstones and names carved in black granite. They communicate to those not there the burden carried by those who were.

I arrived at lists in my own writing through a prolific, long-distance correspondence that I maintained during my dissertation fieldwork. I was an ethnographer living in the burgeoning megacity of Beijing; my correspondent was a creative nonfiction writer living in the small town of Matías Romero.

Wendy Call and I first met in 1999 when we were tossed together as room-mates at a writers' conference. In 2000, when our email began bouncing between China and Mexico, we hadn't seen each other since and had spoken by phone only once. When a call from the wonderfully eclectic, genre-bending, now sadly defunct journal *Chain* came our way, we began crafting our messages into a submission for issue 9 devoted to "dialogue." In what became "Living Elsewhere in 16 Steps," we experimented with the alphabetical series as a means of organization and dialogic juxtaposition. We started with A. Address and ended with P.P.S., with entries along the way like H. History Museum and I. Indigenous Means. Of our method, we wrote, "As 'non-fiction' writers, we find ourselves thinking a lot about what constitutes 'truth,' how to honor the voices of the people with whom we speak, and also about the uncanny, contradictory, parallel, and paradoxical elements of our experiences on opposite sides of the world."[5]

Little of that writing experiment made its way into my dissertation, but during the slow process of revising it into a book, I snuck in a line from A. Address.[6] Slightly altered to account for the passage of time, it now reads:

I made lists, like this one, of what I passed in the daily transit from my apartment to the nearest subway station, of what was there but would likely be displaced, in the wake of demolition, in months or years to come: husband and wife shops selling yogurt, melon seeds, liquor, cigarettes, shampoo, and toilet paper; three competing salons with hairdressers who had repeatedly dyed their hair, waiting behind plate glass for customers and watching TV; the pigeon cage, noisy with flapping wings, on the roof of an enthusiast's apartment; a government family planning clinic; the south entrance to the hospital where victims of the *falun gong* self-immolation in Tiananmen Square were treated a week before their fanaticism showed up on the fruit seller's television set; a couple of dimly lit stores selling bed-side toilets, canes, neck braces, and prosthetic limbs resting motionless under glass; at least four stalls, open night and day, selling funeral clothing and paper money to burn for an afterlife of prosperity; several fresh fruit and flower stands; a Muslim restaurant blaring Uyghur music with barbe-cue mutton for one *yuan* a stick sold out of the kitchen window; three street-side bicycle repairmen with basins of water for finding the leak in a tire; a mishmash of clothing shops crowded with students in baggy pants, leg warmers, and disco t-shirts, trinkets dangling from their cell phones; the gaunt old man staring blankly at them while clipping his fingernails; a string of CD/VCD/DVD stores, with overflowing cardboard boxes of jumbled cellophane-wrapped pirated goods; a hot pot restaurant with showy tanks of doomed fish breathing heavily; a 24-hour Taiwanese-style noodle, dumpling, and soy milk cafeteria; two Adam and Eve™ branch sex shops (nos. 5 and 8), with sales people in white lab coats and advertisements of blond, big breasted blow-up dolls in the window; a store selling light bulbs of all hues and wattage; a trophy store; a roasted chestnut stand; the mandatory dumpling stall; a few old moon-gate entrances to residential alleys; and the homeless woman dragging along the uneven pavement in Cultural Revolution braids and green soldier's uniform.

Fifteen years later, this excessive sentence conjures the sensory, emotional, experiential time and place of my fieldwork and the sense of my daily path through a city undergoing massive physical and social transformation as one among more than twelve million.

I wouldn't know it until I came "home," but as cranes and construction sites riddled the city of Beijing, cancer tumors did the same to my sister's body. As I wrote or didn't write through the years that she was living and dying, I learned from her another list-like form of correspondence, a shared practice of counting, meditation, and making do. Kara had discovered haiku. Its three-line form required only short moments of focus, and the puzzle-like 5-7-5 syllable count was perfect for a boggle-scrabble-sudoku master like my sister. While taking a medication with the side effect of sleeplessness, she sometimes stayed up all night writing haiku after haiku. In the morning, I would find dozens of new poems—tiny blasts of wisdom, anger, insight, and love—in my inbox. I struggled to keep up, sending back mine in exchange for hers. We traded litanies of pharmaceutical peril, televised escape, child-hood joy, and brightly colored games of skill and chance:

drugs yuck I hate them
sutent, temodar, keppra
dexamethasone

but wait there are more
kytril, zofran, marinol
and VP-16

no more morphine no
hate the nightmare dreams it brings
no percocet either

oprah oh oprah
ellen ricki dr. phil
regis and kelly

so who wants to be
our next top reality
star search survivor

you're my monk my house
my crime scene cold case closer
and law and order

spring days carefree sun
shortcuts through neighbors' yards long
for our kid days past

etch-a-sketch lite-brite
chutes and ladders candyland
monopoly life

These simple, ordered lines helped us communicate what had become almost unspeakable. They cut to the quick, the living and dying heart of things. They provided respite along the way toward an uncertain end.

As much as lists rule my life, as they accumulate on my computer, on sticky notes, on crumpled, pocketed slips of paper, I have also learned to listen to lists, to find meaning, poetry, and reprieve in them. They have a rhythm of their own that can sometimes only be heard when read aloud. On a night not long ago, as I read E. B. White's *Stuart Little* to my six-year-old and we neared the end of the anthropomorphic mouse's journey from city to country in search of his missing friend Margalo the bird, I savored the sound of this sentence as it unexpectedly wrapped us in a verdant world of wonder:

> In the loveliest town of all, where the houses were white and high and the elm trees were green and higher than the houses, where the front yards were wide and pleasant and the back yards were bushy and worth finding out about, where the streets sloped down to the stream and the stream flowed quietly under the bridge, where the lawns ended in orchards and the orchards ended in fields and the fields ended in pastures and the pastures climbed the hill and disappeared over the top toward the wonderful wide sky, in this loveliest of all towns Stuart stopped to get a drink of sarsaparilla.[7]

Notes

An earlier version of this essay appeared online in *Savage Minds: Notes and Queries in Anthropology*, September 28, 2015.

1. Sahil Rizwan, "13 Animals Who Are Way More Gangster Than You," *BuzzFeed*, September 22, 2015, accessed September 26, 2015, https://www.buzzfeed.com /sahilrizwan/gangstanimal.

2. Jorge Luis Borges, "The Analytical Language of John Wilkins," in *Other Inquisitions, 1937–1952*, trans. Ruth L. C. Simms (Austin: University of Texas Press, 1964), 103.

3. Michel Foucault, *The Order of Things: An Archaeology of the Human Sciences* (New York: Vintage, 1994), xv.

4. Tim O'Brien, *The Things They Carried* (Boston: Houghton Mifflin, 1990), 4–5.

5. Wendy Call and Sasha Su-Ling Welland, "Living Elsewhere in 16 Steps," *Chain* 9 (2002): 69.

6. An external reviewer of the book manuscript didn't care for this experimental list of a sentence, so out it went again.

7. E. B. White, *Stuart Little*, special read-aloud ed. (New York: HarperCollins, 1999), 100.

3

FINDING YOUR WAY

Paul Stoller

For the Songhay people of Niger and Mali, life is a series of paths that end and then fork off in two new directions. At these forks in the road the traveler must choose her or his direction, destination, and fate. My choices, many of which were shaped by forces beyond my control, miraculously led me to two mentors: the late Jean Rouch, French filmmaker extraordinaire, and the late Adamu Jenitongo, a profoundly wise sorcerer-philosopher among the Songhay people. Both of these men loved to tell stories, the life source of their science and their art. They never told me how to tell a story; rather, they asked me to sit with them, walk with them, and laugh with them. In this way, they said, I would find my own way in the world and my own way to tell stories. They both believed that the story, in whatever form it might take, is a powerful way to transmit complex knowledge from one generation to the next. Like Milan Kundera in his magisterial *The Art of the Novel*, they believed that the evocative force of narrative could capture truths far beyond the scope of any philosophical discourse.

Yet like most anthropologists, I was trained to tell, not to show, to denote the social through analysis, not to evoke it through narrative. Following the path marked by my mentors, though, I have often tried to resist that disciplinary maxim. In most of my writing I've attempted to use narrative to connect with readers through what Jerome Bruner called the narrative construction of reality. There are many elements to Bruner's approach. One central element—at least for me—is that narratives can underscore our human vulnerabilities. In my experience they can bring to the surface deep fears about how we confront misfortune, illness, and death. A second important element of narrative is that it evokes the human dimension of our inextricably intertwined professional and personal lives.

Here's the rub. It is one thing to talk about the important elements of narrative and yet another to know how to express these important themes in our works. It is clear—at least for me—that writing anthropology or anything else is an activity that requires an open-minded and playful approach to exposition, an approach without rules or easy steps to follow. To find their way, writers, like filmmakers or apprentice sorcerers, need guidance from mentors as well as a good measure of existential fortitude. It is not easy to pursue the truth of our stories, but a playful openness to possibility can sometimes show us the way.

When I write or think about writing, which is much of the time, things pop into my consciousness that lead me in felicitous directions. When I sit down to write ethnography, memoir, fiction, or a blog, I move into a different space. When I write, strange things sometimes occur. In the summer of 2013, I read through files trying to find a topic for a talk at a conference on anthropology and the paranormal. After several hours of fruitless perusal, a copy of a *Le Monde* interview, which I hadn't looked at for seven years, fell to the floor. That inexplicable event created a perfect storm, or what Arthur Koestler called a library angel (when browsing through the library you unexpectedly stumble upon a book you've long been looking for), that not only showed me the way to that presentation but also inspired a new book project. These "angels" sometimes appear in other contexts. During a dog walk, a character from a work in progress "talks" to me, telling me that the tone of such and such a passage is wrong or that a particular dialogue is off the mark. Staring at the computer screen, a distant relative or a long-lost friend "visits," reminding me of a turn of phrase that clears a path through the textual thicket.

If we are open-minded and playful, these elements sometimes materialize and can be woven into narratives that powerfully evoke complex social realities. When I sat with Adamu Jenitongo, he told me stories to convey the most important lessons of his being in the world. When I slowly read him the manuscript of what was to become my first book, *In Sorcery's Shadow*, he told me I needed more stories in the text. I asked him if I should recount his story in more detail. He said that would be fine, but "if you want to tell my story, you have to tell your story as well." His personal challenge has shaped all of my professional writing in which ethnographic narrative has been foregrounded, in which an attempt has been made to evoke the texture of intersubjectivity, in which an effort has been made to describe sensuously the nature of place, space, and character. In this way I have attempted to use narrative to evoke the themes of love and loss, fidelity and betrayal, and courage and fear: central elements of the human condition. As in Adamu Jenitongo's example, narratives can sometimes transcend the here and now, which means that they can be fashioned into works that remain open to the world. For me, that is the scholar's greatest challenge and most important obligation.

Note

An earlier version of this essay appeared online in *Savage Minds: Notes and Queries in Anthropology*, September 4, 2014.

THE ECOLOGY OF WHAT WE WRITE

Anand Pandian

One day a couple of summers ago, a caterpillar dropped from the rim of my desktop monitor (see figure 4.1). A peculiar little creature, no more than an inch long, clothed in a jacket of wispy white, a jaunty pair of lashes suspended well behind a tiny black head. The visitation was unexpected. It's not as though I work in a natural wonderland. The walls of the office were made of painted cinder block. The window was fixed firmly in place, completely sealed from the outside. Peculiar odors sometimes drifted from the vent above my desk, possibly from the labs upstairs.

The caterpillar seemed unhappy with the windowsill, where I placed it for a closer look. So I scooped up the errant traveler and stepped outside the building, wondering, for a moment, whether there was anything more palatable in the turfgrass. Then I went back to writing, back to whatever I could forage for my monitor that day.

We tend to think of writing as a lonely task. As Annie Dillard pointed out, "The life of the writer—such as it is—is colorless to the point of sensory deprivation. Many writers do little else but sit in small rooms recalling the real world."[1] There is, no doubt, a limpid truth to so much of her prose. But this colorlessness, though, how could it be? Whether Dillard's venetian blinds slatted against the vista of a graveled rooftop, or some other more porous and inviting space, writing always happens in a sensible world of sounds and

FIGURE 4.1. Caterpillar.

textures, an atmosphere of tangible things and diaphanous beings. How does it matter, this company we keep?

Anthropology is a field science, staked on the value of having been there, somewhere, in the pulsing midst of something. Later, there is the hope of a work that nurtures the same feeling in the mind of a reader, that sense of really having been there too. Do we know enough about what happens between these two moments of palpable and often quite arresting experience? Does the act of description involve turning away from the world, as Tim Ingold has suggested, or, instead, turning more attentively toward an unseen face of its reality?[2] What might the circumstances of our writing, in other words, share with the environments we write about?

Writing, like walking, can be a way of passing through the thick of things, as *Writing Culture*'s famous cover photograph of Steven Tyler might remind us. We write on the fly onto countless surfaces of the world at hand: notepads, napkins, scraps, and screens of many kinds. This sentence, for example—this one right here—came together as I was staring through a sheet of laminated glass, taking in a railway landscape of scraggly limbs, murky water, vinyl siding, and the occasional flock of specks in a winter sky. It came together with the tap of thumbs onto the glassy face of an iPhone, as my thoughts and sentences often seem to do these days. As such screens, frames, and windows proliferate—where, for example, do you see these words?—so does the sense of a yawning gulf between ourselves and the actual world.

Walter Benjamin once wrote that "traces of the storyteller cling to a story the way the handprints of the potter cling to a clay vessel."[3] These words were an elegy for an artisanal unity of life and craft, shattered by our technological modernity. Benjamin's melancholy notwithstanding, what anthropologist can afford to forsake the integral promise of such craft? How else to make sense of that peculiar collusion between fieldwork and writing, their conspiracy to transmit together the force of an experience?

Possession, dream, hypnosis, trance—writing is often likened to such altered states of perception because what happens here is a matter of channeling. Passages are literally passages, openings to a world beyond this one and yet present already within its span. Scattered sheaves of image and paper, the routines of the head and hand, tides of association and digression set into motion by whatever we see and hear, imagine, and recall—writing takes shape through the expansive play of such relays.[4]

Recently, I wrote a book on the making of cinema in India.[5] In that writing I tried to stay true to the sensory depth and richness of the medium, and certain weird things happened as a result. I sat in an opthalmologist's lobby with my laptop and a film, trying to convey the pure sensation of its colors through dilated and unfocused eyes. I tested the patience of my colleagues next door, looping a song hundreds of times over to put something of its rhythm into words. I wrote beside a plate-glass window in Los Angeles, eyes darting between the careening of a car-chase sequence and the glint of passing automobiles outside. That chapter, on speed, took form rather quickly, as a staccato series of eighty-six terse cuts.

How well these techniques have worked, I can't say. But these small ventures in the experience of writing shared their spirit with the process of creation I'd been writing about. Whether a camera operator reacting to the aesthetic potential of light and shadow, a choreographer discerning possible moves in a current of sound, an editor wrestling with his or her body's reaction to a discomfiting scene, or a team of screenwriters slipping into a dream-like space of unruly associations, what I saw, again and again, were diverse ways of acknowledging the creative force of the world at hand. Their openness toward a broader ecology of creative emergence crept into what I do. I've come to believe that something like this happens in our own environments of thinking and writing.

There is a world that writes itself through what we do. Writing is an activity that partakes of the expressive movement of life, borrowing its form and force from the circumstances that make it possible. We write with a multitude of beings, things, and relations, with the complex sensations and unforeseen ideas they put into motion. As Alfred North Whitehead put it, "We finish a sentence *because* we have begun it."[6]

That creature, by the way, took me to *Caterpillars of North America*. Perhaps a spotted apatelodes. I haven't seen another one since.

Notes

An earlier version of this essay appeared online in *Savage Minds: Notes and Queries in Anthropology*, March 2, 2015.

1. Annie Dillard, *The Writing Life* (New York: Harper Perennial, 1989), 44.

2. Tim Ingold, "Anthropology Is *Not* Ethnography," *Proceedings of the British Academy* 154 (2008): 69–92.

3. Walter Benjamin, "The Storyteller: Reflections on the Works of Nikolai Leskov," in *Illuminations: Essays and Reflections*, ed. Hannah Arendt, trans. Harry Zohn (New York: Schocken, 1969), 92.

4. For a sustained exploration of these ideas, see Anand Pandian and Stuart McLean, eds., *Crumpled Paper Boat: Experiments in Ethnographic Writing* (Durham, NC: Duke University Press, 2017).

5. Anand Pandian, *Reel World: An Anthropology of Creation* (Durham, NC: Duke University Press, 2015).

6. Alfred North Whitehead, *Process and Reality* (New York: Free Press, 1978), 129.

5

WHEN DO WORDS COUNT?

Kirin Narayan

Moving to Australia in 2013, I was struck by the blinding intensity of light, the sweetness of fruit, the cockatoos and parrots grazing along median strips as traffic rushed in an unfamiliar direction, and an abundance of acronyms. I was also astonished by the common mention of word count. Was this a local peculiarity, or had a new location sharpened my senses so I might finally notice how academics everywhere had been counting words for a while? Consider this sample of conversations:

"How are you?"

"Excellent! I wrote 2,000 words this morning."

"How are you?"

"I sent out that 10,000-word article for review."

"How are you?"

"The book is going well. I reached 55,000 words this afternoon."

"How is X?"

"She has written 30,000 words in three months!"

I have also heard of writing retreats where gathered graduate students call out their word count at the end, and then the group collectively cheers for the sum total of words they have all written together.

Invited to write a piece between 1,000 and 1,200 words for this collection, I will confess that I first translated the count into pages. This may be my generational default: every one of my college essays and some of my early graduate school writings were typewritten. Just a page a day, I was told; one page, and in a year you'll have a 365-page draft of your dissertation. Yes, we did occasionally count words in those days too, but only in very short bursts—mostly for titles or abstracts—since the exercise required concentration. I remember tapping a pencil against each word in an abstract for my first American Anthropological Association meeting, racking up numbers under my breath. To me, it's still a marvel that a tool menu on a computer can instantly enumerate words and even characters. With the shift to word processing, pages slip away in a constant scroll and word count is on the ascendant.

I am all for word count as an outer limit. It's a boon to know what is expected in a particular setting and to figure out how ideas might be paced. But can we really gauge the worth of words by counting them? Each time I learn of marvelous feats of productivity through word count, I think of the Scandinavian boy whose parents were followers of J. Krishnamurti, and so, although he didn't really know much English, he was sent to the Krishnamurti-inspired Rishi Valley School near Bangalore. I attended the same school some years later, and he was still recalled with wonder. When everyone had sat down to write a history exam, he dashed off page after page. How had he picked up so much Indian history so fast? He was diligently inscribing the same word again and mantra-like again; *blah, blah, blah, blah, blah, blah, blah*. . . . Judged by word count alone, this was a stellar exam.

When I contemplate word count, I imagine the other words that circle around chosen ones throughout the long process of assembling—and reassembling—a piece of writing. In their very resistance to being counted, those other ephemeral words so essential to the writing process are a reminder of what's obscured by a tangible count.

First, what about the seed words developed offscreen? I'm thinking of those words that I wrote inside my head as I walked to yoga class, thinking about this short essay. I'm remembering how, as the teacher instructed us to drop our thoughts, reported word counts thudded around my mat. Rolling up the mat, I gathered these words too, and later I scribbled them on a small lined pad of paper. Now that I've opened up a computer file, this barely legible sprinkle of handwritten words reminds me of various ways this piece might grow. Such seed words, planting ideas, often guide our fingers as we write. Like seed mantras of different Hindu and Buddhist deities, they carry a compressed power we should honor.

Second, what about partly wild, unedited words? For years, I've practiced and suggested freewriting. For such spurts of generative writing, just write forward, allowing the words to spill forth; don't allow the inner editor to intervene. Talk about a rush of words! Freewrites are a chance to play, to kick up inner heels and dash about without clear purpose. I think of the gamboling herd of identical white cows I glimpsed recently beside the highway: was it just the joy of a wide field and spacious skies that had sent them chasing that wintry Australian May evening? Freewrites might be corralled onto a screen or a page, but really, they're moving too fast for a census. The length of a freewrite often just means that one can write (or type) at a gallop.

Third, what about the care that goes into varying words with attention to inflections of meaning, rhythm, and sequence? How do we acknowledge the sorting through and rearranging of alternate words and occasional consultations with a thesaurus, whether online or in the more expansive paper form? All words don't count equally. Like the blahs hypnotically repeated, words that aren't allowed variation can be numbing: punishment for writer and reader alike. I think of a friend who stared out the window in Standard One at the Bombay Scottish School and was required by his teacher to copy the same line 100 times in his notebook: "I will not daydream and look at the crows." Nine hundred resulting words!

Fourth, how do we account for the phantom words that were edited away in a sequence of drafts? Those absent words lurk in the background, adding dimensions of thoughtfulness to the clarity and structure of a piece. If deleting saps the self-satisfaction from word count, then we are in danger of murky, overwritten pieces. Such exiled words could, I suppose, be factored into the industrious accounting of words. Imagine reporting, "I wrote 2,000 words this morning . . . and then I worked really hard to delete 500 unnecessary ones!"

Using word count to measure productivity puts our work into an industrial model of mass production: quantity counts over quality, and in the rush to publish, one can end up saying the same thing over and over (and over) again. It's also interesting to notice that words are counted in rounded numbers, bypassing the quirky, uneven numbers of actual writing. Here too we see a push to standardization: I have never heard anyone virtuously announce the writing of, say, 1,841 words. In an era of metrics and institutional oversight, I understand that letting others know that one has written scores of words is a form of armor. Glinting, impenetrable mention of word count can conceal ideas and insecurities alike. After all, those accumulated words are raw materials for written products that will raise an academic's value.

In the relentless push for production, mentioning skill, craft, and many apprentice-like drafts suggests a slow, quaint world of artisanship.

What is at stake? Care for the words, for the ideas, for the chance to say something distinctively your own, and care for readers too. The work of care cannot be quantified.

I told a New York–based poet friend about the word-count reports that I so often heard. His mouth opened wide.

He was not gaping in awe. Or even astonishment.

He was laughing.

Acknowledgments

With many thanks to Meera Ashar, Shameem Black, Shubha Chaudhuri, Kathryn Dwan, Jane Ferguson, Ken George, Chirag Kasbekar, and Carole McGranahan for insights and stories that helped this piece grow.

SECTION II

WRITING IDEAS

READ MORE, WRITE LESS

Ruth Behar

Years ago, when I started returning to Havana, the city where I was born, I had the good fortune to be welcomed into the home of Cuban poet Dulce María Loynaz. By then she was in her nineties, frail as a sparrow, nearly blind, and at death's doorstep, but enormously lucid.

Inspired by her meditative *Poemas sin nombre* (*Poems with No Name*),[1] I had written a few poems of my own, and Dulce María had the largeness of heart to ask me to read them aloud to her in the grand salon of her dilapidated mansion. She nodded kindly after each poem, and when I finished I thought to ask her, "What advice would you give a writer?"

I'll always remember her answer. It came without a moment's hesitation and could not have been more succinct: *"Lee más, escribe menos"* ("Read more, write less").

That might seem like old-fashioned advice in our world today, where so many of us aspire to write more. But having pondered Dulce María's words, I think I now understand the significance of what she was saying.

It comes down to this: you can only write as well as what you read.

But when we read, we need to do so as writers, assessing the myriad decisions another writer made to produce a text that we loved or hated or, worst of all, that left us totally indifferent.

For those of us who want to write ethnography, the first thing we must do is read ethnographies not as receptacles of information, which is how we are taught to read in graduate school, but in a writerly way.

Read Ruth Benedict's *Patterns of Culture* to learn how she uses the poetic tools of metaphor and repetition, emphasizing a line quoted from one of her interlocutors, "*Our cup is broken*," to evoke the loss and melancholy felt by Native Americans in the aftermath of conquest and colonization.[2]

Read Zora Neale Hurston's *Mules and Men* to learn how to create a talking-at-the-kitchen-table-with-a-friend voice that immediately draws you in as a reader: "And now, I'm going to tell you why I decided to go to my native village first. I didn't go back there so that folks could make admiration over me because I had been up North to college and come back with a diploma and a Chevrolet."[3]

Read Claude Lévi-Strauss's *Tristes Tropiques* to learn how to employ self-deprecating irony in the very first line of your book: "Travel and travellers are two things I loathe—and yet here I am, all set to tell the story of my expeditions."[4]

Read José Limón's *Dancing with the Devil* to learn how to use interior monologue and humor to interrogate the very notion of doing fieldwork: "Been doing it since junior high school in Corpus Christi, Texas, in the late fifties. But I'm not very good at it. . . . Consolation: I'm not here to dance, really. I'm an anthropologist. Forget consolation: Maybe I won't be any good at that either."[5]

In these classic texts, you know who is telling the story and why. There is a strong authorial presence, to the extent that the writers share their misgivings about their writing, bringing you into the intimacy of their thought process. Each has a voice, unmistakable and memorable, impossible to confuse with any other, just like you can tell the difference between Van Gogh and Salvador Dalí. Hard as this is to reconcile with anthropology's strong commitment to cultures, communities, and collectives, the best writers of ethnography are unflinching individualists. They don't write swappable lab reports. They cultivate their sentiments; they attempt to express not just what they think but also what they feel.

But reading ethnography alone isn't enough to make us better writers. Our genre is a latecomer to the literary tradition, so it is necessarily a blurred genre that borrows from many other forms of writing.

We need to read poetry to understand silences and pauses. To challenge the oppression of punctuation. To learn how to make words sing. To liberate ourselves from chunky paragraphs.

We need to read fiction to learn how to tell a story with conflict, drama, and suspense. To learn how to tell a story that leaves us breathless.

We need to read memoir to learn how to write meaningfully about our own experiences.

Children's books should be on our shelves, to keep our souls full of wonder.

We can't read everything, but choose a genre or a set of authors that you put on a pedestal and read with pure awe and write toward that vision of perfection.

But you are no doubt wondering: how to move from reading to writing?

Don't start with the information you want to convey. Ask yourself first what emotion is driving you to write. Anguish? Outrage? Regret? Amazement? Sorrow? Gratitude? Or is it a complex mix of feelings? Begin by acknowledging the heart.

Then dive into all you know with your head, all the things you have carried back to your desk. An ethnographer creates an archive from scratch, drawing on notes, recordings, documents, photographs, videos, and, these days, even emails and Facebook posts. We are the guardians of what we witnessed. But significant as our research is, we shouldn't dismiss memories that surface later when we sit down to write, memories of things we didn't think worthy of being in the archive.

Immerse yourself in your archive in whatever way works for you, whether it's jogging while listening to your recorded interviews or creating a visual narrative by organizing your pictures to tell a story. And spend time thinking about what you left unsaid so that you understand what you put in the frame, what counted and didn't count as knowledge to you.

Write from the specific to the general, choosing images, events, encounters from your archive. Linger, using all the tools that feel right: dialogue, interior monologue, description, metaphor, and sensual details. Also write about the things that didn't make it into your archive, and ask yourself why you left them out. Keep going in this way, illuminating lots of small moments, until you see the shape of the larger narrative emerge. Eventually, if you wish, you can incorporate conversations with scholars and writers who have come before you, doing what is known as the "review of the literature" and "theorizing." But focus on telling the story only you can tell, the story that is your responsibility, your gift.

Every ethnographer reinvents the genre of ethnography when sitting down to write. Our genre will always be quirky because it comes about through the magic of a unique intersection in time and space between a set of people and a person who wants to tell their story. This moment of shared mortality is improvised and fleeting, won't ever be repeated. There is something so spiritual about ethnography. We try to honor, with accuracy and poetry, a fragment of what was revealed to us.

Keep in mind that uncertainty will haunt you during the whole process of writing. Even after numerous revisions, you will likely fail to live up to the ideal of what you hoped to be able to write. When you finish, admit to yourself it's flawed, but feel blessed that you told a story that was yours alone to tell.

Always remember, if you get stuck, your teachers, other writers living and dead, are right next to you. Your beloved authors are ready to show you how they resolved a problem that is vexing you. Those authors you hated, they'll help you too, teaching you through counterpoint what kind of writer you want to be. As for the authors you found forgettable, let them go gently into that good night. Keep learning and keep trying. Read more, write less, and you will write better.

On several occasions I have been asked to teach workshops in ethnographic writing. Over the years I have put together some writing tips. People have found these tips helpful, so I thought I would share them here.

Ruth's Writing Tips

1. Take care of the Spirit first:
   Before sitting down to write, get in the zone.
   Do yoga. Take a walk.
   Listen to an audiobook. Read a poem.
   Light a candle.
   Summon the ancestors and all your guardian angels. Say thank you and begin.

2. Understand your voice. What kind of observer are you? What compels you?
   Understand how you are seen by those you are observing. Who do they think you are? Why have they accepted you?
   Understand the mutuality of gazes.
   You have a unique story to tell.
   The ethnographic encounter is specific to you and the people who have received you.

3. When you are doing fieldwork:
   Don't judge or self-censor. Be a sponge. Collect more than you need.
   Let yourself be led by your intuition and sensibilities.
   Keep notes about the setting. Not general notes, but specific. What does it feel like to be in that place day to day?

4. Create the archive for your writing.
   Gather notes, clippings, documents, recordings, recipes, receipts, letters, emails, photos.
   Be methodical and tactile. Put things in a binder or a folder so that you can see and touch them.
   Your archive is unique. No one else has this archive.
   It is your well. Dip into it.

5. Share: in the field and later when you are writing, share your thoughts and ideas with the people and communities that have received you.
   Integrate their responses into your work.
   Create dialogic scenes where you can address different points of view.

6. Write about revelatory incidents. This is a concept I learned from James W. Fernandez when I was a graduate student, and it's been one of the most useful in my writing.
   A revelatory incident is a moment when things came together or didn't.
   Paradoxes. Ironies. Surrealism.
   Show these moments by creating scenes with protagonists who speak their mind.
   Show season of the year, time of day.
   Show setting and how being in that place felt in the body.

7. Pay attention to *conflict*, both internal and external.
   Why am I telling this story? (your conflict)
   A young woman is on the verge of emigrating to another country, leaving her mother behind (another's conflict).
   Connect the two in your writing (your conflict and another's conflict).

8. Learn to listen. Learn to borrow.
   Transcribe. Translate. Be a scribe.
   Use the language of those who you are writing about.

Seek out their metaphors, their way of telling a story, and put it down as accurately as you can.

Add your voice as another layer, but let their voices resonate and be heard.

9. Ideas for when you're stuck:
Write fragments. Small stories. Small moments.
Trust that you'll find a purpose for them later.
Experiment with tenses.
Write not just in the past or present tense. Try writing in the future tense too.
Write in first, second, and third person.

10. All ethnography is *memoir*, a looking back on an experience that is over.
Understand that you are offering a *chronicle* of a moment that is gone and cannot be repeated. It is unique.
All ethnography eventually becomes *history*.
We think of ethnography in *spatial* terms.
But we must also think of it in *temporal* terms.

11. Storytelling *and* context: Move back *and* forth. Evoke *and* explain.
No territory is virginal.
Acknowledge your intellectual guides.
Use footnotes creatively to carry on a parallel conversation apart from the main text.
Blend quotations into your text as if talking to your predecessors.
Think of citations of the work of others as a conversation with those who came before.

12. Have faith. And learn to *revise*.
Is your writing stilted? Rewrite so it sounds like you're talking to a friend at the kitchen table.
Read your writing aloud. Does it sing? If it doesn't, change it.
Does your writing feel like something you'd want to read? If not, fix it.
Is every person in your story capable of both love and hate? Give everyone that complexity.
Feel blessed every time you rewrite.
You will think you are done long before you actually are.
Always revise a few more times after you think you have finished.
And then, let it go.

Notes

An earlier version of this essay appeared online in *Savage Minds: Notes and Queries in Anthropology*, February 2, 2015.

1. Dulce María Loynaz, *Poemas sin nombre* (Madrid: Aguilar, 1953).

2. Ruth Benedict, *Patterns of Culture* (New York: Houghton Mifflin, 1934), 22.

3. Zora Neale Hurston, *Mules and Men* (Philadelphia: Lippincott, 1935), 2.

4. Claude Lévi-Strauss, *Tristes Tropiques*, trans. John Russell (New York: Criterion, 1961), 17.

5. José Limón, *Dancing with the Devil: Society and Poetics in Mexican-American South Texas* (Madison: University of Wisconsin Press, 1994), 141.

7

PRO TIPS FOR ACADEMIC WRITING

C. Anne Claus

I weaseled my way into a writing class as I was finishing my PhD. Others had advised against taking the course ("Just finish your dissertation and worry about its readability later"). But Orwell (1946) had convinced me that good writing reflected clear thinking. If clear thinking emerged through writing with clarity, shouldn't we all be required to take at least one class about the craft of writing before we inflict our thinking on others?

The professor had taught writing for years and was on the editorial board of the *New York Times*—a real professional.[1] His (The Pro's) over-enrolled class was pitched to future journalists, but that seemed insignificant to me. "Anthropologists are also writers, without proper training or hope," I pleaded with him for a spot. "Isn't it important to make academic writing more compelling, more accessible?" I argued and implored and won.

The Pro's task was enormous. We students were formidable, with our ingrained use of dull verbs that arrange and present, our anxious prose with its superfluous connective tissue, our obfuscating descriptions of abstractions. He started small, with sentences. A third of the way into the class we progressed to paragraphs and then finally to thousand-word pieces.

I wish that more anthropologists could luxuriate in a writing class. I'm certainly not a pro, but if you're reading this we conceivably share a set of literary aspirations. Perhaps the lessons I learned will be useful for your ethnographic compositions too?

Writing Tips from a (Real) Pro

Cover Less Ground

Ask yourself, what will make my sentence as simple and clear as it can be? Be economical and efficient. Your sentences are most likely too long, too crowded. Revisit each sentence—are your ideas moving too quickly in the space you have given them? Look for the incomplete thought and clarify. Rephrase, reword, recast. Often this work will open a new pathway for writing and thinking.

Every single sentence should captivate. The weight of your sentence does not make it more valuable. Allow each sentence to do a tiny part of what you want it to do. Believe that a slow build over time will convey your message.

Resist the semicolon. It will tempt you to overstuff your sentence with ideas.

Enliven Your Prose

How many consecutive lackluster words can the reader tolerate? Avoid any turn of phrase or cliché that is used thoughtlessly or out of habit. Someone else's phrases will rot in your sentence. Writing is a series of choices, and it *shouldn't* just flow or come easily. If it does, we ought to be suspicious. Are we submitting to rhetorical convention and therefore relinquishing our freedom of choice?

When you're submerged in theoretical explications, try to make just one sentence shorter, clearer. Is the subject of your sentence capable of performing the action that you're attributing to it? Move away from abstractions by adding a sentence about actual actors performing actual actions.

Please don't *replace* real, live action with noun phrases (i.e., don't participate in *the replacement* of real, live action with noun phrases).

Structure Sentences Dynamically

Occasionally our writing is marred by longueur. For me, writing about the policy context of coral conservation can produce bland but necessary text. In that case, isn't it better to just lay down the details as quickly and succinctly as possible?

When tedium sets in, I turn to John McPhee (e.g., 1977). Where a less skilled writer might depend on a personal anecdote or a vignette to seduce the reader, McPhee creates structural variety. Even when writing about policies, McPhee's prose is energetic. He does this by changing the patterns of his sentences. Or he upends his prose, introducing a pulse. And each sentence's structure is different from the previous and following sentences. McPhee changes the rhythm and sustains the reader's attention.

Trust Your Reader

This lesson is the hardest to implement, and it requires a bit more discretion than the others. Although it may seem that academic writing is different from other writing we do—letters, emails, blog posts—it *isn't*. Set the cap and gown aside when you sit down to write. Writing that sounds oratorical, stiff, and formal is unclear and opaque and difficult to understand, whoever the audience is. Introduce some levity—throw in a contraction or two! Because we take our writing seriously and hope that others do too, our prose conveys anxiety. Our citations betray us here ("Look, these other people agree with me"), but alongside these attributions that academic convention requires, we fill our paragraphs with unnecessary navigational markers. We *clarify*, we *indicate*, we *argue*, we *summarize*.

You aren't responsible for your readers' ignorance or inattentiveness. You *do* have to tenderly bring their attention along. This should not include using terms such as *while, therefore, as, when, since*: terms that illustrate that we think the reader is dull. *But, nevertheless, yet, however.* Convey negation through luminous prose, and forgo those insipid grammatical markers.

Joan Didion (e.g., 1969) does this well. She is quietly assured about the information she presents. Instead of hierarchical sentences, she builds a rhythm by lengthening her sentences one fragment at a time. By the end of her paragraphs we have followed along without feeling like we've been led to a predetermined conclusion. She structures her paragraphs so they build cumulative power.

Final Thoughts

Clearly, The Pro's tips are impossible to implement all the time. How many of them did I disregard in this short piece? . . . Fewer here than in the draft. The Pro constantly reminded us that clear writing emerges from careful editing. The initial work of making words appear on your screen is the most frustrating and torturous. Spend more time revising. This is where your ideas are shaped and refined. Even incremental changes will inject clarity and liveliness into your ethnographic prose.

Anthropologists identify as fieldworkers, archivists, researchers, and teachers, but seldom as writers. Would we be more likely to do so if we explicitly studied the craft of writing, if we were more confident about our technical skills? Taking a writing class will likely sharpen your thinking and make your writing more vivid and accessible to others. I advocate sneaking into one of your own.

Notes

An earlier version of this essay appeared online in *Savage Minds: Notes and Queries in Anthropology*, February 16, 2015.

1. For more extensive tips from The Pro (Verlyn Klinkenborg), see Verlyn Klinkenborg, *Several Short Sentences about Writing* (New York: Vintage, 2012).

MY TEN STEPS FOR WRITING A BOOK

Kristen R. Ghodsee

When I was first asked to write an essay about ethnographic writing, I wasn't sure exactly what I was going to write about. I'd recently finished my fifth book and was in the early stages of a sixth manuscript, so it seemed like I should have something to say about how to get a big project done.

But I never realized I had a process until I started writing this essay. To get the creative juices flowing, I sketched out a flowchart of how I tackle a project from start to finish. The chart surprised me. My quirks and old habits turned out to be a defined system, one that I have implemented for each of my books without even knowing it.

1. Produce an Imaginary Table of Contents

When I have an idea for a book, I type out an imaginary table of contents (TOC). I think about the overall argument and how to best organize the material I will need to substantiate that argument. At this stage I make a preliminary plan about the number and the style of the chapters. For more traditional academic books, I go with fewer but longer chapters that are organized thematically. For projects aimed at undergraduate students or general readers, I have a greater number of short chapters and prefer a more intuitive chronological organization of the manuscript. Although this outline changes, the intellectual work that goes into its initial production helps me think through the big questions of audience, tone, and length before I start writing.

2. Create Electronic Files

After I have the TOC, I create a separate document file for each of the chapters, as well as for the front matter, the acknowledgments, and any appendices. Then I cut and paste in any preexisting writing that I've done. I call this "found text," and I include everything that might be relevant to the chapter: journal articles, essays, book reviews, field-note excerpts, emails, outtakes from previous books, etc.

3. Write Crappy First Drafts

Whether I'm building around "found text" or starting from scratch, I write a crappy first draft (CFD) of each chapter. I don't always do them in order, but I don't edit any individual chapter until I have CFDs of all chapters. These first drafts are appalling, but writing a chapter draft from start to finish without worrying about the grammar or coherence allows me to concentrate on the ideas and emotions that I want to convey. No one ever sees these drafts; I delete them all once I start revising.

4. Print Out and Line Edit Each of the Chapters

I edit by hand (with a fountain pen) on paper. Editing on screen is more efficient and environmentally friendly, but it makes for lazy writing. Line editing in print forces me to read through the entire chapter before making changes to the electronic file. This allows me to keep the larger structure of the chapter in my head and to see how the pieces might work better in a different order. This round of line edits is tedious because it is my initial crack at correcting the serious deficiencies of the crappy first draft.

5. Print Out and Line Edit Again

I repeat the process above. The chapters are still rough, but after this round of line edits, they start to become readable. At this stage, I focus on grammar, syntax, and narrative flow. I start watching for typos and think about topic sentences and paragraph length. I also consider how my arguments develop over the course of the chapter and what additional material I might need to substantiate my claims. Only after I have everything down on paper do I input the changes into the computer.

6. Combine the Chapters into a Manuscript

After the second round of line edits, I go back to my TOC and think about the overall structure of the book. Some chapters have outgrown themselves and must be divided in two. Orphaned chapters find new homes or get cut altogether. All of the text that gets slashed is dumped into an electronic "outtakes" file. This serves as a reservoir of "found text" for future projects. All of the chapters are now combined into one big electronic document.

7. Print Out and Line Edit

Call me a murderer of trees. I print out the entire manuscript and do a full round of line edits by hand once more. I concentrate on overall coherence and clarity, and look for more material to cut. The manuscript begins to feel like something that I can share with the world without dying of shame.

8. Find Friendly Readers

My mom, my partner, my friends, and nonjudgmental colleagues are my first line of readers. At this point, I've usually been working too intensely and for too long on the project. I need some critical distance. Giving the whole manuscript to a few trusted interlocutors allows me to take a break and get some much-needed external input. Are my arguments clear? Is there still surplus prose? How many typos have I missed?

9. Listen to Stephen Hawking Read My Words

Once I have incorporated all of the friendly suggestions, I use the "speech" function in Microsoft Word to have my computer read me the entire manuscript. Unwieldy syntax, overused words, and even simple typos are more easily heard than seen.

10. Complete References and Send It Off

The final task is to organize all of the references and the bibliography. Careful attention to the references allows me to review the overall structure of the book and think about the literature to which I will be contributing. Only after the references are in order will I begin to contact editors. At this point, the manuscript is ready for blind review. I say a little prayer, send it off, and start work on my next project.

Note

An earlier version of this essay appeared online in *Savage Minds: Notes and Queries in Anthropology*, February 24, 2014, and this text was drawn upon and expanded from a chapter included in my book *From Notes to Narrative: Writing Ethnographies That Everyone Can Read* (Chicago: University of Chicago Press, 2016).

9

SLOW READING

Michael Lambek

Instructors on the front lines report that undergraduate grades are falling into a bimodal distribution rather than the comfortable old bell curve. The majority do poorly, it is said, because they do not know how to write. I suggest the source of the problem lies one step behind writing, in reading.

Writing presupposes reading. To write, one has to know how to read, and to write well, one has to read well. Whether or not we write in order to be read, as Mary Murrell asks in her essay "What Is an (Academic) Author?," at the minimum we are our own first readers. We read in order to own our writing, to confirm and assert it is ours, that it is what we want to say and the best way we know how to say it. Even before the copy edit and the proofing, we read what we write; reading is part of the very technique of writing. I am reading these lines as I write them.

The relation of this function of reading to the practice of writing has changed over time. Word processors enable us to revise with ease. We read and reread our work in progress, write and rewrite, and cut and paste with abandon. Writing with a word processor has become a different skill than it was with a typewriter or a ballpoint pen. And before those inventions, the writer with ink and pen or brush had to know exactly what she wanted to say and how to say it before she put it to paper or parchment. Space was also limited, the end of a page imposing the same tyranny as the boxes with fixed character limits on recommendation forms.

As the allusion to calligraphy suggests, writing is an art. Anyone trying to write—a letter, novel, dissertation, poem, or ethnography—knows that it is a skill to be cultivated and to be learned through the sheer doing. This cultivation occurs in part by means of reading, and it is thereby not fully deliberate or self-conscious. The fact of intertextuality, that texts connect and respond to one another in multiple ways, implies that writing is, to a degree, mimetic. It is mimetic not only explicitly of what we are trying to represent but also tacitly of what we have read. Hence the reproduction of style and genre from text to text. Literary theorists have had much to say on all this.

As for anthropology, we teach by having students read exemplary works. In the M.A. seminar called Critical Issues in Ethnography that I have sometimes taught, I expose students to a wide range of ethnographic writing styles. I do not reserve my admiration exclusively for the kind of first-person writing that Ruth Behar advocates in her essay "Read More, Write Less" (which uncannily preempted my decision to approach writing through reading). Yet I like to start my course with a text that raises the writing stakes or challenges the conventions of genre, a book such as Jamaica Kincaid's *A Small Place* or W. G. Sebald's *The Emigrants*. Both these books are like and unlike conventional ethnography in provocative ways; both address anthropological topics; both offer superlative powers of observation; both complicate the positionality of writer, reader, and character. It is a striking fact to discover that, just like Kincaid, Malinowski begins *Argonauts* in the second person, but with very different affective consequence. Sebald uses photographs just like the "writing culture" folks would say ethnographers do, but in a completely different relation to the text. Both Kincaid and Sebald write in exquisite prose, and each of them sets and stays true to a particular tone and rhythm. When I set out on a new writing project, I try to cleanse my palate by reading a piece of really good fiction. (It may not have the desired effect, but there is always a horizon to aim for.)

I am afraid that reading is becoming a lost art or one limited to that privileged small percent at the top end of the bimodal distribution. Marilynne Robinson, surely one of the best American writers, whose novels range from the surreal (*Housekeeping*) to the simple sublime (*Gilead*), gave a book of her essays the pointed—and quite wonderful—title *When I Was a Child I Read Books*. How many of our students can now say that of themselves?

We all know what the issues are. First, the shift in the venues and means for imaginative experience, from private reading to electronic gaming and various forms of rapid-fire and simultaneous online communication. Second, the shortening of texts. This is as true for "high culture" as it is in the popular sphere, as novels slim down from the hefty tomes of Dickens or Tolstoy. Ethnography has also shrunk. Evans-Pritchard's supreme *Witchcraft, Oracles and Magic among the Azande* is taught in abridged form. The original doesn't sell because instructors don't assign it; instructors don't assign it because students won't read it. Students won't read it for "lack of time" and for want of sufficient attention span. There is a risk that the works that do sell pander to these students.

Third, there is the substitution of images for text and even of text received as image. "Good teaching" is now supposed to be produced through orchestrating sound and image bites, in which PowerPoint summaries can be captured on cell phones. What get lost are the slow reception, translation, and absorption of ideas over the course of a lecture, the disappearing classroom arts of listening and note taking. In effect, what professors are now expected to provide for students are not lectures themselves, in all their depth, idiosyncrasy, unpredictability, and provocation, but the professors' own notes—as if the instructors were the ones receiving instead of giving the lecture. Listening, reading, and writing on the part of students are effectively short-circuited, and the professors get high marks both on student evaluations and from the institution's teaching and learning center for their innovative use of technology. A further approach, cheerfully called "experiential learning" at the University of Toronto, does afford some real benefits, but it also avoids silent reading and writing or a situation in which a student might actually be forced to be alone with his or her thoughts.

The subjectivity cultivated in silent reading or in letter writing and journal keeping is once again restricted to a small proportion of the population. Such reflective subjectivity was a significant component of the modern self or subject, the self that is displayed and reflects on itself in nineteenth- and twentieth-century fiction, philosophy, and social theory, the self that is presupposed, exemplified, and enacted by most authors we value, even by those poststructuralists who claim to deny or subvert it. (Post-structuralists read too.)

Our profession and our own writing have been based (among other things) on the art of quiet reading (perhaps: the quiet art of reading), of reading to ourselves and for ourselves, and communing with ourselves by means of the text. The question is, what kind of writing can we expect when we no longer read this way?

We have not yet reached a fully postliterate society. Certainly, technology enables lively new genres of writing, shorter and less formal, like the blog where this essay first appeared, with the request for eight hundred to a thousand words that I am now over (I write; therefore I count). The art of reference letters flourishes—and is beautifully sent off in Julie Schumacher's epistolary novel *Dear Committee Members,* which should be on every (aging) academic's bookshelf. A forward-thinking editor at the University of Toronto Press, Anne Brackenbury has been keen to commission graphic ethnography. And less *is* sometimes more. We read and admire Geertz and Sahlins more for their essays than their monographs, and we should give as much attention to the crafting of articles as we do to books.[1] I salute the journal HAU and its former editor, Giovanni da Col, for trying to enliven the style of academic articles without dumbing them down.

As the number of texts increases, it is only right that most of them should be shorter, enabling a more equal reception among a limited audience. But we need to resist the reduction of books and lectures to the compilation of information (or misinformation) or the status of executive summaries. Just as the slow food movement promotes good eating (and irrespective of any elitism), we need to advocate slow reading. Good writing will follow, as surely as food lovers become cooks.

Notes

An earlier version of this essay appeared online in *Savage Minds: Notes and Queries in Anthropology,* March 9, 2015.

1. For a lovely example, see Donna Young's "'The Empty Tomb' as Metaphor," *Religion and Society* 5, no. 1 (2014).

10

DIGGING WITH THE PEN

Writing Archaeology

Zoë Crossland

Like fiction, archaeology allows us to visit other worlds and to come back home again. So it can be a useful exercise to juxtapose archaeological texts with historical novels, poems, and other forms of writing. Just as a novelist does, a writer of archaeology has to attend carefully to the conventions that shape the stories we tell. The written past demands some kind of narrative coherence: a consistency in our compositional form and in the internal logic of the world we bring into being. Like poets, we have to choose our words carefully. In this comparison we can identify the shared techniques used by archaeologists, novelists, and poets to evoke other worlds and to draw in the reader. We can also consider the narrative possibilities that are excluded from our archaeological writing and ask what opportunities might be opened up by allowing different forms of voice and language.

Going further than comparison, how might experimenting with different forms help us find new ways to conjure stories from the material traces of the past? There is an intimacy to archaeological excavation that is rarely captured in our narratives: the rasp of a trowel over granular soil, the vegetative odor of damp roots stripped green and white by a spade thrust, or the cold, polished feel of porcelain, smooth beneath the fingers. Much is gained in the translation from earth to text, but what is lost? How might we find narrative space to include some acknowledgment of affect and emotion, as well as the texture and grain of encounters with the stuff of the past?

These are questions that we work through in my Writing Archaeology class, which I first taught in spring 2014, when I also wrote the blog post on which this essay is based. In the class we explore how archaeological evidence can evoke particular affective responses and how novels and poems work to do something similar. What enlivening techniques might we learn from fictional accounts, and how might they encourage us to think more critically about the role of the reader in bringing a text to life? It's clear that the practice of archaeology is as much about writing as it is about field-work. The texts we compose are fundamental to translating artifacts and sediments into stories about the past, yet we pay relatively little attention to the craft of writing, preferring to train students in techniques of excavation and field survey. This is not to say that archaeologists have not thought critically about writing.

We began the class by reading some of the many experimental texts in archaeology. These include Rosemary Joyce and colleagues' dynamic *Languages of Archaeology*, Janet Spector's pioneering *What This Awl Means*, and Carmel Schrire's unflinching and evocative *Digging Through Darkness*.[1] There are a surprising number of archaeological texts that play with form, positioning, and language. Many of those scholars who experiment with fiction also take an autobiographical approach, working to situate their experiments within the context of their own frustrations with the limits of conventional archaeological texts. Poetry is rare, however. A beautiful contribution has been published in the form of the book *Stonework*, by Mark Edmonds working with the artist Rose Ferraby.[2] Given the doubt that lies at the heart of archaeological endeavor—that moment when one must leap from the material signs that lie within our experience to the projected past that we read from and in them—how is archaeological writing approached? Do we attempt to hide or minimize this doubt, to embrace it, or to elaborate upon it? What is noticeable in many texts is the need for a framing device. Archaeologists rarely let a fictionalized or poetic piece stand on its own terms. In order to think about this more closely, we also read novelists who write about the past or material traces, such as Raymond Williams and Orhan Pamuk.[3] We read poets too. Seamus Heaney, of course, but also Peter Riley's *Excavations* and Armand Schwerner's *The Tablets*.[4] Riley and Schwerner both play with the boundaries of fact and fiction in ways that are normally forbidden to us archaeologists. Since I first taught the course, I've supplemented the syllabus with the wonderful 2015 collection *Subjects and*

Narratives in Archaeology, edited by Ruth Van Dyke and Reinhard Bernbeck, which brings together a range of different writing forms to explore many of these questions.[5]

The Writing Archaeology class is a small seminar designed for students who are working on substantial writing projects—whether a senior thesis or a doctoral dissertation. As part of the class the students undertake weekly writing assignments that work to better understand an author's aims, his or her successes and failures. So, for example, in reading and discussing Janet Spector's classic text *What This Awl Means*, I also asked the students to write a similar narrative about their own research. Spector's text has at its heart an imagined relationship between a bone awl and the adolescent girl who made and owned it. This was one of the first attempts to write an archaeological history as a story: a biographical account that centered on a named and historically documented person. I asked the students to write about their own projects in semi-fictionalized form, using a voice that was as close as possible to the one that Spector deployed.

This is an exercise designed to prompt students to think about language with precision. I asked them to consider the language choices that Spector made. For example, what verb tenses does she use, and how do they shift at different moments in the story? I also asked them to think about how Spector's word choices affected their response to her story as readers. What kind of narrative mood is evoked by the text, and how is this accomplished? What kind of adjectives and verbs are used? Do they give the effect of a story quickly told, words piled up in haste, or does the narrative seem stretched out, slow and unhurried, or perhaps more evenly paced and evenly treated? Perhaps something else entirely is achieved? Finally, what do the students bring to the text as readers? Does the account resonate with other stories they've heard and, if so, how?

We workshop everyone's writing in the second half of each class. I ask students to identify one thing that they like or are proud of in the piece they've submitted and one thing that they feel didn't work or that they struggled with. We discuss our responses, make suggestions, and note other points that we enjoyed or that might need a bit more thought. What has been revelatory for me in this exercise is the very different tone and topics of discussion that this approach elicits. By starting to take sentences apart, word by word, we've been finding out more about our own reading and writing practices. The writing exercise also gives students some insight into the terrain that the author was negotiating. Why did she make particular choices, and how might different styles of writing change how they read the text? To write a short piece that attempts to inhabit someone else's authorial voice encourages close reading: attention to the exact words chosen and to the difficulties of experimental writing. What comes out of this class on writing is a more generous reading experience.

Let me offer some of the responses that the students gave me when I asked them about their thoughts on the class as I was writing the original blog post in 2014.

Michael Merriam suggested that the exercise worked as an "excavatory tool" into the texts we read. In emulating a writer's style, he pointed out that one has to figure out the boundaries that separate homage, pastiche, and parody. As Courtney Singleton put it, in writing such a response to the text you "have to sit with the author" and face the difficulties and challenges that the author faced. Valerie Bondura noted that it is an uncomfortable process to force yourself "out of your narrative comfort zone" and into other voices. When imitating an author's voice, the students must make similar decisions about how to characterize the past people that they inhabit in the text. Courtney and the others noted how uncomfortably transgressive this can feel, enhancing their awareness of the ethical issues around representation and the control over narrative. This was felt especially strongly by those students working on the recent past or who were telling a story about another nation or people's histories. To acknowledge this is to recognize that these writing exercises are steps along a path. Not an end in themselves, they are meant to make visible the assumptions that we bring to our writing, as well as to open up new ways of thinking about our archaeological evidence and to hopefully prompt insights that we might not otherwise have had. What's important here is to create a safe workshop space to engage with one another's work and to acknowledge that failure is always possible. It is in this place of creative risk that the generative potential of failure emerges, eliciting insight into the writing process and prompting growth as a writer and reader of anthropology.

Acknowledgments
Contributions by Lindsey Bishop, Valerie Bondura, Charles Garceau, Emma Gilheany, Michael Merriam, Maud Reavill, Maura Schlagel, Dianne Scullin, and Courtney Singleton. With thanks to Severin Fowles for bringing Armand Schwerner's poetry to my attention, and to Carole McGranahan for her kind invitation to contribute to the *Savage Minds* blog and to this volume. Finally, I must acknowledge the overt theft of Seamus Heaney's poetry in the title of this piece.

Notes

An earlier version of this essay appeared online in *Savage Minds: Notes and Queries in Anthropology*, March 3, 2014.

1. Rosemary A. Joyce, *Languages of Archaeology: Dialogue, Narrative, and Writing* (Oxford: Blackwell, 2002); Janet D. Spector, "What This Awl Means: Toward a Feminist Archaeology," in *Engendering Archaeology: Women and Prehistory*, ed. Joan M. Gero and Margaret W. Conkey (Cambridge, MA: Basil Blackwell, 1991), 388–406; Carmel Schrire, *Digging through Darkness: Chronicles of an Archaeologist* (New Brunswick, NJ: Rutgers University Press, 1995).

2. Mark Roland Edmonds and Rose Ferraby, *Stonework* (Orkney: Group VI, 2012).

3. Raymond Williams, *People of the Black Mountains,* vol. 1, *The Beginning* (London: Chatto and Windus, 1989); Orhan Pamuk, *The Museum of Innocence* (Toronto: Knopf Canada, 2010); Orhan Pamuk, *The Innocence of Objects: The Museum of Innocence, Istanbul* (New York: Abrams, 2012).

4. Seamus Heaney, *Opened Ground: Selected Poems, 1966–1996* (London: Macmillan, 1999); Peter Riley, *Excavations* (Hastings, UK: Reality Street, 2004); Armand Schwerner, *The Tablets*, vol. 1 (Orono, ME: National Poetry Foundation, 1999).

5. Ruth M. Van Dyke and Reinhard Bernbeck, *Subjects and Narratives in Archaeology* (Boulder: University Press of Colorado, 2015).

SECTION III

TELLING STORIES

11

ANTHROPOLOGY AS THEORETICAL STORYTELLING

Carole McGranahan

Anthropologists are storytellers. We tell stories: others' stories, our own stories, stories about others' stories. But when I think about anthropology and storytelling, I think also of something else, of anthropology as theoretical storytelling.

What is anthropology as theoretical storytelling? Several things. A discipline engaged in explaining, understanding, and interpreting cultural worlds as well as in developing theoretical paradigms large and small for making and making sense of cultural worlds. This is not something new to anthropology. Looking across generations of anthropological scholarship, theoretical storytelling appears repeatedly. From Zora Neale Hurston's tales and lies to Muchona the Hornet to the Balinese cockfight to Rashīd and Mabrūka and Fayga in Lila Abu-Lughod's *Veiled Sentiments* and on and on. Stories stay with us. People stay with us. Esperanza. Adamu Jenitongo. Uma Adang. Gloria. Miss Tiny. Charles and Morley and Nick Thompson. Angela Sidney. Valck. Mr. Otis. Bernadette and Eugenia. Tashi Dhondup. And so many more. Anthropology as theoretical storytelling may be a method of narration by both ethnographer and subject, a means of organizing writing, a way of arguing certain ethnographic points, and an ethnographically grounded way of approaching theory. This is not then a singular approach or description, but a term that captures a range of anthropological sensibilities and strategies.

As with many before me, in the field I found myself to be a recipient of stories. Yet not all was narrative. Some moments in the field were more staccato or fragmented, confusing or obscure; some were just talk about this or that, about the minutiae of everyday life or about nothing at all (and those are deeply cultural moments indeed). But many days included storytelling, official and not, almost always told over shared food and drink. Some of these stories I asked to hear in the context of my research, and others people told me for reasons both known and unknown. Turning these stories into a written ethnography or a spoken one in the classroom involves analytical and narrative labor. This process is about both ideas and story.

IT WAS A DARK and stormy night. People were gathered in Lhasa's Twentieth Park (*nyi shu'i gling ga*) to celebrate '*dzam gling spyi bsangs*, the Universal Smoke Offering Day. Throughout the day, people picnicked and gambled in tents set up throughout the park. The weather was bad, but the atmosphere was festive, with people eating, drinking, and enjoying themselves; it was a party after all. Beer maids roamed from tent to tent singing, flirting, and refilling *chang* (beer) bowls. Much of Lhasa's high society was there. The flaps of their tents were down, perhaps as much as to prevent prying eyes as to provide shelter from the weather. Inside one tent, dimly lit by oil lamps and candles, a group of important men played mahjong and drank chang. As they played, a thunder and lightning storm developed. Outside the tent, two men huddled, nervously preparing for their own festival activities. Then, as one or another of the men inside the tent contemplated his next play, there was a ferocious roar of thunder, followed by a flash of lightning. The lightning illuminated the tent, and through chang-glazed eyes, the men inside saw that one of their mates had fallen over. Outside the tent, the two other men were already gone, swiftly making their escape through the back alleys of Lhasa. The man who had fallen was dead, murdered with just one shot fired precisely at the time of the thunder, so as not to be heard and thus giving the assassins enough time to make their getaway. This was 1921, and the murdered man was Pangda Nyigyal, the head of the newly powerful Pangdatsang family, an eastern Tibetan (Khampa) trader settled in Lhasa and a favorite of the Thirteenth Dalai Lama.

It was a dark and stormy night.

For real. This is not an entry in the annual Edward Bulwer-Lytton "dark and stormy night" sentence contest, but the way numerous people told this story to me. Dramatically. Voices lowered. Voice and tone matching what a dark and stormy night feels like. Narrators who've never heard of Edward Bulwer-Lytton but who instead narrated the story as it was told to them. Narrators who reproduced oral framings as much as cultural and political ones. Anthropologists who then retell in English these stories originally told in Tibetan.

When I sat down to write my dissertation and faced the question of where to start, my advisor, Ann Laura Stoler, gave me a piece of advice I now share with my graduate students: start with a story you know must be in there, one that can't be left out. What stories can't be left out? As I wrote those stories and beyond, and as I continued to write and teach, the place of storytelling as theoretical strategy in anthropology became clearer to me. We tell stories to make theoretical arguments. We use narrative to convey both story and theory. Renato Rosaldo makes these points beautifully in *Culture and Truth:* narrative is key to social analysis.[1] As Kirin Narayan writes of *Culture and Truth* and of what she learned in Rosaldo's Stories and Culture graduate seminar, "Stories are inherently analytic, and . . . in the sequence of reasoning, analysis has narrative form."[2] Years of reading good, well-written ethnographies in which the argument is built in part through narrative structure demonstrate these points. Yet narrative drives much of our theoretical work in underappreciated ways.

Anthropologists specialize in thick description. When Clifford Geertz, for example, suggests that it's turtles all the way down, this is commentary on the simultaneously bounded and limitless aspects of ethnographic interpretation. To say our descriptions are thick is to say they are concerned with meaning and not only description. We don't just work to describe turtles but to get at why turtles matter, why it's turtles rather than elephants, and why the fact that it's turtles all the way down does not close down our interpretations but rather provides a foundation for them. Describing turtles, including why turtles are culturally meaningful, is a key component of theoretical storytelling. Description itself may be a nonnarrative form of prose, but thick description is narrative. It involves characters, a plot, a story line, a form, a goal. In thinking about the place of interpretation within anthropology today, it has in some ways been folded almost seamlessly into ethnography. Interpretation is now unmarked, assumed, expected, and often narrative in form. This has become so true that experimental ethnography is now that which is nonnarrative; the pendulum has swung back in the other direction. As a vehicle for theoretical argument, narrative provides both form and content. As Hayden White might say, theoretical storytelling is content, and it is form; it is both.

Storytelling's theoretical powers are not neutral. They are important conceptually and cognitively, and they always need to be situated in specific contexts: historical, ideological, political, cultural. And, as Hayden White does say, "Narrative is an expression in discourse of a distinct mode of experiencing and thinking about the world, its structures, and its processes."[3] In that sentence, one could replace *narrative* with *ethnography* in order to see how contemporary ethnographic writing in anthropology relies on storytelling. When we write and when we teach, we do not just share information; we also tell stories to bring material, data, beliefs, and theories to life. Walter Benjamin differentiates between information and stories by claiming that "the value of information does not survive the moment in which it was new. It lives only at that moment; it has to surrender to it completely and explain itself to it without losing any time. A story is different. It does not expend itself. It preserves and concentrates its strength and is capable of releasing it even after a long time."[4]

In this current moment, our Zora-inspired "spy glasses of Anthropology" are focused on stories more than on information. In temporally shifting away from a focus on the ethnographic present, we have also shifted away from information in this Benjaminian sense. Instead, what we are in search of and what comes to us are stories—stories that do not expend themselves but take new shape in our retelling of them.

Our telling of stories told to us is itself a theoretical exercise. Narrative helps us "translate knowing into telling"—that is, narrative provides us with a means for "fashioning human experience into a form assimilable to structures of meaning that are generally human rather than culturally specific."[5] Death, for example, is generally human. All humans eventually die. All societies have some sort of funerary rites. Yet not all people encounter tragic deaths. Not all deaths come as thunder roars.

THE DRAMATIC STORY of the murder of Pangda Nyigyal is still told today by Tibetans in exile. Eyes wide, voices lowered, narrators almost one hundred years distant from the event drape their narration in suspense and conspiracy that is enabled first by the fact that the murder was never solved and second by the controversial place of the Pangdatsang family in modern Tibetan society and history.[6] Who shot Pangda Nyigyal? We don't know. Or do we? Some people know. Some names are whispered into the ears of anthropologists. Some names are kept secret, tucked away for other times and other stories. Kirin Narayan writes that "storytelling, after all, does nothing except shuffle words, and yet through the words' arrangement, new worlds are built and filled with an imaginative wealth."[7] The worlds built through stories create truths; they do not just hold or represent them. Stories give frameworks to hopes, to morals, to politics, to ethnographies. And yet.

Anthropology as theoretical storytelling needs to dwell more in the connection between the documentative and the generative. In referring to an earlier moment in the discipline, Michael Taussig claims that "anthropology is blind to how much its practice relies on the art of telling other people's stories—badly. What happens is that those stories are elaborated as scientific observations gleaned not from storytellers but from 'informants.'"[8] In missing storytellers, we also miss the power of stories even as we tell them. Anthropology relies on both. We tell stories to get to the point, to make our points. We miss that the stories are the point. They are the getting, and they are the there. Julie Cruikshank and many others have demonstrated poignantly how people live storied lives. Anthropology is a storied discipline. This is one of our truths.

Notes

An earlier version of this essay appeared online in *Savage Minds: Notes and Queries in Anthropology*, October 19, 2015.

1. Renato Rosaldo, *Culture and Truth: The Remaking of Social Analysis* (Boston: Beacon, 1989).

2. Kirin Narayan, *Alive in the Writing: Crafting Ethnography in the Company of Chekhov* (Chicago: University of Chicago Press, 2012), 8.

3. Hayden White, "Storytelling: Historical and Ideological," in *Centuries' Ends, Narrative Means*, ed. by Robert Newman (Stanford, CA: Stanford University Press, 1996), 59.

4. Walter Benjamin, "The Storyteller," in *Illuminations: Essays and Reflections*, ed. Hannah Arendt, trans. Harry Zohn (New York: Schocken, 1969), 90.

5. Hayden White, "The Value of Narrativity in the Representation of Reality," *Critical Inquiry* 7, no. 1 (1980): 5.

6. Carole McGranahan, "Sa spang 'mda gnam spang 'mda: Murder, History, and Social Politics in 1920s Lhasa," in *Khams Pa Local Histories: Visions of People, Place, and Authority*, ed. Lawrence Epstein (Leiden: Brill Academic Publishers, 2002).

7. Kirin Narayan, *Storytellers, Saints, and Scoundrels: Folk Narrative in Hindu Religious Teachings* (Philadelphia: University of Pennsylvania Press, 1989).

8. Michael Taussig, *Walter Benjamin's Grave* (Chicago: University of Chicago Press, 2006), 62.

12

BEYOND THIN DESCRIPTION

Biography, Theory, Ethnographic Writing

Donna M. Goldstein

How do we write about people in a way that does not flatten them out? Or write in ways that don't overrepresent what we know about a person and claim to account for all of their deep motivations and interior thoughts and feelings? Whether I am writing about ordinary people who are subjects of inquiry "in the field" or individuals who are public figures, I have come to realize that one key mechanism of writing involves how we bring together biography and ethnography.

I subscribe to a form of "doublethink"[1] when it comes to praising the virtues of ethnography, or ethnographic writing. Ethnographic writing can make the fuller context come alive by providing insights into specific and grander histories. It can establish certain forms of motivation and aid the narration of biographical information. Ethnography struggles to be more than just narrative substance, but what exactly is that "something more"? Over time my feelings of unease with ethnography have been growing, even while I continue to embrace it. This unease is produced by some of the usual reasons—representational politics and the many things we discussed in the 1990s, but perhaps also from the other side—that is, from claiming to know too much. Too much and too little information are both problematic, but in different ways. That is, it is not just that many of our ethnographies are formed within contexts and power dynamics rife with colonial politics and racism but also that our ethnographic work suffers from the opposite, from a still somewhat thin form of depth (based on discourses located in the present) and flat character development, a sensibility noted by authors speaking to questions of interiority of a variety of sorts.[2] As ethnographers, we often lack the skills and the actual affectual relations with those we come to know. That "lack"—whether it is skill or connective tissue—makes it hard for us to create representations of both fuller-bodied and multidimensionalized individuals with their complex and muddled life histories, their current and past thoughts, and the *longue durée* of living that generates any individual. For many of us, we need to accomplish our ethnographic goals while rejecting easy psychological analytics. Too little information flattens our characters; too much information can potentially reveal more about the author than the character described.

These individuals we bring to life in our ethnographic creations—whether famous or simply people we meet in the course of fieldwork—are often central to our ethnographic work even when they are just one individual among many. It is unfair, I suppose, to compare our ethnographic work with great literature or great film or television. At this point in time I read more ethnographic work than I do great literature (a regret, I should say!). And full confession: I have also taken to watching film and television in the late-evening hours, and I am often deeply envious of the ethnographic richness of these creations. Take, for instance, the Swedish television series *30 Degrees in February*, which is focused on Swedish and Thai characters caught in the world of East/West tourism in Thailand.[3] The characters develop over a period of years, motivations are revealed, character flaws are made known. The series is still a mere snapshot of a world, but it is one that covers a few years, and the portraits created from these human encounters are memorable. The characters have depth and make sense to the viewer in their context. By comparison, in our ethnographies the portraits of temporality, the passage of time, and the movement of individuals on their life journeys can often seem a bit thin.

These issues present themselves in our work, both in our longer ethnographies and in shorter, more analytical articles. I am personally drawn to biographical portraits—however problematic—that are richly detailed and that do not simplify the motivations of character. In my early work,[4] I revealed fragments of biographical material of my friend and informant in the field, Glória, who aided so much of my work in urban Rio and who schooled me in the proper contextualization of her own life. I have also written about the geneticist and (honorary) biological anthropologist James V. Neel[5] in his work with the Atomic Bomb Casualty Commission (ABCC) in postwar Japan and then the Amazon, as well as his later critical scientific debates about the effects of ionizing radiation with a rival scientist whose training took place in the former Soviet Union and Ukraine.[6] I have also analyzed the gestures, comedic style, and entertainment value of Donald J. Trump the candidate[7] and then again the peculiar and surreal forms of nostalgic racism the man actively promotes in the postelection as president.[8] In writing about Trump, my coauthors and I have had to consider the overwhelming amount of material produced not just by other academics but also by journalists writing daily in a media-saturated environment. I have to agree with Sherry Ortner when she resists the temptation to associate the intellectual value of anthropology—in what she characterizes as a reductionist division of labor—solely with the ethnographic. As she writes, "I seek to reappropriate a larger anthropology in which ethnography, theory, and public culture are held in productive tension."[9] Ortner points to the centrality of theory, and I think she is right.

But perhaps we should also add to this list the productive tension that the representation of individuals presents to us in our ethnographic writing.

It is ultimately our analytics—our productive use of theory—that saves us. Perhaps it saves us from being judged solely as creative writers! We are already doing more than simply narrating human relations. We tend to believe we offer "more" than in-depth journalism (and there is nothing wrong with thinking that), a parallel field that suffers with us in corresponding ways. In-depth journalism also enters into the problematic areas we have ourselves been grappling with for years. Take, for example, a recent *New York Times* front-page article by Ellen Barry titled "How to Get Away with Murder in Small-Town India." Barry remarks on her own tensions as a journalist, revealing her struggles with the following words: "Over the past decade, in Russia and then India, I have been asked versions of this question hundreds of times: Who are you to come here and tell us what is wrong with our system? And it's true, the whole enterprise of foreign correspondence has a whiff of colonialism."[10] Her article and her attempt to reveal the mechanics of a murder in a rural Indian setting condense and explain many of our own tensions and challenges as ethnographers.

But we carry on with our work, even with its challenges.

Many eloquent anthropologists have written about the process of working with life histories; clearly the ethnographic process today involves the use of both individual and collective biographical fragments. A few years ago I taught a graduate course on the place of biography in ethnography. In that context and along with the graduate students in that class, I took in some valuable lessons from the parallel exploration of professional literary biographies and anthropological approaches to biography. Anthropologists have had some great successes with providing deep, if fragmentary, biographical portraits of informants. However, we have done so not by simply imitating literary biography but at times by writing against it, keeping portraits aligned with increasing levels of contextualization and with our theory and analyses. In that course, we arrived at a few insights about ethnography and biography that I want to share.

Contrary to literary biography, successful contemporary anthropological biography immerses the reader deeply within a social, cultural, historical, and political context rather than deeply within the psyche of an individual. Some ethnographic productions—perhaps unknowingly—enter dangerous, even obsessive territory when they look too deeply at one informant rather than focusing on the fuller context, meaning, and social and political world that contextualizes that same informant. We found ourselves less enamored of projects that become focused on idiosyncratic personal details and that essentially cause the author to lose sight of more collective biographic contextualization and more clearly ethnographic goals. But there is no single formula for success or failure.

Finally, it is worth recalling to anthropologists engaged in biographical work that judging individuals and their actions from the comfort of the present is problematic. In other words, it is still good to be reminded that the historical context of the biographical subject does matter and that most biographical subjects themselves grow and change over time. Ethnography requires both biographical rendering and theoretical analysis. It is clear that ethnography expects more than simply narrative: it requires the ability to weave social context and a kind of dense evidential analytics—theory—within its form. A key aspect of ethnography is thus its narrative capability to embrace simultaneously the intimacy of biography in social context while delivering sufficient theoretical explanation. This strange amalgamation sets ethnography apart from other art forms.

Notes

1. George Orwell, *Nineteen Eighty-Four* (New York: Penguin, 1949).

2. Kathleen Stewart, *Ordinary Affects* (Durham, NC: Duke University Press, 2007).

3. *30 Degrees in February*, directed by Anders Weidemann, SVT, 2012.

4. Donna M. Goldstein, *Laughter out of Place: Race, Class, Violence, and Sexuality in a Rio Shantytown* (Berkeley: University of California Press, 2003).

5. Donna M. Goldstein, "'*Experimentalité*': Pharmaceutical Insights into Anthropology's Epistemologically Fractured Self," in *Medicine and the Politics of Knowledge*, ed. Susan Levine (Cape Town: HSRC, 2012), 118–51.

6. Donna M. Goldstein and Magdalena E. Stawkowski, "James V. Neel and Yuri E. Dubrova: Cold War Debates and the Genetic Effects of Low-Dose Radiation," *Journal of the History of Biology* 48 (2015): 67–98.

7. Kira Hall, Donna M. Goldstein, and Matthew Bruce Ingram, "The Hands of Donald Trump: Entertainment, Gesture, Spectacle," *HAU: Journal of Ethnographic Theory* 6, no. 2 (2016): 433–47.

8. Donna M. Goldstein and Kira Hall, "Post-election Surrealism and the Hands of Donald Trump," *HAU: Journal of Ethnographic Theory* 7 (2017): 397–406.

9. Sherry B. Ortner, "Generation X: Anthropology in a Media-Saturated World," in *Anthropology and Social Theory: Culture, Power, and the Acting Subject*, ed. Sherry B. Ortner (Durham, NC: Duke University Press, 2006), 82.

10. Ellen Barry, "How to Get Away with Murder in Small-Town India," *New York Times*, August 20, 2017.

13

CAN'T GET THERE FROM HERE?

Writing Place and Moving Narratives

Sarah Besky

One of my favorite *Saturday Night Live* skits from the mid-1990s is a game-show parody called "What's the Best Way?"[1] The premise is simple: a group of New Englanders jockey to give fast, accurate driving directions. Phil Hartman plays an old man with an airy Downeast Maine drawl, Adam Sandler plays an electrical contractor from Boston, and Glenn Close plays an upper-class Connecticut resident. The host, played by Kevin Nealon, asks questions about how to get from one place to another within New England. For example, "Who's got directions from Quincy, *Maass* to the *Jahdan Mahsh* department store in Bedford, New Hampshire?" Contestants buzz in, quiz-show style, with their directions, directions that are loaded with quirky geographical references, including a "wicked huge Radio Shack" and a *fahm* that offers a chance to pick fresh Maine blueberries ("but only in the *summah*").

I love this skit because it satirizes my own predilection as a native New Englander for giving overly detailed directions that orient the asker to the contours of the road, the colors and shapes of houses, and places that "*youstah* be there" (instead of supposedly conventional things such as the number of traffic lights or street names).

But I also find this rather esoteric parody instructive for thinking about how to write place ethnographically. For many anthropologists, navigating field sites that are out-of-the-way or otherwise marginalized, Phil Hartman's character's resigned answer to one directional challenge might ring a little true: *yah caahn't get theyah from heeyah*. Beyond writing about place, how can we use our writing to recall visual, material memories of getting from one place to another (or failing to do so)?

Doing fieldwork involves moving through and experiencing space in ways particular to our projects and the places we work. In my research on Darjeeling tea plantations, I climbed up and down steep Himalayan foothills, pulling myself through the tightly planted, gnarled tea bushes that gripped the slopes. But a trip down to the plantations each morning first required a consideration of the eating schedules of the families of macaque monkeys, who would descend from the temple, where they spent their evenings, to the road below to munch on offerings left by morning walkers and whatever else they could mug off of passersby. If I could not find an old Tibetan woman on her circumambulation of the temple complex to cling to for protection as we weaved through the gauntlet of hungry monkeys, I made elaborate detours. When I write, I recall these everyday movements. As ethnographic writers, these remembered images and descriptions from our field notes are "data," as important as material from interviews or other punctuated events.

Why should we care about how (or whether) one can "get there from here"? Perhaps because, as Kirin Narayan reminds us, "Reading transports us." She frames the project of writing place with a question: "How do ethnographers enhance this journey so that readers glean facts about a place and something of the feel of being there?"[2]

The "arrival trope" is, of course, the most common of ethnographic devices. I have one. You probably do, too. But the arrival trope has been rightly criticized for fetishizing the state of finally *being* somewhere *else*, ready to begin anthropological fieldwork. We probably all recall Malinowski's directive to "imagine yourself suddenly set down surrounded by all your gear, alone on a tropical beach close to a native village, while the launch or dinghy which has brought you sails away out of sight."[3]

This impulse to recount arrivals speaks to the fact that ethnographic narratives are concerned with movement—from place to place.

The primary means by which I move from place to place, both in the field and closer to home, is walking. When I work in Kolkata, the act of winding my way through pedestrian congestion, in and out of markets, and through that city's metro is a constant sensorial overload. When I write about Kolkata or Darjeeling, I use the local equivalents of the "wicked huge Radio Shack" to draw readers into these movements—and importantly the sensations of these movements. As Alex Nading has argued, "trailing" the movements of people and other creatures can be a way of carrying place seamlessly from fieldwork into narrative.[4]

When I write about place, then, I close my eyes and reimagine walking. This is less visualization exercise and more constructive daydreaming. What does it smell like? What does it sound like? What does it look like? What does it feel like? How *do* I get there from here? How many Dunkin Donuts (or their Himalayan or Kolkatan analogues) do I pass on the way? I find that on my first couple of drafts, these descriptions are *way* overwritten, but with more editing, place starts to tighten and even serves to bolster historical and theoretical elements of books and articles as well.

When I read an ethnography, I want to know where I am in the world. When I write, I want to communicate not just stories about people but also stories about landscapes.

Most anthropological monographs begin with a field-site chapter as the first substantive section after the introduction. (I would add that many proposals and articles allow for a field-site/background section after the introduction as well.) Sometimes these chapters can be a total slog to write (and read). Perhaps we tell ourselves that we need to get a lot of historical and contextual material across so that the (more fun to write) subsequent ethnographic material makes sense.

We should bring our creative ethnographic writing skills to these chapters, but we should also work to pepper the remainder of our narratives with more place descriptions. Such descriptions can serve as a medium to convey forward what might otherwise be an episodic tale. Amitav Ghosh beautifully accomplishes this kind of conveyance, both in his intimate fluvial story about life, work, and uncertainty in the Sundarbans, *The Hungry Tide*, and in his epic account of Mandalay, Calcutta, and the spaces in between, *The Glass Palace*.[5] An unfolding landscape—of plants, animals, infrastructures, and histories of change and perturbation—can be as much a "character" in an ethnographic narrative as a human interlocutor, as encapsulated in ethnographies by Julie Cruikshank, Laura Ogden, Hugh Raffles, and Anna Tsing.[6]

While I was writing my dissertation, Kirin Narayan, who was my dissertation advisor, reminded me on multiple occasions that "all quotations need context." We all know that quotations don't just happen, yet they often seem to magically appear in the narratives we craft. We need to ask ourselves: *Where* was I? What was going on during this conversation? Was I plucking tea? Was I making tea? Was I drinking tea? Was I holding a baby while someone else performed similar labors? Or were we walking?

Without a grounding in place, narratives don't flow. They *caahn't get theyah from heeyah.* Voices appear out of nowhere. Ethnographic narratives, then, are like New Englanders giving directions. Where to turn? Certainly, "two lefts and a right" will get you there, but what about that kid on the corner selling fireworks? Turn here? At the place you can get a good peach cobbler—but not on Sundays, lest you be overrun by the after-church crowd? This kind of context building—the folksy chatter that can seem so superfluous to the weighty, critical questions we're asking—provides an excellent opportunity for giving stories a physical medium in which to live.

Notes

An earlier version of this essay appeared online in *Savage Minds: Notes and Queries in Anthropology,* March 23, 2015.

1. "What's the Best Way?" SNL Transcripts, accessed April 22, 2017, http://snltranscripts.jt.org/92/92ibestway.phtml.

2. Kirin Narayan, *Alive in the Writing: Crafting Ethnography in the Company of Chekhov* (Chicago: University of Chicago Press, 2012), 30.

3. Bronislaw Malinowski, *Argonauts of the Western Pacific* (Long Grove, IL: Waveland, 1922), 4.

4. Alex Nading, *Mosquito Trails: Ecology, Health, and the Politics of Entanglement* (Oakland: University of California Press, 2014).

5. Amitav Ghosh, *The Hungry Tide* (London: HarperCollins, 2005); Amitav Ghosh, *The Glass Palace* (New Delhi: Ravi Dayal, 2000).

6. Julie Cruikshank, *Do Glaciers Listen? Local Knowledge, Colonial Encounters, and Social Imagination* (Vancouver: UBC Press, 2005); Laura Ogden, *Swamplife: People, Gators, and Mangroves Entangled in the Everglades* (Minneapolis: University of Minnesota Press, 2011); Hugh Raffles, *In Amazonia: A Natural History* (Princeton, NJ: Princeton University Press, 2002); Anna Tsing, *In the Realm of the Diamond Queen* (Princeton, NJ: Princeton University Press, 1993).

14

ETHNOGRAPHIC WRITING WITH KIRIN NARAYAN

An Interview

Carole McGranahan

In January 2014 I interviewed Kirin Narayan through email, she in Australia and India while I was in the United States. Inspired not only by her writings, but also by an ethnographic writing workshop she led for faculty and students at the University of Colorado, I wanted to share her insights and inspiration with others. Here is our conversation:

CAROLE MCGRANAHAN (CM): One of the things so unique about your writing are the many genres and forms you write across: academic prose, fiction, memoir, creative nonfiction, writing about writing, storytelling, editing, books, articles, and so on. What has your writing path in anthropology been like? How much have you purposefully shaped what and how you wrote versus how much have you embraced what invitations and opportunities have serendipitously come your way?

KIRIN NARAYAN (KN): My writing path in anthropology is for me part of a longer journey that began as a child discovering the magic transport of words: the chance to reach out beyond immediacies to share insights, experiences, imagined spaces, and also to record what I learned from others. My mother kept my old notebooks, and once every few years I leaf through. I find a range of genres, trying this, trying that, a form of play as I found new forms through reading. Of course, this was all parallel to what was being expected in school. I learned to take stock of form and produce what a good student was expected to do, though also trying to keep this somehow mine in a jaunty choice of words.

For me, this question about purposeful shaping versus the serendipity of outward forces pushing work into form goes back to this early tug between writing what I wanted and writing what was expected or demanded. Outward expectations—invitations and deadlines—can be a great galvanizer, forcing words into form and especially pushing one to finish. It's a painful and mysterious alchemy to transform what one is *supposed* to write into what one *wants* to write. Frankly, I've been encountering the same difficult challenge after agreeing to respond to these questions!

With the big press and procession of outward professional and institutional demands, it's ever more of a challenge to pay attention to a welling of inspiration separate from all the Have to Do's. As a beginning assistant professor, I was lucky to have received some talismanic advice from Professor A. K. Ramanujan, a great figure in South Asian studies, who was a poet, a linguist, a folklorist, a translator, and more. He told me that he wrote first thing in the morning. He staunchly held to the need to listen to one's own creativity. If he felt a poem stirring, he said, and instead insisted to himself that he should write an article, neither the poem nor the article were likely to get written. But if he allowed the poem to come to him, then later he could do the article with greater energy. I wish I had written down his exact words, but I have often inwardly re-created them.

CM: What changes have you seen in anthropological writing over the last several decades?

KN: It seems to me that anthropology grows ever more capacious, allowing for multiple kinds of intellectual projects and forms of writing. The critiques of the 1980s, when I was a graduate student, have, I believe, left the lasting legacy of more room to write in, more references as armor to justify an innovative style. Thanks especially to feminist anthropology, we also have had the chance to recover the fuller range of experimental forms that our anthropological ancestors worked with, forms that were earlier not recognized as a bona fide part of our legacy. There has been a greater acceptance of more openly embracing collaborations—writing with rather than writing about—and to write with the urgency of ethical and political engagement for wider audiences.

CM: Your books are populated by characters the reader really gets to know, including yourself—from Swami-ji in *Storytellers, Scoundrels, and Saints* and Urmila-ji in *Mondays on the Dark Night of the Moon* to your mother, father, and brother in *My Family and Other Saints* and then Anton Chekhov himself in *Alive in the Writing*. I see this attention to character rather than to a person's status or category or role in a society as a hallmark of the new post-1980s ethnography in general, but also as something you have in particular really developed for the field. Why does a fully fleshed-out individual speak so strongly to ethnographic knowledge? Why do you think this has mattered so much in recent decades?

KN: Simply as a literary device—engaging readers—the chance to evoke other people and their stories is a real gift for ethnographers. The best ethnographers and those writing for popular audiences in particular have always known this, and you can look back into the history of anthropology to find all kinds of memorable characters, especially in fieldwork memoirs and life histories. But I think that more than a literary device, portraying people in their complexity is theoretically and ethically important.

Writing about individuals known through long periods of shared time with an attention to their many facets doesn't allow us to contain them or pin them down in Schutz's memorable phrasing as "homunculi of theory." This keeps us honest about other people's creativity, transformations, and quirky unpredictability, and grounds intellectual missions within human encounters that can allow different readings. Fully fleshed-out individuals bring light to the complexity of lifeworlds that ethnographers try to make sense of and enhance a sense of compassion, a feeling for stakes and difficulties. Yet writing with a sense of character also demands a nuanced sensitivity as sometimes the most fascinating things can be embarrassing or harmful.

CM: What are you working on now?

KN: Most immediately I have just finished an essay for the new journal *Narrative Culture* about the stories told among artisan communities in different regions of India and the embedded commentaries on the creative process, on shifting relations to materiality, and a wariness toward patronage. I am letting that essay settle a little as I look forward to learning more about memory and forgetting of artisan stories at a moment that many hereditary artisans have shifted occupations. In different ways, this is related to *My Family and Other Saints, Alive in the Writing,* and also my ongoing work with oral traditions in the Himalayas.

CM: What book or article of someone else's do you wish you had written?

KN: I'm often filled with admiration for other people's writing and can marvel at how much they are able to write and publish, but I don't wish that I'd written what they have. I know that I could never duplicate another writer's particular experience, insight, and skill. So I try to learn something for my own writing from what I really like in someone else's.

CM: Do you write in the field, or perhaps a better question: *what* do you write in the field? Only field notes or also drafts of things?

KN: Whether I write and what I write in the field really depend on the fieldwork circumstances: the project and the people around me. No matter where I am, I try to do freewriting in a journal each morning. Sometimes that material can form the basis for notes.

In addition to talismanic field notes, because of my interest in oral traditions I am usually working on transcriptions to be folded into further discussions. I am often writing letters or now emails when I can. I sometimes get a flash, seeing how the materials in notes could be made into a chapter and might try my hand at that.

The biggest separate project I've taken on in the field was writing *Love, Stars and All That.* I was in the Himalayan foothills of Kangra in 1990–1991, with many people around me pouring out sorrowful commiserations over how old, unmarried, and unmarriageable I had become. Writing a comic novel in the evenings, after field notes and transcription, and summoning up the company of faraway friends who might laugh, was for me a form of staying sane.

CM: Whom do you write for? To what extent are anticipated readers (individuals and community of readers) a part of your writing?

KN: Of course, this changes with every project and genre. Mostly, when I can think of my writing as sharing something I care about with someone I care about, that can help loosen a big freeze of self-doubt into a flow of words. My anticipated readers are both people I can give a face to—like my mother or friends in various locations—and also an amorphously imagined interested, smart, friendly, and hopefully somewhat forgiving person whom I might not yet have met but who I will become connected to through these written words. Especially for books, I am writing for the widest circle of potentially interested readers, whether or not they are professional anthropologists.

CM: What would Chekhov make of *Alive in the Writing: Creating Ethnography in the Company of Chekhov*?

KN: I like to hope that Chekhov would be amused rather than appalled. As a doctor, he could playfully invent imaginative ailments, and he liked to say that he suffered from "autobiographophobia." So there's a chance that all the details I assembled might have brought on a related case of "biographophobia" even as he might have found all the earnest advice giving a little plodding. As someone who loved absurdity, he might have been entertained to find his quirky brilliance reframed and set into dialogue with all these other figures living in different times. And as someone with a strong sense of social justice he might have given his blessings to portions of *Sakhalin Island* being read afresh and perhaps seeding ideas for further ethnography.

CM: Why ethnography?

KN: For the discipline of paying attention, for learning from others, for becoming more responsibly aware of inequalities, for better understanding the social forces causing suffering and how people might somehow find hope, and most generally for being perpetually pulled beyond the horizons of one's own taken-for-granted world.

CM: The postscript to *Alive in the Writing* is such a gift to writers. You have wonderful, encouraging, and concrete suggestions for writing: getting started, moving forward, moving past writer's block, revising, and finishing. Do you follow your own advice? What are the hardest parts for you as a writer?

KN: I'm so glad that you found that postscript helpful. Writing is always hard for me, and yes, I try to follow my own cheery advice—

sometimes more successfully than other times. Every part of the process can be painful and burdened by self-doubt. Writing along with others is a wonderful way to get past the sense of one's own crushing limitations. All of *Alive in the Writing* and especially the postscript was a way of conjuring up companionship with the hopes that this might help others as it has for me.

Thank you for including me!

CM: It is my pleasure, Kirin. This is such wonderful food for thought, from reflections on anthropology and ethnography to reassurances about writing, and all in between. Thank you for *your* quirky brilliance, catalytic energy, and the permission to write what needs to be written, to let—for example—a poem pause the writing of an article so that you may come back to it refreshed and ready. May it be so!

Notes

This interview first appeared online in *Savage Minds: Notes and Queries in Anthropology*, February 3, 2014.

15

ON UNRELIABLE NARRATORS

Sienna R. Craig

The idea of a decision is a decision.
We build arguments around impermanence
But are not the sort of people to admit
To inconstancies.
—Tsering Wangmo Dhompa, from *In the Absent Everyday* (2005)

I have been thinking about the idea of the "unreliable narrator" and what it might mean for ethnographers, careful raconteurs of intertwined stories: ours and others. The idea of the unreliable narrator emerges in literature, theater, and film as a tool of craft that plays with senses of credibility or believability, sometimes to trick the reader or the audience, other times to push the boundaries of a genre or challenge the cognitive strategies that a reader might employ to make sense of the story she is being told. Although unreliable narrators may materialize through a third-person frame, they are more commonly first-person renderings. In the most facile sense, an unreliable narrator is biased, makes mistakes, lacks self-awareness, tells lies not of substance but of form. But the device can also be used in a revelatory vein: to twist an ending, to demand that readers reconsider a point of view, to leave an audience wondering. Like our anthropological propensity to classify, literary theorists have done the same for the interlocutors of our imaginations. Types of unreliable narrators include the Madman, the Clown, and the Naif, to name a few. Others posit that the unreliable narrator as a device is best understood to fall along a spectrum of fallibility, beginning with the contours of trust and ending with specters of capriciousness.[1] This is the shape of a character as she defies the expectations of a reader, who then may well pass judgment on this scripted self.

In medicine the figure of the unreliable narrator emerges—perhaps too often—as the patient: that suffering middle-aged woman whose pain seems to be located at once nowhere and everywhere, the veteran who describes his sense of displacement upon return from battle in ways that fail to align with the *Diagnostic and Statistical Manual*'s latest definition of PTSD but simply *must* be that. Equally possible, though sometimes more difficult to capture, is the physician as unreliable narrator: the resident, credentialed as culturally competent, who presumes an immigrant family is "clueless" as they take in the diagnosis of a rare genetic disorder that presents in their toddler, or the oncologist who strives for optimism in the face of the latest clinical evidence, suggesting aggressive, experimental chemotherapy against the indications that his patient should prepare for death. Each presents a distinct form of unreliability that has to do with the vulnerable spaces that arise in narrating suffering.

I HAVE KNOWN Karchung[2] for more than two decades. Still, her quick wit arrests me. Over spiced tea and biscuits, we chat about the past and future of her high Himalayan home. In speaking of migrations and the transformation of local lives as many decamp from mountain villages to the global village that is New York, she remarks, "I remember visiting a cousin in Brooklyn about ten years ago. She was fresh from the village and couldn't read in any language. When she gave me directions to her apartment, she told me to go in the direction of the *tap je*, the frying pan! She meant the direction marked with 'Q'—for Queens." We laugh, seeing a cast-iron skillet emerge from the contours of a foreign alphabet, handle and all. I marvel at the human skill to not just read signs but to read *into* signs and, in the process, to make sense of an unfamiliar landscape. Far from being an unreliable narrator, my friend's friend created a reliable interpretation of an unreliable world.

My phone rings. The number signals Nepal. It is another friend who happens to be from the same village as Karchung, someone whom I have also known for many years. He and his wife live comfortably between Kathmandu and his rural village. All of their children now reside in the United States. Through social media posts, he knows that Karchung and I are about to gather here in New York with other people originally from their Himalayan homeland, a region that is culturally and geographically contiguous with Tibet but home to Nepali citizens. The timing of this call is significant. My friend knows that Karchung and I are together. He knows that I value his opinions but also that I trust Karchung and that they tend to tell different stories about change and stability in their village, and their village in the world. Whereas Karchung speaks often of cultural disorientation, empty-ing hamlets, plays of power and influence between Nepal and New York, he emphasizes continuity, if not permanence. "There is no place like our village in the whole world," says my friend over the phone, impassioned. This is the tail of a speech whose body was actually a request that I help him craft a narrative for potential foreign donors about supporting a local Himalayan convent. Once we are off the phone, Karchung quips that he is disingenuous: "His own daughter was a nun, and he helped her escape those obligations to come to America." True enough. But does the space between lived reality and social ideals undercut his narrative and affective claims, his desire to live up to community obligations?

The following morning, I gather with a group of Himalayan friends now living in New York, in part to share data from a recent stint of fieldwork in Nepal—an effort at my own reliable narration, this looping back. The con-versation skirts the borders of language loss, identity confusion, the chal-lenges of caring for elders between here and there, and possible futures. In an effort to become Americans, some people from this region use the frame of Tibetan identity as a pathway for seeking political asylum. There is exis-tential certainty to their "Tibetanness." They speak a Tibetan dialect, practice Tibetan Buddhism, and are subject to forms of oppression that being Tibet-identified can produce in today's Nepal. Yet they are citizens of Nepal. They risk becoming unreliable narrators as they relate stories of exile, even as other currents—of truth, of violence, of need, of desire—run through the body of their stories. Theirs are not "bogus" or frivolous claims.[3] Still, their narratives endeavor to sculpt the messiness of identity and belonging into a neat shape, drawing clean lines around social and political suffering such that they might be recognized—and, in that recognition, believed.[4]

After a long time in the immigration *bardo*, that in-between realm be-tween one paper life and the next, permanent resident status may materialize. A green card may arrive in the mail. But where once stood a Nepali with land to his name and a country to call home, the reliable unreliability of asylum as narrative strategy may bear new weight. Under "Place of Birth," official documents may now read *People's Republic of China*. In these efforts to claim a new place as one's own, people who once lived between this river and that mountain, who belonged to a village and a district but who were marginalized members of the Nepali nation-state, have entered into a new kind of exile: a narrative split between that which is lived and that which is documented.

And yet . . . these twists and turns of identity prompt different questions about unreliable narrators. Do these asylum stories, which live within alternative experiences of diaspora, bespeak larger collective truths about political upheaval, socioeconomic precariousness, and cultural connections? What veracity do the stories gain by being told and retold? When does the bitter taste of gossip—a form of unreliable narration—become the bite of lived experience?

AS THE CHILD of a contentious divorce, I came to see my parents as unreliable narrators. Their perspectives often felt too fraught, too invested. Troubled truths, like riptides. But to question the story was to balk at allegiance, if not to reject love. This childhood work—navigating, tacking between— has shaped my ethnographic sensibility.[5] Today more than ever, family truth has become emotionally charged terrain: uneven, unpredictable, viscerally contested. But reliability is not synonymous with truth. Like Karchung and other friends who maneuver between Nepal and New York, we make our way, feeling out spaces of trust. This, too, is a form of reliability in an unreliable world. We all carry emotional inheritance. Part of mine is to be a generous listener, to resist taking sides. This, in turn, has coaxed me toward the tools of fiction in writing ethnography because they are strategies for trustworthy storytelling. Does this make me an unreliable narrator more than a cultivated critical voice might? I am not sure. I tell the stories as best I can.

To be clear: being an unreliable narrator is not the same as being unbelievable. Rather, unreliability raises questions about what and whom we can count on. Whether a reader or a patient, a key informant or a collaborator, a new immigrant or a native, we want to feel supported. This is an anodyne to our potential unmooring. In contrast, unreliable narration is the rug being pulled out from under the story. It shirks the everyday investment required to believe in the possibility of someone else's truth, however shape-shifting that reality may be. Perhaps this is what Veena Das means when she talks about anthropology as the work of acknowledgment against the pretense of understanding.[6] What do we come back to? Where do we hold on?

Notes

An earlier version of this essay appeared online in *Savage Minds: Notes and Queries in Anthropology*, February 10, 2014.

1. Greta Olsen, "Reconsidering Unreliability: Fallible and Untrustworthy Narrators," *Narrative* 11 (2003): 93–109.

2. This is a pseudonym.

3. Bridget M. Haas, "Citizens-in-Waiting, Deportees-in-Waiting: Power, Temporality, and Suffering in the U.S. Asylum System," *Ethos* 45 (2017): 76.

4. Judith Butler has helped me to understand this concept of "recognition." See Judith Butler, *Giving an Account of Oneself* (New York: Fordham University Press, 2005).

5. See Carole McGranahan, "Ethnography beyond Method: The Importance of an Ethnographic Sensibility," *Sites: A Journal of Social Anthropology and Cultural Studies* 15, no. 1 (2018): 1–10.

6. Veena Das, *Life and Words: Violence and the Descent into the Ordinary* (Berkeley: University of California Press, 2007).

SECTION IV

ON RESPONSIBILITY

16

IN DIALOGUE

Ethnographic Writing and Listening

Marnie Jane Thomson

"How do we write anthropology in a way that does justice to the stories we tell?" It weighs on me, this question. There it is, staring at me from the introduction to this volume. It is the question that paralyzes me when I sit down to write. Sometimes it prevents me from even making it into the chair. How can I portray the complexities of the stories that people have shared with me?

I have convinced myself that I am a better listener, a better researcher, than I am a writer. I have been cultivating this research persona since 2008, when I first visited my primary field site, a UN camp for Congolese refugees. I have spent years listening and dutifully recording what I heard. Yes, I was an academic writer long before that first trip, but now it feels different. Graduate school papers and written exams are different from writing ethnography. Until the dissertation, I never had to distill so many personal and cultural details into a document that will do justice to the many stories I have collected.

Some Congolese refugees have told me that listening is enough. Listening to their stories of the war, the chaos of fleeing, and the hardships of life in the camp is enough. A few have told me that listening in itself was a gift. Others have told me that neither listening nor writing is enough. They want to know what I can contribute that is more material, more tangible, that will contribute to their political goals. But either way, everyone is interested in how I will portray them on paper. Even more than portrayal, however, they are concerned with how they will be perceived by those who do not know them.

"What do Americans think of us?" Nia asked me.

We were sitting in wicker chairs in Nia's home in the camp, looking at the photos I had printed from my visit the previous year. I told her I had taken these photos for personal reasons, not for my research, so I had not presented them anywhere in a formal fashion. I could not remember if I had shown them to anyone, actually. I told her maybe just a few friends and family members had seen them.

"What did they say—do they think we are dirty people?"

I turn to dialogue when I feel stuck or paralyzed in writing. My field notes are full of dialogue. Conversations are so much of what we do as anthropologists. I do not know how to do participant observation without dialogue. We may observe discussions, but we also participate: we ask questions, we respond, we joke, we empathize, we sometimes say the wrong thing. In this way, dialogue returns me to my research. I attempt to recreate the words that were spoken—via the most accurate translation I am able to muster—and also the context in which they were uttered. Something about reading, writing, and translating conversations takes me back to the ethnographic moment I had attempted to capture in my field notes. Such moments seem to be the crucibles in which ethnographic knowledge is collaboratively produced.

"No," I said quickly. "But my friend in Dar es Salaam, a Tanzanian, looked through the entire stack of pictures I brought with me. She stopped at a picture of you and then at one of your husband. She asked who each of you were, not knowing you two were married. When I told her you are Congolese refugees, she said she was surprised. She called you both smart."

Nia smiled. "Really? She did not think we were refugees?"

I had found Nia bathing her youngest daughter in a basin outside when I walked up to their home that day. She often does this before I come to her house, anticipating that her daughters will follow us inside, climb onto my lap, and perhaps even ask to take some pictures. She cleansed them of the red dirt that inevitably finds its way onto everything and everyone. Marougé, it is called, combining the Swahili prefix ma-, found in words like matope (mud), with the French word for red. Marougé is the color of life in the camp.[1] In the dry season even the highest leaves on the trees are dusted with it. In the rainy season the brick walls of the houses melt back into the mud they were before they became bricks.

Yet even without describing this scene, the simplicity of our words conveys our anxieties and vulnerabilities. The story of my Tanzanian friend, while true, implied that Nia and her husband were "smart," in contrast to other people in the camp who, presumably, were not. Nia's relief and disbelief that a Tanzanian did not immediately recognize her refugee-ness meant she was pleased by this distinction. We were both flirting with an idea we hoped to transcend in our lived and written expressions: that refugee was a dirty word.

"Nope. Besides no one could call you dirty. Americans typically shower once a day. How many times a day do you bathe?"

Nia was laughing now. "At least twice, even three times many days."

Jitahidi, Nia's husband, did not laugh. "It does not matter if we are clean or dirty. Do you think if Europeans cared we would still live in these conditions? Do you think there would still be war in Congo if the US cared about it?"

Jitahidi's comment strikes at the heart of my paralysis: that no matter how many stories I listen to, I will not be able to write in a way that makes people care. That the war in Congo will continue, that refugee camps will always be permanently temporary solutions to structural and other problems. This is why I try to faithfully render dialogue in my writing. Jitahidi's and Nia's words speak to social theory. Their comments are critiques. They pry open the silence that shrouds the conflict in Congo, unearth the muddiness of camp life, and connect their plight to global politics. My hope is that dialogue invites listening into the text and welcomes readers to the conversation.

Notes

An earlier version of this essay appeared online in *Savage Minds: Notes and Queries in Anthropology*, September 22, 2014.

1. Marnie Jane Thomson, "Mud, Dust, and *Marougé*: Precarious Construction in a Congolese Refugee Camp," *Architectural Theory Review* 19, no. 3 (2015): 376-92.

17

WRITING WITH COMMUNITY

Sara L. Gonzalez

Writing is a responsibility in the academy. Through our writings we enter into dialogues with one another. From undergraduate thesis to dissertation, scholarly articles, and monographs, our writing marks the trajectory of our careers. It forms the basis on which our peers and colleagues evaluate the contributions we make to the discipline. But writing is more than a job responsibility of an academic. In writing anthropology, and in my case archaeology, there is an added responsibility to scrutinize how the histories we produce are connected to the lives and futures of the communities we study. Although we often write in a singular voice, as I do here, I advocate for writing with community. By this I mean not coauthoring with community members but conducting research with community such that the writing which follows—collaboratively or singularly authored—is part of a broader effort to disrupt settler colonial narratives and to decolonize the practice of researching and writing Native histories.

The formation of anthropology as a discipline in North America occurred at the same time as European and American governments dispossessed indigenous nations of their homelands. Coinciding with the closing of the Indian wars in the late nineteenth century, the Bureau of Ethnology, later renamed the Bureau of American Ethnology, sponsored ethnographic and linguistic research on Native American communities. These salvage ethnographies documented the cultural traditions and lifeways of Native American tribes under the presumption that the combination of assimilationist policies and exposure to American lifeways would cause them to vanish entirely. Archaeologists followed suit, recording ancestral sites and collecting artifacts, as well as human remains, in their attempt to document the cultural history of tribal nations. The objects and ancestors uncovered by archaeologists and others—often through dubious means—became specimens of national history; they are representations of a past that purportedly ceased to exist following the arrival of Europeans and their colonization of the continent. Given this colonial history, how can the work of these disciplines be used to disrupt settler colonial relations in the present?

As an archaeologist who works with tribal nations in California, Washington, and Oregon to develop culturally sensitive methods for studying, managing, and representing tribal heritage, remembering this legacy of settler colonialism is an important step in confronting injustices today. Approaching archaeology as a tool for restorative justice, Chip Colwell-Chanthanphonh (2007, 25, 34) asserts the value of using archaeology to reveal the material truths of colonialism and its impact upon indigenous communities. The process of remembering and retelling history is an important element of healing, but justice also comes through asking and interrogating how the legacies of colonialism continue to unfold through the ways in which we investigate the past. Connecting archaeology to issues of social justice is a bold prescription for our discipline, one that asks us to understand how the pasts we produce are connected to the present lives and futures of the communities we study.

In the case of my work with the Kashia Band of Pomo Indians,[1] restoring justice to the act of researching and writing the history of the Kashaya starts with the recognition of the fundamental human and cultural rights of the community to tell its own history. From this starting point, the Kashia partnered with the California Department of Parks and Recreation and archaeologists from UC Berkeley and the University of Washington on the development of the Kashaya Pomo Interpretive Trail Project (KPITP) at Fort Ross State Historic Park in Sonoma County, California. The goal of this public interpretive trail is to introduce visitors of Fort Ross to Metini, the ancestral homeland of the Kashaya. Visitors to the park have a unique opportunity to directly experience archaeological heritage through the on-site reconstructions of the former Russian American Company mercantile colony, which was occupied from 1812 to 1841. The represented landscape of Fort Ross fosters images of the park as a singularly Russian place even though the vast majority of the colonial outpost's workforce was indigenous

FIGURE 17.1. Fort Ross Cultural Heritage Day, July 2011. Photograph by Sara Gonzalez.

(Native Alaskan and Native Californian) and the fort and workers' villages were themselves settled in the heart of Metini, which has an archaeological history that goes back at least eight thousand years. This erasure of Metini's indigenous—and specifically Kashaya—heritage inspired the development of the trail, which features on-site interpretation of Kashaya history and heritage places located on the coastal terraces of the park.

According to Reno Franklin, the first Kashia Tribal Historic Preservation Officer and the former Chairman of the Kashia Band of Pomo Indians (pers. comm.), the purpose of the Kashaya Pomo Interpretive Trail is to show the public "how Kashaya have learned to walk in two worlds." This message is a direct confrontation of colonial narratives that envisioned tribes as relics of the past, fully acculturated. So strong was this latter perspective that archaeological studies of Native societies during the historical period measured the degree of "Indianness" of a community through a ratio of discovered Native versus European-manufactured artifacts (Quimby and Spoehr, 1951). Counteracting this narrative, KPITP integrates Kashaya voices, perspectives, and tribal history into the interpretive content of the trail so that the public may witness the deep connection of the tribe to its homeland, from time immemorial to the present.

Achieving these goals also involves restoring justice to the process of history making. Interpretations created for the cultural heritage trail are the

FIGURE 17.2. Fort Ross State Historic Park Reconstructed Landscape: Native Alaskan Village Site. Photograph by Lee Panich.

FIGURE 17.3. Sharing stories with Kashaya tribal elders. Photograph by Jim Betinol.

final product of a community-based research protocol that frames research as a process that should, ultimately, be of benefit to both researchers and communities. In practicing community-based research with the Kashaya, project members moved away from generating knowledge about the Kashaya to creating knowledge with each other (Tamisari 2006, 24). Producing knowledge with a community is distinguished by the formation of personal, reciprocal relationships between researcher and community, in which both researcher and community acknowledge the individual contributions and shared knowledge of collaborators. This approach stands in contrast to extractive models of research that position researchers as the sole authorities and arbiters of knowledge. In approaching the research partnership from a place of mutual respect, honesty, integrity, and trust, KPITP fostered an openness of communication so that tribal elders, scholars, and community members could remember and, importantly, share histories of Fort Ross and Metini.

Public representations of Native American history typically rely upon data generated through archaeology, ethnography, and historical documents. Although each of these sources adds dimension to our understanding of Metini and Fort Ross, alone they offer incomplete glimpses of Kashaya history. For example, representations of Native history and heritage in archaeology often focus solely upon the context or function of artifacts and sites. This type of representation obscures the social and cultural contexts that made these places, and the archaeological remains we recover, meaningful for the people who used them and who remain connected to them today. For example, archaeologists classify CA-SON-1889—a stop on the interpretive trail—as a thousand-year-old shell midden and low-density lithic scatter. We have meaningful archaeological data for this site, where material traces document more than six thousand years of human settlement on the coastal terraces of Metini as well as the changing relationship between people and their lands. Yet places such as this rock outcrop with its associated midden and scatter of tools are as marked by the activities that we can see materially as they are by those we only know through traces of memory and history (see figures 17.1 and 17.2).

Kashaya stories about how shellfish were gathered, or the stories you tell children when visiting the rocky coastal terrace, or about the kinds of plants you would use to ward off a cold are used with empirical evidence related to material practices and the local environment to add to the depth of interpretation of Kashaya history and heritage at CA-SON-1889. Viewed in these terms, the Kashaya Pomo Interpretive Trail transforms the picturesque vista of the terrace into a community space. It is a schoolhouse where you brought children to learn, a place that reminds the contemporary community of its past and future, and part of a living heritage and landscape.

On December 10, 2015, the Kashia Band of Pomo Indians closed the acquisition of the Kashia Coastal Reserve, which gives the tribe access to and ownership of their coastal homelands after they were removed from them more than 150 years ago (Bay Area Open Space Council 2015). This event is a watershed moment and reminder of both the things the Kashia have lost and gained since the Russian American Company came to Metini. There is the potential through the kind of collaborative, community-based work represented by KPITP that archaeology can leave positive, lasting legacies so that in the future we can see the practices and communities such as the Kashaya in our contemporary imagination (see figure 17.3).

In writing the past, we also write the future. This carries with it a deep responsibility to do justice to these stories and, importantly, to the people connected to them in the present.

Notes

An earlier version of this essay appeared online in *Savage Minds: Notes and Queries in Anthropology*, December 23, 2015.

1. The Kashia Band of Pomo Indians of Stewart's Point Rancheria is the official, political name of the federally recognized tribal government. Tribal members and anthropologists also commonly use the alternate spelling "Kashaya" to refer to the tribal community. For the purposes of this paper, I use Kashia to refer to the tribal government and Kashaya or Kashaya Pomo to refer to the tribal community.

18

TO FIELDWORK, TO WRITE

Kim Fortun

Sometimes, to do fieldwork is to write. This was the way that fieldwork first went for me in the years in the early 1990s when I was working in Bhopal, India. My research was at the site of the "world's worst industrial disaster," resulting from a massive release of toxic chemicals over a sleeping city (from a US-designed pesticide plant). The devastation was horrific but debatable from the outset. Dead people and animals were strewn across the city, rows of the dead covered in white sheets paved hospital courtyards. The sounds of coughing and grief were overwhelming and unforgettable. Disaster was blatant and flagrant, yet it was still a struggle to account for it in words and politics.

It was years later that I was told and read about the sounds and sights of Bhopal in the days just after December 3, 1984. Journalists, activists, academics, poets, and many who were tangles of all these had helped with the accounting. Stories about the plight of gas victims were also, always, stories about cover-up and denial. Even the basics—the numbers of dead, the number exposed, the number injured—were (and remain) in dispute. At the thirtieth anniversary of the gas leak in 2014, activists were still mobilizing to revise the death record.

I was in Bhopal six years after the gas leak, when the legal case was before the Indian Supreme Court. It was a politically fraught, discursively troubled time. The Indian state was neoliberalizing, Hindu nationalism was on the rise, and leftist activists were mobilized against an increasingly ominous state-multinational complex, working to connect an array of people's movements linking farmers, fisherpeople, tribals, and those working against big hydroelectric projects in the Himalayas and Narmada Valley. Early use of computers in and on behalf of the grassroots animated and increased the sheer volume of writerly output.

I spent my time writing legal documents, press releases, and pamphlets for students and journalists on behalf of gas-leak survivor organizations. I also helped a former plant worker, T. R. Chouhan, write his account of what went wrong in the factory; he wanted his story in English so it could be widely read around the world. Bhopal had already been extensively written about. The challenge was to figure out what more needed to be said, in what forms, and with what timing. Writing required thinking about the discursive terrain we were operating within and about how different forms of argument, evidence, and symbolism were likely either to work or to go awry. Writing was a way to work alongside my research "subjects" (emically) and a way to work together to understand the political and discursive conditions within which we worked—collaboratively producing "etic" perspective. Ethnography thus had to loop: to figure out what to focus on and write about, one had to have already paid deep ethnographic attention.

But I have written about this before. Indeed, writing was both the subject and the challenge of *Advocacy after Bhopal* and of the PhD dissertation that came before: a dissertation painfully shaped, chapter by chapter, around the different genres in which advocacy in Bhopal was carried out. I wanted to convey how form mattered, encoding how fiction works differently from the legal affidavit or field reporting in the style of human rights activists. The memorably harsh stories of Mahasweta Devi, which reading Spivak had taught me to read, were an important catalyst that powerfully demonstrated what different genres can deliver.

Writing Late Industrialism

What more needs to be said and written now, about writing as fieldwork, and writing in and about disaster? Maurice Blanchot's book *The Writing of the Disaster* has been an important touchstone for me for many years, conveying how writing—especially of disaster but also beyond—is always violent, involving cutting and slicing that attends to some things and ignores others. Haunted by world wars, Hiroshima, and the Holocaust, Blanchot places his insistence on writing, nevertheless. A challenge I pose for myself is to temporalize this injunction, to put it in our particular historical moment as a call to responsibility and critical, creative practice.

I think it can be said that writing is an especially important way to participate in and observe the conditions of our times, times I have written about as "late industrial,"[1] characterized by discursive density and risk, expertise of remarkably high order, oiliness, and slow as well as fast disaster. Neoliberalism and fundamentalism now saturate the discursive terrain rather than work as oppositional terms. Computation enables both surveillance and slick-to-the-point-of-slimy PR while also providing fundamentally new ways of accounting for and connecting people and problems. Big data, informatics, and new visualization capabilities both feed the monster of commercialism and provide ways to see and address problems previously discounted or disavowed.

New modes of producing and working with data pose special challenges for ethnographers. We must learn to read the formative influences on and of data and informatics, and learn to use data and informatics as we have learned to use ethnographic writing: tactically, reaching across scale, working against dominant systems of representation, working otherwise.

Consider, for example, how ethnographers might learn to read and make use of newly available "smart city" data—data about transportation flows, air pollution, and environmental public health—to better understand how a city works, how urban imaginations and planning are directed, and how (late industrial) cities are data interpolated. Then we must consider how to leverage, animate, and travel with such data in our own ethnographic expressions— building our own data-enriched visualizations, mapping data pathways— where and how differently configured data can move and possibly redirect social formations.

Writing Against, Writing Forward

It is thus a time of writing against, and of writing forward: writing against the present, and writing the present forward, to futures underdetermined by it.

Ethnographers can write against the elisions of public-relations machinery that (still, decades later) tells us that toxic sludge is good for you,[2] that industrial chemistry is "essential2life,"[3] and that high concentrations of ground-level ozone are good for business.[4] And they know what they write against more acutely in the very crafting of sentences and claims, through which we understand how deeply commercialism and what I think of as "industrial logic" have saturated available concepts, terms, and the very way we think about and practice language. Industrial logic is a ruthlessly essentialist logic, bounding meaning and responsibility in ways out of synch with the saturated, soiled grounds on which "life" is now figured (see figure 18.1).

Writing against challenges hegemony (vernacular and theoretical); it enacts "anthropology as cultural critique." Writing forward without overdetermination is even harder, depending on mixes of forms, deeply experimental sensibilities and practices, and technical as well as rhetorical creativity: creativity that literally creates, putting different issues, scales, data, and types of analysis together in new ways. Creativity that puts people—across geography, discipline, and social standing—in new formations, leveraging different kinds of code (social as well as technical), literally reordering things.

Philosopher Dan Price's work points to the kinds of creative remixing I am calling for. Author of *Without a Woman to Read* and *Touching Difficulty*, Price is an amazing reader of reading, writing, and formations of the ethical. He has also helped write the maps at the center of the Houston Clean Air Network.[5] Houston has long had difficulty with its air, but it has taken high-end technology to make that difficulty more visible and accountable. And the difficulties are far from over. The state of Texas is leading an effort today to discredit the science supporting stricter ozone standards that would again put Houston (as well as many other cities) out of compliance with federal standards.[6] Price is not simply pushing information about levels and health impacts of ozone out to the public, merely correcting an information deficit. His goal in mapping Houston, with plans to draw in new data sets in coming years, is to refresh and reorder the semiotic field, and the ways people relate to both knowledge and one another: rebooting possibilities for sense making. The ends are thus underdetermined and inconclusive with purpose. It is arche writing, with political purchase.[7]

This, I think, is what it will take to write out a world that isn't overdetermined by what has come before. It will take new kinds of work and writing, and an expansive sense of what writing can be and do. Old oppositions—between the theoretical and the practical, the literary and calculative, the hermeneutic and definitive—must shift and reformulate.

Writing Futures

As I write here, for example, my student Pedro de la Torre also writes, in keeping with the work of Hanford Challenge and other organizations working to shape the cleanup and long-range stewardship of the Hanford Nuclear

FIGURE 18.1. The 1995 book *Toxic Sludge Is Good for You* describes how the waste management industry sponsored a contest to come up with the name *biosolids,* then "went about moving the name into the dictionary and insuring that the dictionary definition of the name would not include the word *sludge.*" The name stuck. PR Watch reported in 2013 that the U.S. Composting Council (USCC) (partnering with companies like Waste Management) now sponsors "International Compost Awareness Week," calling for "gardeners to celebrate by joining the USCC's Million Tomato Compost Campaign, which connects community gardens, compost producers, chefs, and food banks to grow healthy soil, healthy food, and healthy communities." Sourcewatch describes the U.S. Composting Council as "a front group for dumping sewage sludge onto gardens and farms." The linkages are complicated, and this is what ethnographers need to parse and write-out. *Biocycle,* a magazine published by the USCC, also (according to deeply credible ethnographic interlocutors), "legitimately advocates for organics recycling on every level, so hard to say if they are purely a front for the biosolids industry or if it's just part of it." The image here was the widely circulated poster for the campaign, promoted by celebrity chefs like Nathan Lyon.

Reservation, where the United States produced most of the plutonium used in its nuclear arsenal, including the plutonium used in the atomic bomb dropped on Nagasaki in 1945.[8] Today, Hanford Nuclear Reservation is the most contaminated nuclear facility in the United States and also the nation's largest environmental cleanup effort.[9] Like Bhopal, Hanford can and should be connected to an array of issues and movements focused on nuclear weapons and power; on rights of indigenous nations, downwinders, downstreamers, and exposed workers; and on what the US Department of Energy calls "long term stewardship"[10] and "legacy management."[11] Just imagine (or just imagine how hard it is to imagine) what needs to be written for this—for stewardship of forever toxic sites over the very *longue durée*—on the order of thousands (or tens of thousands, or millions) of years. There is a large plume of iodine-129 in Hanford's groundwater; its half-life alone is 15.7 million years. What kind of writing can address this?

De la Torre has blogged for Hanford Challenge, has helped develop materials for educational campaigns, and has given presentations about future land-use maps and the challenge of visualizing Hanford's past, present, and future. Like Bhopal, Hanford has been extensively photographed,[12] mapped,[13] filmed,[14] drawn and painted,[15] and written about.[16] And much of the effort has been recognized as cultural work aimed at changing the way that people think about the problems at hand, at possibilities for collaborative action, and about how the future can and should be configured. There are enduring conflicts of interest and interpretation. Together with one of Hanford's unions, for example, Hanford Challenge recently announced a legal action against the Department of Energy that calls for DOE to finally deal with workers' exposures to toxic chemical vapors from Hanford's aging high-level nuclear waste tanks—after decades of reports, discussion, and disavowals.[17] Hanford Challenge is thus writing against, while writing forward; de la Torre studies and writes about the dynamics of this by helping Hanford Challenge write. Ethnography loops, with critical intent.

Many of Hanford's injuries aren't blatant and flagrant; the violences are slow and insidious, and make no sense in usual terms. De la Torre, as an ethnographic fieldworker, is writing in many ways to make sense of this, in process mapping and helping refigure discursive terrain. Such is what is called for by the many slow disasters of our times: Bhopal, Hanford, and so many others. Ethnographers need to be in the mix, not only writing about but also writing alongside those we work with, building code, big data, and play with visualization into ethnographic practice, as a way to better understand, write against, and write past the formative conditions of our times.

FIGURE 18.2. Photos of people missing in the aftermath of the Bhopal gas leaks.

A crude board of photographs (see figure 18.2) of people missing in the aftermath of the Bhopal gas leak haunts and guides the work I describe here. The board—a crude information technology—was a sad representation of loss and was grossly inadequate for the task at hand. Upgrades are needed. The hazards signs that today mark Bhopal, Hanford, and other toxic sites also point to a challenge for ethnographers. Identifying and calling out hazards continue to be critically important. But more needs to be said and done. We need to write back but also forward.

Notes

An earlier version of this essay appeared online in *Savage Minds: Notes and Queries in Anthropology*, September 14, 2015.

1. Kim Fortun, "Ethnography in Late Industrialism," *Cultural Anthropology* 27, no. 3 (2012): 446–64, http://www.culanth.org/articles/135-ethnography-in-late-industrialism.

2. Rebecca Wilce, "Trade Group Offers Free Sewage Sludge 'Compost' to Community Gardens in 'Million Tomato Campaign' for Food Banks," PR Watch, May 9, 2013, https://www.prwatch.org/news/2013/05/12103/trade-group-offers-free-sewage-sludge-compost-community-gardens-million-tomato-ca. Also see Center for Media and Democracy, "Portal: Toxic Sludge," May 2015, https://www.sourcewatch.org/index.php?title=Portal: Toxic_Sludge.

3. Kim Fortun, "Essential2life," *Dialectical Anthropology* 34, no. 1 (March 1, 2010): 77–86, https://doi.org/10.1007/s10624-009-9123-8.

4. Jamie Smith Hopkins, "Battle over Smog Standard Heats up, with Dueling Arguments over Cost," Center for Public Integrity, March 17, 2015, accessed August 20, 2019, https://publicintegrity.org/environment/battle-over-smog-standard-heats-up-with-dueling-arguments-over-cost/.

5. Houston Clean Air Network, Houston, Texas, accessed August 18, 2019, https://houstoncleanairnetwork.com/.

6. Jamie Smith Hopkins, "Texas Aligns Itself with Industry in Fight against Tighter Smog Standards," Center for Public Integrity, March 17, 2015, accessed August 20, 2019, https://publicintegrity.org/environment/texas-aligns-itself-with-industry-in-fight-against-tighter-smog-standards/. See also Tony Barboza and Priya Krishnakumar, "Does Your County Violate the EPA's New Smog Limits?," *Los Angeles Times*, November 25, 2014, accessed August 20, 2019, http://spreadsheets.latimes.com/epa-tightens-regulations-ozone-pollution/.

7. See Jacques Derrida, *Of Grammatology* (Baltimore: Johns Hopkins University Press, 1998).

8. Pedro de la Torre III, "An Unsettled Future," Inheriting Hanford Blog, May 31, 2015, accessed August 20, 2019, https://inheritinghanfordblog.com/2015/05/31/an-unsettled-future/.

9. Taylor Kate Brown, "25 Years on at America's Most Contaminated Nuclear Waste Site," BBC News Magazine, June 11, 2014, accessed August 20, 2019, https://www.bbc.com/news/magazine-26658719.

10. Long-Term Stewardship Resource Center, Office of Environmental Management, U.S. Department of Energy, accessed August 20, 2019, https://www.energy.gov/em/services/communication-engagement/long-term-stewardship-resource-center.

11. Office of Legacy Management, U.S. Department of Energy, accessed August 20, 2019, http://energy.gov/lm/office-legacy-management.

12. Declassified photos, "Safe as Mother's Milk: The Hanford Project," accessed August 20, 2019, http://www.hanfordproject.com/photos.html.

13. PNNL Hanford Online Information Exchange (PHOENIX), Pacific Northwest National Laboratory, Richland WA, U.S. Department of Energy, accessed August 20, 2019, http://phoenix.pnnl.gov/apps/gisexplorer/index.html.

14. *Arid Lands*, directed and produced by Grant Aaker and Josh Wallaert, Sidelong Films, San Francisco, CA, 2007, accessed August 20, 2019, http://www.sidelongfilms.com/aridlands/film.html.

15. "Particles on the Wall," From Hiroshima to Hope, Green Lake, Seattle, WA, accessed August 20, 2019, http://fromhiroshimatohope.org/particles-on-the-wall-exhibit.

16. Shannon Cram, "Becoming Jane: The Making and Unmaking of Hanford's Nuclear Body," *Environment and Planning D: Society and Space* 33, no. 5 (2015): 796–812, doi: 10.1177/0263775815599317.

17. Hanford Challenge Press Releases, Hanford Challenge, Seattle, WA, accessed August 20, 2019, https://www.hanfordchallenge.org/press-releases.

19

QUICK, QUICK, SLOW

Ethnography in the Digital Age

Yarimar Bonilla

In his contribution to this volume, Michael Lambek offers some reflections on the virtues of "slow reading." In an era of rapid-fire online communication, as images increasingly substitute text, Lambek argues that we would be well served to revel in the quiet interiority and reflective subjectivity made possible by long-form reading.

I would like to think more carefully about this claim and to consider whether we might want to make a similar argument regarding the shifting pace of academic writing. If, as Lambek and others suggest, the temporality of reading has been altered by the digital age, can the same be said for research and writing? How have new digital tools, platforms, and shifts in technological access transformed the temporality of ethnographic writing, and is this something we necessarily wish to slow down?

I recently had occasion to experiment with sped-up academic pacing when offered the opportunity to contribute a piece to *American Ethnologist* about the protests surrounding the killing of Michael Brown in Ferguson, Missouri. In brainstorming our article, my coauthor, Jonathan Rosa, and I asked ourselves hard questions about what we could contribute to the unfolding discussion about Ferguson. Both of us had produced academic "slow writing," the product of years of careful research, analysis, drafting, and editing. We had also engaged in some forms of "fast writing." For example, I had published journalistic pieces on social movements in Puerto Rico and Guadeloupe. But these pieces focused on events not being covered in the mainstream media and for which informed journalism was necessary. The same could not be said of Ferguson. Despite an initial lag in journalistic coverage, by the time we were drafting our article, Ferguson had reached a point of media saturation; indeed, it had become a challenge to keep up with the numerous thought pieces and editorial columns emerging at a feverish pace during this time.

In plotting our article we thus asked ourselves: How can we contribute to this fast-moving conversation while still producing a piece that might hold up over time? That is, how could we produce something fast but not ephemeral?

The result was an exercise in mid-tempo research and writing.[1] It was not the product of long-sustained fieldwork, and it was very much written "in the heat of the moment," but it nonetheless tried to anticipate how anthropologists might look back on Ferguson over time—how they might use this event to teach and write about broader issues of racialization, longer histories of race-based violence, the racial politics of social media, and the shifting terrain of contemporary activism.

This process forced us to think about the challenges of being not just fast writers but fast ethnographers. How can we speak to fast-moving stories while still retaining the contextualization, historical perspective, and attention to individual experiences characteristic of a fieldworker? Also, how can we engage with emerging digital platforms such as Twitter with the cultural relativism characteristic of our discipline?

The latter requires us to take seriously the narrative genres and political possibilities afforded by new forms of digital communication without assuming that their speed robs them of their social complexity. For example, although some might see the prevalence of "memes" and the seeming dominance of image over text on the internet as an inherently negative development, as anthropologists we are well poised to recognize that shifts in communicative practices are neither inherently virtuous nor corrosive. Rather, they speak to, and are themselves generative of, a new set of social and political possibilities.

In the case of Ferguson, the fast-moving pace and ease of access afforded by Twitter helped activists and supporters bring heightened awareness to what would have otherwise been an underreported story. Moreover, it allowed many individual users for whom slow writing is not a possibility or a desired practice to engage in forms of creative expression and reflective activity that could challenge, contest, and contextualize mainstream print narratives in which they rarely see themselves adequately represented. The tweets, images, memes, and hashtags that circulated during this time (and which continue to circulate) should thus not be seen as cheap and fast substitutes for artisanally crafted modes of personal reflection. Instead, they need to be understood as complex texts, worthy of the same kind of close reading and critical analysis that scholars usually devote to other forms of prose.

Ethnography in the digital age requires us to avoid conflating the fast with the ephemeral or the vacuous. The aggregative and cumulative dimensions of social media, as well as its far-reaching scope, force us to rethink what constitutes an enduring or transformative social action. Attention to these practices also requires us to think more carefully about how we, as academic writers, can contribute to fast-moving conversations without giving short shrift to the kind of historical and analytical contextualization that is often absent in quickly changing public debate.

Notes

An earlier version of this essay appeared online in *Savage Minds: Notes and Queries in Anthropology*, March 30, 2015.

1. Yarimar Bonilla and Jonathan Rosa, "#Ferguson: Digital Activism, Hashtag Ethnography, and the Racial Politics of Social Media," *American Ethnologist* 42 (2015): 4–17.

20

THAT GENERATIVE SPACE BETWEEN ETHNOGRAPHY AND JOURNALISM

Maria D. Vesperi

For some time I have been trying to craft a narrative piece about post-traumatic stress disorder. I have the title, "Welcome Home Jimmy," words emblazoned on a homemade sign stretched over a celebratory backyard barbeque. I have the subject—a decorated US Navy pilot just back from three combat tours in a place that bore no familiar coordinates for his happy hometown crowd. I have the time line, critical because this scene spiraled out in signifiers that were clear to me only in retrospect. I have a broad set of readers in mind, and I know I can speak to them by conjuring up the smiling faces of relatives, friends, and friends of friends from that hot summer day. These are the folks who cut the grass and load the grill to welcome a loved one home from war. I even have an opening sentence: "No one mentioned that something was wrong with Jimmy."

Jimmy sweated in the modified dress blues he had donned for this occasion, game to please his combat veteran father and his older brother, a high-ranking reservist. Antiwar types in the group tried hard to look beyond the uniform, speaking with him of his bright civilian future or reaching back for anecdotes from high school and college. But despite his best efforts to be gracious, Jimmy looked strained around the eyes.

I am moved to write this account because I was "there" in Clifford Geertz's sense,[1] a guest at the event, an unwitting participant in a wounded young man's ultimately fatal realization that his pain could not be made visible. Questions of form bring me up short, though. I am confident in my ability to represent what I saw that day, and confident that Jimmy's distress points to something directly as a natural signifier, the way smoke points to fire. Linguistic anthropologist Alessandro Duranti puts this well: "The smoke does not 'stand for' the fire. . . . The actual smoke is connected, spatio-temporally and physically, to another, related, phenomenon and acquires 'meaning' from that spatio-temporal connection."[2] As Duranti and other linguists know, however, more nuanced indexical processes are also at work. These are best summarized for me by the old *New Yorker* cartoon where a Washington matron socializes near a window with the Capitol dome framed in the distance. Drink in hand, she remarks, "Where there's smoke, there's mirrors."[3]

I noticed Jimmy's eyes and promptly filed the information away, framing it only too late. The smoke in this case referenced signs that have since joined the cultural vernacular and are recognized collectively as post-traumatic stress disorder. But there was no name for his disquiet, not really, when Jimmy came home from Vietnam.

I was once an editorial writer and columnist, assignments that required training my sight on a goal and keeping IT there. I might be pushing an audience of one, the governor, to veto a pro-golf-course bill on Monday, after telling the newspaper's Sunday readership of 500,000 about the impact of stormwater runoff just the day before. The root danger, toxic chemicals, was the same, but the signs pointing to harm were not. The governor faced swift retribution from angry developers if he used his veto pen. The citizens faced long-term unease about harm to themselves, their children, even their pets, if he didn't. In each case, context, perspective, and the underlying, under-stated gift of tools—some might call them theories—for interpreting the story were key.

I haven't decided if I should cast "Welcome Home Jimmy" as narrative journalism or as an ethnographic account. A piece I wrote some years back for *Anthropology News* keeps coming to mind: "Anthropology and Journalism: Attend to the Differences First."[4] A news platform would require Jimmy's full name and biographical details, a requirement I understand and accept but that his family might find troubling. In addition, Jimmy's ontological position as an individual at a unique moment is not the point. Jimmy's story is most tragic because it is so routine, so everyday life in the modern world: Henri Lefebvre's serene breakfast table with a nuclear bomb detonating in the background.[5] There are so many like Jimmy, stretching decades before and decades after, so many welcome-home barbeques, so many missed signs.

I write to share anthropological knowledge with wider audiences, to bring anthropological theories and research methods to bear on telling everyday life. In my own writing and in my term as general editor and current executive editor of *Anthropology Now* and its related projects, my goal has been to present anthropological findings, theories—and, most important, practical approaches for understanding the world—in ways that well-informed general readers can apply and make their own. For these reasons I am leaning toward a form of narrative ethnography that shares its sturdy models and methods as well as its story, delivering all in an accessible style that can capture the immediacy, openness, and, I would say, vulnerability of strong journalistic writing.

In the English edition preface to his ethnography on urban policing in the Paris suburbs, *Enforcing Order*, French theorist Didier Fassin provides a cogent description of what ethnography can add to the understanding of how police function in relation to the state and to their subjects in contemporary society. He questions this at first, writing reasonably, "After all, we have excellent accounts by journalists, vivid memoirs of former officers, and remarkable fictions in crime novels, detective movies and television series."[6] He adds that social scientists already participate in "the production of public representations of police work." But for Fassin, as for me, it is what he describes as "the combination of presence and distance"—being there for an extended period and then "bringing the larger perspective into being" through historical, social, political, and economic context—that gives ethnography its power.[7] Fassin explains that he privileges a narrative style with theory embedded in a way that doesn't halt the reader, making use of a structure I would describe in journalism as "long form" or "literary." He modestly refers to his book as "a tentative application of the art of storytelling to the monotony of routine."[8]

With Jimmy's story, I hope readers will walk away wondering, "Do I know that guy?" Here my goal is not to gift the certainty of recognition—as if I could—but to share the tools to see and interpret, to spot fire and give it a name. In thinking through ways to do this I keep coming back to *The Best Years of Our Lives*, a powerful 1946 film about returning from war. It was based on a book-length narrative poem, "Glory for Me," by journalist and World War II veteran MacKinlay Kantor. The poem, the screenplay adapted from it by Robert E. Sherwood, and the resulting feature film can be traced to a 1944 no-byline account from *Time* magazine, "The Way Home."[9] Firsthand reporting, blank verse, screenplay, and film—a big story in four genres united by themes of home, kinship, cultural values both shared and shattered. These themes thread through ethnographic narratives as well, and anthropologists share related challenges in how to shape them: time distortion in the construction of chronologies; the slippery, sometime ephemeral nature of dialogue; the effects of pseudonyms versus named individuals; and the implications of now-mainstream techniques of new journalism for transparency and claims to authority. But there are generative spaces between such obstacles, and those willing to explore them will find tools to welcome so many stories home.

Notes

1. Clifford Geertz, *Works and Lives: The Anthropologist as Author* (Stanford, CA: Stanford University Press, 1988).

2. Alessandro Duranti, *Linguistic Anthropology* (Cambridge: Cambridge University Press, 1997), 17.

3. Victoria Roberts, "Where There's Smoke, There's Mirrors," *New Yorker*, February 9, 1998.

4. Maria D. Vesperi, "Attend to the Differences First: Conflict and Collaboration in Anthropology and Journalism," *Anthropology News* 51, no. 4 (2010): 7–9.

5. This truly arresting cover image appears in Henri Lefevre, *Everyday Life in the Modern World* (New York: Harper and Row, 1971).

6. Didier Fassin, *Enforcing Order: An Ethnography of Urban Policing*, trans. Rachel Gomme (Cambridge: Polity, 2013), xi.

7. Fassin, *Enforcing Order*, xi-xii.

8. Fassin, *Enforcing Order*, xi.

9. "The Way Home," *Time*, August 7, 1944.

SECTION V

THE URGENCY OF NOW

21

WRITING ABOUT VIOLENCE

K. Drybread

After enduring the watery beans and undercooked rice served in Brazilian prisons for nearly three years, my taste buds couldn't wait to reencounter the restaurants of New York City when I returned from the field. It was a surprise to find that even the spiciest chana masala tasted insipid.

I was numb. Kind neighbors had to remind me to put on a coat when I left my apartment to walk to the library, even though the sidewalks were covered with ankle-deep snow. My nose didn't even twitch when I was forced to wait for a train on a piss-drenched subway platform.

Well-meaning friends recommended therapy. Graduate advisors suggested writing as a strategy for self-care. I watched movies instead.

One night, I selected Ônibus 174 (Bus 174), a slick documentary directed by José Padilha, which tells the story of a Rio bus robbery that turned into a nationally televised hostage situation. The film manages to vilify both impoverished black favela youths who turn to violence out of desperation, and the police officers who are tasked with keeping the violence that these young men perpetrate out of the neighborhoods where privileged Brazilians like Padilha live. I left the movie theater with hot tears in my eyes and cried for six hours. Then I opened a brand-new notebook and wrote without pause until I'd completely filled its pages with the seemingly endless reasons my fieldwork experiences led me to despise Padilha's film.

No one but me will ever read those pages. The writing they contain is too raw to share. I confirmed this a little while ago, when I pulled out that notebook to verify that the writing was as awful as I remembered; it was. Sure, I'd vividly described a few places and had jotted down the kernels of thoughts that have since ripened or that I'm still cultivating. But, overall, the prose was too emotional and self-absorbed to be ethnographic.

Unfortunately, that private notebook reads a lot like some of the texts I've recently read from emerging ethnographers who've studied violence in the field and have rushed to write publicly about their experiences before they've had the time to think them through. I commend these individuals for having the courage and the discipline to write, but I also worry that their writing might start a trend in which ethnographers of violence begin to privilege writing as a therapeutic, rather than a theoretical, endeavor.

Ethnographers of violence who are far, far more accomplished than I am have argued that writing can be a healing exercise; even as it plunges the anthropologist back into the field, it also offers a way to move beyond personal experiences of horror to arrive at larger conclusions about the human condition.[1] But the movement from therapy to theory is not as simple as this statement implies. It is only over time, and via multiple drafts, that writing permits the ethnographer to tease out the ways that intensely felt personal experiences of fear or suffering jarred their previous understanding and challenged them to rethink troublesome problems and uncomfortable truths from unexpected angles.

When we read Victoria Sanford (2003) or Jason de León (2015)—or many, many others who write about violence with style and grace—we don't always notice the intellectual labor that went into producing their work; instead, we feel the immediacy of the ethnographic encounter. The grit and urgency of the writing belie its polish. Many of us aspire to write so vividly, so personally.

Yet it is crucial to note that when we read texts such as Philippe Bourgois's *In Search of Respect* (2003), Michael Taussig's *Law in a Lawless Land* (2005), or Donna Goldstein's *Laughter out of Place* (2013), we are compelled by what the author tells us about the people and the places they have studied, not by what the author reveals about himself or herself.

This turning outward can make writing ethnographically about people who perpetrate egregious violence exceptionally hard. Not only do those of us who do this kind of work have to cautiously avoid slipping into so-called pornographic representation; we must also find a way to convey the humanity of people who do "inhuman" things, while also doing justice to the victims of their violence. Writing in the first person compounds these difficulties. How does one insert themselves, as ethnographer, into such a narrative?

In writing up my research on prison rapes and murders, I've struggled with the competing desires of wanting to present myself as a likable protagonist and wanting to honestly relate the ways that my ethnographic practice could not help but become entwined with the forms of violence that I've studied. As I've attempted to navigate between these two treacherous poles of representation, I've worried that my writing would become either disastrously self-exculpating or unnecessarily self-flagellating.

To solve this problem, I've tried positioning the ethnographer in the stories I write about violence as a character rather than as a robust and authentic representation of me. Rereading these drafts, I often feel like I've turned the violent events of my fieldwork into fiction. And then I wonder: Is turning into ethnographic fiction events that I experienced as being too real (and as having too-real consequences) just another way to avoid confronting their ethical ramifications?

These thoughts have led me to entertain a simpler solution: to pretend that the violence I either witnessed or experienced in the field did not happen at all. I would not be the first to elide physical violence in my ethnographic writing. In fact, I've admittedly written much less about the violent events that were central to my fieldwork than I have about the forms of structural violence that have shaped the ethnographic contexts in which I studied precisely because I find doing so to be less fraught than writing about specific instances of physical aggression or pain. But blood, bullets, and torn flesh were so prevalent in my research that I would feel dishonest if I wrote them out of my work.

Another course I've considered steering in writing about my ethnographic encounters with perpetrators of violence is to unequivocally position myself as observer rather than participant. But, to me, this would hearken back to the late nineteenth century, when ethnography was decidedly about the "other," not about the complex relationships that entangle us with people we might—especially when acts of murder or torture are involved—prefer to refer to as "them."

The choice I've made is to directly acknowledge both my discomfort with and my complicity in the violence that I've studied. The subsequent challenge is how to write this way without dipping into the egocentrism that sometimes plagues writing about ethnographic encounters with violence.

Moving from therapy to theory in writing about personal experiences of violence is intellectually demanding work, especially when the difficulty of the task is exacerbated by the imperative to publish quickly and often. But reflection, and time, must intervene to create enough distance between the visceral and the emotional aspects of certain ethnographic encounters if the ethnographer is going to successfully think through the ways that personal experiences of fear or suffering can illuminate larger patterns or problems.

When we privilege writing as a therapeutic exercise, we run the risk of forgetting that, at least for the ethnographer, writing should lead to analysis, not just catharsis.

Note

1. Kimberly Theidon, "'How Was Your Trip?' Self-Care for Researchers Working and Writing on Violence," Drugs Security and Democracy Program, DSD Working Papers in Research Security (New York: Social Science Research Council, 2014), https://kimberlytheidon.files.wordpress.com/2014/04/dsd_researchsecurity_02 _theidon.pdf.

22

WRITING ABOUT BAD, SAD, HARD THINGS

Carole McGranahan

Writing is not always easy. Sometimes the writing flows, and sometimes it doesn't. But writing about things that are emotionally weighty, heavy, and disturbing is a different kind of not easy.

Monday morning at my home in Colorado, I wrote a political asylum report for a victim of political violence in Nepal. Monday afternoon, bombs exploded near the Boston Marathon finish line, killing several people, in-juring hundreds, and stunning many (including me, a runner and native of Massachusetts). The next day, I read about a twenty-year-old Tibetan mother who self-immolated and died in Tibet, and I wrote two more Nepali political asylum reports, one especially gruesome, and then collapsed on the couch, paralyzed in a sort of grief and shock and despair at the bad things that human beings do to other human beings.

Writing felt necessary but debilitating. I could write about the particularly horrific asylum case only in short increments, writing a sentence or two, then turning to something that would allow me to breathe freely, breathe in some goodness and hope, and then exhale the horror. Write the horror down. Make sense of the horror for a judge. Or at least try to.

How is it that I have unconsciously developed a relative scale for how "bad" another's suffering is? Yet some asylum cases are just unbearable to read, to sit with, to know. I can't even imagine the "to live" part. What is the responsibility of the writer, of the anthropologist, when stories of people's suffering are in our hands? How do we meet that responsibility when we feel melancholy in the writing?

I've long written about politically charged topics: Tibet, guerrilla warfare, the CIA, menstrual blood and bullets, and so on. However, it wasn't until I started serving as an expert witness in Nepali political asylum cases that I came to experience other people's suffering in a deeply personal way. As expert witness, my role is to testify that the claimed details of political persecution in an asylum petitioner's case are consistent with the political conditions in the country. As an anthropologist, my job is also one of testimony, of speaking truth to life (not just to power), of representing and interpreting people's lives as ones mired—for better and for worse—in cultural systems composed of contradictions. Both of these require the ability to get at insider and outsider understandings of any given situation, to make the one understandable or minimally translatable to the other.

In April 2012 the journal *Cultural Anthropology* published a special collection of essays on the self-immolations in Tibet. Duke University anthropology professor Ralph Litzinger and I edited the collection, working over a two-month period with eighteen other scholars and writers to write about the thirty-some Tibetans who had set themselves on fire and died. One year later that number was 120, as 80 more Tibetans had self-immolated in just one year. Today, as I update this essay in August 2019, 164 Tibetans have self-immolated as a form of protest against Chinese rule in Tibet. Both painfully and poignantly, the contributors to the essay collection collectively tried to speak to this unfolding phenomenon, attempting to provide context, background, acknowledgment, and recognition, and to provide answers to questions that we knew we could not answer. One day, after having spent seventy-two hours straight reading and editing the final versions of the essays, I realized a depression had set over me. The weight of so many stories of death, of bodies burning, of political intractability, and the feeling of being so small in the face of all this were overwhelming. Yet the collective power and strength and compassion of the writers was also there, especially the unanimous sense among the contributors that our writings were needed, could contribute something, were meaningful in some way, including, but not limited to, our own individual feelings of humanity and obligation as we witnessed individual after individual setting themselves on fire. And still, the heaviness of it all.

What are the stakes of writing about emotionally difficult topics? The social and political stakes are clear to me; I write about issues that I believe to be important, issues that should be better known, issues on which we collectively need to hear new and valuable perspectives. The personal and emotional stakes are not always as clear. I still feel unprepared for my own deep-felt reactions. The emotions generated from writing on hard, sad topics are real and need tending to. I have multiple strategies for addressing them: stepping away from the computer, reaching out to friends and family, going for a run, focusing on positive things, reading poetry, finding music that feels right in the moment, turning to a ritual such as making a pot of homemade chai, reminding myself that what I feel is but a tiny fraction of the pain felt by the person who experienced it firsthand.

I am grateful for those anthropologists and other writers who have led the way, whose works on violence and suffering I have read and I have taught and I have learned from: Val Daniel, Gina Athena Ulysse, Veena Das, Michael Taussig, Ruth Behar, Donna Goldstein, and so many others. I am grateful I have knowledge that sometimes can be used to help others. And I am grateful for the power of writing, for when I return to it after pausing, writing always ultimately enables me to address, to engage, and to remain undefeated by bad, sad, hard things.

Note

An earlier version of this essay appeared online in *Savage Minds: Notes and Queries in Anthropology*, April 18, 2013.

23

WRITING TO LIVE

On Finding Strength While Watching Ferguson

Whitney Battle-Baptiste

I am a writer.

This simple statement is a recent revelation. Although I am a scholar who reads and interprets, thinks critically about theory, and teaches many aspects of writing, those actions have never made me a writer. Claiming "writer" was never something I thought about. The strength I pulled from writing was from reading the words of others, not writing my own. When I was a child, books kept me grounded and helped me to imagine. As I matured, books became a source of the familiar, tools I used to orient myself and keep connected after I left home. I was born in the early 1970s, on the island of Manhattan, and grew up in the shadows of tall buildings with concrete at my feet. I read about survival but never wrote about it. I was one of those folks who could never maintain a journal for more than a week. I always leaned on the strength of others to work through life's ups and downs. These words were always healing, grounding, necessary for survival.

In the early years of graduate school, I felt lost and out of place. I was far from home physically and mentally. I was leaning on the words of others again. Yet I saw the opportunity to begin to weave my own history into my scholarship, probably a reason that I chose anthropology. Today, I use words to help me understand the world around me, the cyclical rhythm of time and space. I now know the difference between the words of others and the words I pull together; they have become my method of healing and grounding myself.

I am a writer even when the words escape me.

Recently, I have not been able to pull my words together, for they don't come very easily. Making sense of the world around me is getting more complicated. When I search for the healing properties that words held in the past, I only find pain, hurt, and sorrow. I sense a disconnect between my identity as scholar and my identity as writer. As an archaeologist, I focus my scholarship on the material aspects of race, gender, and class within the fluid boundaries of the African diaspora. My work is settled firmly in the past, yet these days my thoughts are stuck in current moments of injustice, racism, and death. The murders of Michael Brown, Ezell Ford, John Crawford, and countless others were making my research feel hollow. And I knew I was due to contribute a blog post about writing. I was paralyzed because I could not shake this hollow feeling. As I watched the events unfolding in Ferguson, Missouri, through social media, I began to understand why I felt disjointed. Life is connected to our scholarship; that is why I am a writer.

I write about issues of race, gender, and class in the United States and parts of the Caribbean. I teach about slavery, colonialism, racism, and the realities of oppression throughout the world. And when one thinks globally, it is hard not to see the connection between the wars abroad and the wars at home. As I watched the militarization of a place such as Ferguson, I turned to my father, a veteran who toured during the post–Korean conflict, to shed some light on how this could happen here. I could not believe that even as someone who grew up in a place where we could not trust law enforcement, I had never seen it like that, so obvious and so transparent. I felt traumatized but in a different way. The conversations with my father helped me to think more critically about how I study and teach about race and gender and the lived experiences of people "on the ground." Why was I surprised that I was looking at full-on military accessories being used to combat unrest and dissent on the streets of Ferguson? Why was I surprised that, according to my brother, a veteran of Desert Storm, the spoils of war had made it into the vaults of a local police station? For there are many people all around us who live with the wars they left behind and keep these memories close to their chests. I had to fill the emptiness in order to write, so I looked to the people close to me to help make sense of it all. You see, almost every man in my family has been in the military. I felt as if I was seeing the wars come home, as my father and brother helped me to find those missing words. I was able to pull strength from their words in order to reconnect my multiple identities. The writer and the scholar, or maybe the scholar-writer within.

I learned more than I expected from these two men. I began to think differently about race and trauma from the men in my family, and I learned just how close the effects of post-traumatic stress disorder (PTSD) were to me. These conversations made me understand why Ferguson affected me so deeply. For when PTSD and race come together, a different story emerges. It also cut deeper because I now have two sons of my own to raise in this country that is so committed to violence. I am also able to expand my understanding of the intersection of racism, gender, trauma, and pain through their eyes and words. The work of a writer is hard at times. But when you pull those words together, perhaps, in some small way they can be used to heal, ground, and recuperate yourself and others. Thank you to my father and my brother; you helped me to fill the emptiness and find the words again.

I write to understand. I write to heal. I write to teach. I write to live.

Note

An earlier version of this essay appeared online in *Savage Minds: Notes and Queries in Anthropology*, November 26, 2014.

24

FINDING MY MUSE WHILE MOURNING

Chelsi West Ohueri

February is the worst month of the year. I keep repeating these lines in my head as I stare at the blank screen. I struggle to think of anything else to say. The beginning of this month is now becoming some sort of a routine.

My dad taught me to write in the early-morning hours. "When I was your age," he used tell me, "I went to bed early so that I could wake up around 4 a.m. and do my homework when the house was quiet." Around age eleven or twelve I began to emulate this practice, although I never quite got a handle on the waking-up-early part, so instead I just developed late-night writing habits. To this day, I usually produce some of my best work between midnight and 5 a.m. When I think about it, my dad helped me to craft much of my approach to writing.

Whenever I wrote papers for school assignments, he corrected them for mistakes, or, as I remember more vividly, he dismantled them. He always asked questions aloud too, the kind of questions where the first time I might answer and he would quickly add that the question was rhetorical and did not require an answer but then the second time, if I remained silent, he would look at me with a "Well, I'm waiting for an answer" type of face. "What kind of sentence is this?" he often asked. "And, and, really? Who is teaching you that you can begin a sentence with and?" Inside of my seventh-grade mind, I recalled that people often began sentences with "and" during everyday conversation. What was different about words on paper? I smile when I think about the so-called rules of writing like this one because when I consider some of my favorite pieces, they are usually ones in which the rules are pushed, bent, broken, or rewritten altogether. My dad, though, just wanted me to succeed, to excel. He read my college essays and listened to each talk that I gave. He wanted me to be the best: he wanted me to shine. His energy, his cheer, his hope all became my muse.

He died without warning on February 1, 2012, on a crisp Wednesday afternoon, with not a cloud in the sky. He was buried exactly one week later, on February 8, an unwieldy day soaked with invasive rain, the kind of rain that pesters, slowly creeping into every inch of your being. His birthday is February 23. I tried to quit graduate school after he died. I put on a pair of his old pajamas and planted myself in his chair, announcing to the world that I had no intention of ever leaving, which did not last long because my mother made me return to school later that semester.

There is a certain melancholy that lingers after a loss, a feeling in which you want to remember every single thing so that you will never forget, but simultaneously never wanting to recall any memory or thought because it might torment. For me this feeling is intensified in February. The entire month is one long spastic sequence, a reckless oscillation between laughter and agony, between motivation and stagnation. It is exhausting. During this time, writing can morph from excruciatingly painful to liberating in such a short span of time.

I think back to many sympathy cards that we received, ones that begin with lines such as "There are no words . . ." or "When words fail . . . ," and this has me thinking: Why have I never seen a greeting card with an expression of words working or doing their job? How exactly are words failing? At times, I am overwhelmed with moments of dense, sharp silence, but there are other periods of relentless chatter, swelling with nonstop sentences and an inability to control my utterances. I am not sure if words are necessarily always failing during grief because at times it feels as if they are successfully betraying me. They fool me, they tease me, and then sometimes they slap me in the face. I think that more often than not I am just uncertain of what to do with my words, and I panic when they materialize in some unrecognizable form on paper.

"Why don't you try to write through this?" I have been asked this question many times, and I still cannot make much sense of it. I have never been too sure of my position or role as a writer. However, I do know that it has been impossible to write *through* whatever this grief is. Whenever I have tried to write *through* it, the erratic emotions erupt all over again. Just when I think I am "keeping it together," I start to fall apart. I experience long, wordless lulls that give birth to gaps and pauses that I neither recognize nor comprehend. Sometimes my words make no sense at all. Other times I write with a maniacal fury, composing pieces that make me jump up with an enormous energy for a spontaneous dance break, the kind of celebration that rivals the response to a one-handed touchdown grab. I write while laughing. I write while crying. However, to whatever other side I am supposed to be writing *through*, I do not know where that is.

Therefore, this February and for every February that follows, I think it may be time for me to abandon this idea of writing *through* and instead try writing *with* this grief. The grief hangs with me, and as long as I am trying to write *through* it, I think I will be disappointed when it is still there. And sometimes, the fear of failure stops me from writing anything at all, just as the fear of never finding my muse again holds my hands hostage when I try to write. I smile now, though, because I know that somewhere my dad cringed when I began that sentence with and. I smile too because I know I carry my dad's voice, his corrections, his thoughts, his smile each time I write.

My muse is not missing. I think it just transformed. Perhaps those of you reading may also have experienced deep hurt or traumatic loss along your writing journey, and if so, I share this with you today to begin a dialogue about the ways that we carry these pains along with us. Writing, like grieving, is very much a process, and neither happens in a linear fashion. I think what is important for all of us to remember is that while we try to make sense of it all, we remember just that: we are all learning how to navigate. We write. We shape. We cut. We ache. We dream. We create.

Note

An earlier version of this essay appeared online in *Savage Minds: Notes and Queries in Anthropology*, February 9, 2015.

25

MOURNING, SURVIVAL, AND TIME

Writing through Crisis

Adia Benton

"Everyone identifies with the survivor." The man, whose name I have yet to learn, wore a sage-colored newsboy cap. We were sitting next to each other at my neighborhood café. A half-hour before, he was several feet away, sketching, occasionally eyeing my copy of Frantz Fanon's *The Wretched of the Earth*. "Pardon me," he said, as he approached my table. "I couldn't help but notice that you're reading. . . ." Within minutes, our conversation about radical anti-imperialist writing and secret societies had devolved into a meditation on how humans cope with tragic and sudden death.

"Everyone identifies with the survivor," he repeated, as he adjusted his sketchpad in his lap.

"I don't," I said.

The man paused for a moment and raised his eyebrows as if he didn't believe me. I recounted the story of an old work buddy, James (a pseudonym), who had died in a helicopter crash in West Africa about ten years before. At the end of the story, I repeated a peculiar tidbit I had heard from a mutual friend about the last moments of James's life: "He was so committed to the organization that he threw his papers and laptop out of the window so that no important documents would be lost."

As I talked, the memories of working with James at an international nongovernmental organization (NGO) in Sierra Leone came flooding back:

James demanding that we consume beers at "the last station" during his field visits from the capital, all-employee chats on the staff guesthouse roof, and sober meetings in the dust-covered office on the main floor of our rural office building. And there were memories that were figments of my imagination: a frightened and determined James tossing office memos, reports, and contracts out the window of a rapidly descending aircraft. It didn't matter if the memories were real or not; they haunted me. For far too many nights in those weeks after his death, I was startled awake by dreams that placed me on the helicopter: dreams that had me convinced that I had been substituted in his place.

The man in the newsboy cap smiled sympathetically. I had proven that I identified with the dead. He said I had told a "great story." But I felt embarrassed and self-conscious. A decade had gone by, and I hadn't raised a glass in James's memory. I think he would have liked that. I had not really even told this story—not in this way. Perhaps I had shied away from retelling this story and from the rituals of memorialization because the circumstances of his death felt too raw; they reminded me of my vulnerability, that thing I wanted to forget and denied daily as I toiled away, psychically and spiritually impaired, in a place haunted by war.

It occurs to me that the man in the newsboy cap had nudged me toward an uncomfortable truth. Although I was at first convinced that I didn't strongly identify with the survivors, my uneasy relationship to James and his place in my story revealed a hitherto sublimated, yet profound, discomfort with being a survivor. But it was only in writing this essay, during an escalating Ebola crisis in West Africa, that I was able to get to the point of processing and acknowledging this discomfort, of interrogating my insistence that I didn't identify with the survivor, that I wasn't like everyone else. It had taken me years to write about James's death—though he had appeared in my writing in allusion to other, mundane things—and it had taken weeks to extricate meaning from the chance café encounter sparked by a shared interest in Fanon.

In some ways I remembered something that I have known for quite a while: certainly we can all write things on the fly, and those things might even be smart, insightful, or poignant. In fact, sometimes we are compelled to write in the moment, driven by an ethnographic sensibility and knowledge. This writing in the moment is motivated as much as by anger and grief as it is informed by ethnographic encounters. It is not the same as the slow ethnography to which so many of us have become accustomed.

Time, especially for the ethnographer, can help to tease out uncomfortable truths and challenge deeply held notions of others and ourselves. The passage of time can encourage fuller reflection on the chance encounters that move us to think differently about the human condition. With time, intimate encounters and significant moments are relived and reimagined. They are reinvigorated as they are transformed from field notes and faint recollections into words on a page or coalesce into an argument. For me, this is what gives ethnographic writing its potential. Writing is reflection and presents an opportunity to do things with time. Ideas and images can bounce around in my head for weeks, months, or even years, making connections to one another, before I can finally write them down. Once the ideas, people, and places are there in front of me, vividly described and thoroughly undressed, they gradually regain their materiality. These figures, places, things, and their evocation in the written word smooth a path for identification with survivors and survivals, both real and imagined.

As an ethnographer who has conducted fieldwork in Sierra Leone and previously worked in the region where Liberia, Sierra Leone, and Guinea meet, it was probably no coincidence that the memory of James resurfaced there and then; that was the place where James died. It was also a region that was experiencing the worst outbreak of Ebola in the thirty-eight years since the disease was first identified. As I wrote essays about Ebola in West Africa and the United States—and watched my Twitter time line fill up with news about Ferguson, Gaza, and Syria—I found myself drawn to arguments about whose deaths were grievable, whose lives mattered, and how such calculations were made manifest in the actions of an international "community." I was reminded of how writing, no matter the tempo, had helped me to remember the dead, and the conditions of their living, in a way that settled uncomfortably between identifying with and being a survivor and empathizing deeply with the oppressed, the dispossessed, the policed.

There was little time to reflect and write about the unfolding events in the slow motion that ethnographic writing often requires. Yet I continued to write, supported not by the luxury of time but by the desire to make use of grief and anger. Writing lets me, for just a fleeting moment, pin down—perhaps even slow down—and make sense of an unfolding crisis. It may also help those of us who identify both as survivors, and with the dead, come to terms with our own grief.

Note

An earlier version of this essay appeared online in *Savage Minds: Notes and Queries in Anthropology*, October 20, 2014.

SECTION VI

WRITING WITH, WRITING AGAINST

26

A CASE FOR AGITATION

On Affect and Writing

Carla Jones

We are living in affective times. In anthropology, affect is in the air. We see it in journal themes, conference panel titles, and numerous other measures of anthropology's current interests. This feels relevant for thinking about writing. Feeling seems central to the reasons we write, even if we rarely say that out loud. We need to feel in the mood to write, feel ready to say something, feel safe to say it, feel passionately about saying it, and feel proud of it once we've said it. These sentiments undergird the conditions for ethnographic writing. These feelings contrast with the supposed objectivity of a social science based on only certain sorts of data and facts. In recent decades, supposed truths have been some of our favorite to critique, such that we now have a robust disciplinary critique about the fundamentally political and subjective nature of knowledge production. But, ironically perhaps, our feelings about these critiques are largely positive. Critique is affect at work.

I want to suggest that a key motivation to write is irritation. This may seem contrary and cranky. I don't mean for it to. For me it is empowering. I increasingly find that the nudge that takes me from mental idea to written word is much more than a deadline. It is a feeling that might be impolite. I find that I am most in the mood to write when I am agitated. Perhaps irritation sparks my desire to write anthropology because, at their best, anthropological conversations can turn agitation into attachment.

My research is about gender, style, and politics in contemporary Indonesia. These may seem like superficial topics to publics here in the United States. Instead, these topics open to issues timely in both countries and, in combination with race or religion, to issues of fear, violence, and discipline. But in the United States, Indonesia is far too little known a place for such connections to be made. The piety, for example, and the meaning of such piety of my predominantly Muslim friends and informants in Indonesia are not recognizable to most Americans. In Indonesia and in the United States, the zeitgeists in which my friends in both places currently live frame them as radically other to each other. They are depicted as so different that they could not share anything meaningful in common. However, while they certainly would disagree with each other on many things, I also know they would recognize fundamental familiarities between them. Some examples: most of my friends, in both places, are disappointed with their current political choices. They question their place in an imbalanced class system. They worry about getting ahead. They worry about looking good. They are stressed. They are bored. They worry about their parents, their partners, and their kids. In short, they have lots of feelings, and those feelings are often very similar. They often turn to similar forms of sociality to soothe these worries, like cooking, celebrating holidays with family, or going shopping.

Affect theory has emphasized that affect is about public feelings, not just personal emotions. Yet it is precisely public feelings that frame personal feelings as mutually unintelligible. And, if personal feelings are unintelligible, then the individuals holding them are similarly unrecognizable in nuanced or even human ways. In the United States, public representations of Islam currently position it as singular and sinister. Indeed, in these depictions Islam is threatening in large part because its adherents are imagined to be incapable of keeping their religious beliefs to themselves. In Indonesia, representations of the United States are similarly alien, frequently depicting a place where atheists have great wealth, few kin, and empty lives.

If ethnography is the antidote to misrepresentation, then stories about similar families, worries, and pastimes can say something humane in a sea of fearmongering. Stories can shorten cultural distance, even if only for a short time. Narrating similarity is something that anthropology does well at times, but we also know that anthropology has relied on categories of difference for its role in translation and narration. Our own stories of how things should be shape how we recognize humanity.

I am often asked a simple question: why did I choose to study Indonesia? Indonesians, Americans, students, and family members ask me this innocent, reasonable question. It isn't easy to answer. As I suspect is true for most anthropologists, the answer is a mix of choice and luck. I was lucky to be born to parents who raised me in Southeast Asia (in Hong Kong, the Philippines, and Singapore). Although I probably would have become an anthropologist even if I had not grown up abroad, I likely would not have focused on the countries in which I was raised: they were too familiar to me. As a college student in California, I had little interest in studying the places I already knew. I wanted to study a place that was just unfamiliar enough to still be a bit exotic. My university had an excellent program in Indonesian studies, so that is the place I chose. If I had gone to a different college, I might have chosen another place. Selecting Indonesia was both choice and luck.

Sharing a background story of that sort is vulnerable because it appears to threaten the emotional foundation that anthropologists are supposed to have with their research communities. We are supposed to fall in love with a place and a people, and have sentimental explanations for our choices. This is not always the case. Yet in spite of my own nonromantic journey, over the decades I have felt more and more connected to my Indonesian friends' feelings. Here or there, when a friend gets married, has a child, gets divorced, or loses a parent, these all cause me joy or pain. If I am truly lucky, I am able to be present for some of these events. Small things connect me, too, like being able to wander through a market arm in arm with a dear friend, bargaining and chatting with vendors. Or gossiping about cousins and colleagues while sitting in interminable traffic.

These small delights could be enough. The little joys of feeling close to people who, like me, are sorting out life as it comes to them, making sense of the contours as they emerge. But they aren't enough. It should be sufficient to simply want to relate those recognizable insecurities that we all share, but it isn't. I want anthropology to do more, and I want my writing to do more. So, instead, I find that nothing sends me to the keyboard faster than reading regrettably common and acceptable descriptions of Muslims in general, and Indonesians in particular, as provincial and anachronistic and dangerous. No writing block can endure the irritation born of my reaction to radical difference. Being agitated is truly empowering. And if writing is in any way a small solution to the continued circulation of conventional wisdoms that reproduce exclusions, then maybe getting cranky is good because it produces more writing. I would really like to live in a world where writing about the small things were enough. I would like to find myself in a world where I wasn't provoked, but until that day comes, here's to turning to the keyboard. Here's to feeling.

Note

An earlier version of this essay appeared online in *Savage Minds: Notes and Queries in Anthropology*, October 26, 2015.

27

ANTIRACIST WRITING

Ghassan Hage

To the people of the bus

In my recent work on racism I have differentiated between the "racism of exploitation" (e.g., toward slaves and migrant workers) and the "racism of exterminability" (e.g., anti-Semitism). I argue that the latter is more prevalent today in the racist modes of classification of Muslims in/by the non-Muslim West. As such, it requires a specific form of antiracist writing.

Inspired by certain dimensions of Eduardo Viveiros de Castro's multirealism, and the teaching of a seminar around Mauss's *The Gift*, I have tried to show that the racist experience of the other as exterminable involves the projection of complex layers of affective and existential angst that takes us beyond the dominant domesticating mode of existence in which we live and where instrumental classification thrives.[1] It invites us to perceive the experience as pertaining to a multiplicity of other realities and human modes of existence. The first is the reciprocal mode of existence classically explored in the work of Marcel Mauss on the gift. I read *The Gift* as pointing to a whole order of existence where people, animals, plants, and objects stand as gifts toward each other. The second is what I will call, after Marshall Sahlins, the mutualist mode of existence.[2] It highlights an order of existence where others are "in us" rather than just outside of us. Central here is Lucien Lévy-Bruhl's work on "participation": a mode of living and thinking where the life force of the humans and the nonhumans that surround us is felt each to be contributing to the life force of the other.[3]

Despite some facile claims to the contrary, neither Mauss nor Lévy-Bruhl claimed something as simplistic as "look at us: we are modern, instrumentalist, and rational, and look at those others who are so different from us living in a world of gift exchange, or a world of participation." Both emphasized that the logic of the gift and the logic of participation were more pronounced in those societies than they were in our own but that they were not as foreign to us as we might first think. They continue to be present along with, sometimes in the shadows of, the dominant domesticating mode of existence. They exist as minor realities. Thus, everything in our environment that we relate to is always simultaneously for us (domestication), with us (gift exchange), and in us (mutuality), even if we are less conscious of our enmeshment in the last two of these forms of relationality. I might decide to cut a tree on my property because I need its wood or simply because it is in the way. In so doing I am letting instrumental exploitative reason prevail. But does that mean that this instrumentalist relation of domestication is the only relation I have with the tree? What Lévy-Bruhl and Mauss encourage us to think is that even when a relation of domestication has prevailed, other forms of relationality between us and the tree are still at work. I might still feel that the tree and I were in a relation of "gift-ness" toward each other. I wake up in the morning and thank it for being there, and I might even feel that the tree itself is happy to see me there too. I might even experience a mild relation of mutuality with the tree, feel that not only is it a gift but that it is actually enhancing my existence: something about the way it is growing and deploying itself in the world actually pumps life into me.

In my work I have shown how important it is to see that the racism of exterminability is itself enmeshed in these three modes of existence. To classify people as exterminable is not only to see them instrumentally as harmful and useless. It is also to want to have "nothing to do with them," thus negating their "gift-ness." It also involves a "negative participatory" experience: rather than seeing in others a life-enhancing force, the racist sees in them something that sucks life away.

Because its articulation to this multiplicity of worlds is what makes racist exterminability what it is, antiracism itself needs to work at this multirealist level. Up till now, antiracism has been far too centered on combating racism at the level of domestication by deploying rational arguments and statistical knowledge that try to show the empirical falseness of the racists' assumptions. This is so despite a long history that shows how immune racists are to rational and empirical argumentation. Consequently, I argue that antiracism, without vacating this empirical/rational ground, should also move to think of itself as affective, and even as magical, in ways that speak to the racist sentiments and affects generated in the realm of reciprocity and mutuality.

It is here that we come to the question of antiracist writing. For what is true about antiracist practices in general is also true of antiracist writing. Writing is also enmeshed in a multiplicity of worlds with their corresponding forms of otherness. One can write "about" the racialized, treating them as passive subjects of analysis. There is no doubt that such a form of antiracist writing can be overanalytical, treating racism, racists, and the racialized as objects of what amounts to analytical domestication. This is when all writing aims to do is to "capture" reality, a concept with an impeccable domesticating pedigree. But this is not all that antiracist writing does or can do. One's writing can take the form of a gift to the racialized. There is a long tradition of sociological and anthropological writing reflecting on how to write "with" rather than just "about" one's informants. This is particularly true of ethnographies of indigenous people, where anthropologists have an established history of being sensitive to questions of reciprocity. Antiracist writers can learn a lot from these ethnographies. Finally, a piece of antiracist writing can be in itself a form of life that participates in enhancing the being of the racialized, aiming to speak to them in the sense of speaking into them and participating in their being. Sometimes this can be a question of style: it is hardly a revelation for antiracist activists that one can write something like "one in three African Americans will go to prison" as either a mere "depressive" confirmation of marginalization or as an invigorating call to arms stressing the racialized's agency and capacity for resistance. I think that the poetic/phenomenological tradition, such as what one finds in the work of Michael Jackson, can offer an inspiration for a more consciously mutualist writing in this domain.[4]

The question then becomes what it means to become more conscious of antiracist writing as enmeshed in this plurality of modes of existence. I would like to think that, at the very least, such consciousness would widen the writer's antiracist strategic capacities and render antiracist thought more efficient at combating racism. This opening of the strategic horizon is crucial as antiracist political forces face the lethal neoliberal forms of exclusion meted out on the racialized today. For example, the ease with which asylum seekers are radically expelled and disallowed to set a footing in society appears at one level as a form of instrumental/rational/bureaucratic decision making, even if judged as extremely harsh. Yet such extremism is impossible without a culture of disposability and exterminability in which this exclusion is grounded, and one that is far from being entirely instrumental/rational/bureaucratic. It goes without saying that from a disciplinary perspective it is this culture that is by definition the appropriate domain of anthropological investigation and writing. It so happens that, politically and ethically, this culture is also the most important to address, understand, and struggle to transform.

Notes

An earlier version of this essay appeared online in *Savage Minds: Notes and Queries in Anthropology*, October 27, 2014.

1. Eduardo Viveiros de Castro, *Cannibal Metaphysics: For a Post-structural Anthropology* (Minneapolis: Univocal, 2014); Marcel Mauss, *The Gift: The Form and Reason for Exchange in Archaic Societies* (London: Routledge, 1990).

2. Marshall Sahlins, *What Kinship Is—and Is Not* (Chicago: University of Chicago Press, 2013).

3. Lucien Lévy-Bruhl, *How Natives Think* (Princeton, NJ: Princeton University Press, 1985).

4. Michael Jackson, *At Home in the World* (Durham, NC: Duke University Press, 1995).

28

WRITING WITH LOVE AND HATE

Bhrigupati Singh

Reading precedes writing. Today, in this era of right swipes and social media selfhood, some say that the art of reading, and the kinds of commitment, attention span, and patience with words required for scholarship, is itself becoming endangered. What does the future hold for us scholars? To be a soothsayer, that is to say one who can comment on the changes that drifts may bring, one must look not only to today but also to yesterday and to the day after tomorrow. There was a time, for instance, when scholars primarily wrote not in the form of the essay but in a more difficult and older art of texting—namely, sutras or aphorisms.

LET US NOT underestimate the new forms of attentiveness that are emerging. Instagram, for instance, which for some discerning readers, in its minimization and subordination of text, creates new possibilities for thinking images serially and for enabling independent associations.

SOME ASSOCIATIONS AND FORMS of sociality can turn one into a misanthrope, like the saccharine affirmations and modes of self-presentation made commonplace by a semipublic sphere like Facebook. These affirmations are no more likable than the variably anonymous, obnoxious negations of trolling. To say yes and no, to examine our account of ourselves and others: that is what we learn to do in writing. And thus, with the hope of retaining these measures we attach ourselves, perhaps too securely, to the length of the essay rather than to the strip of the sutra.

READING PRECEDES WRITING. A senior colleague in this volume suggests that before writing he picks up a good book to read, even for a few minutes. That's fine, but there is a crucial qualification. Just because food is necessary for life, we don't run around stuffing our faces with the first thing we find. The crucial question is one of diet. What is our food for thought? For two years or so my diet consisted mainly of Nietzsche. As you can see, for good and for ill, it had an effect. Even now, I am careful about what texts I come near to, in terms of sustained exposure. For instance, Heidegger inflates me in a way that I always regret and cringe at, once enough time has passed, and I have returned—to what? To think is to be beside oneself. Dependably so. And when then of independence?

FOR A MOMENT, here, I am free of the necessity of citations. And yet I keep quoting. When are we not quoting? Often we read books that are merely echoes, a few local colors re-creating a picture we already had. A different line or circle, or a new joining of disconnected dots is a kind of revolution.

LET ME NOT overstate the difference between the essay and the sutra. Emerson's essays, for instance, are sometimes aphorisms lined up alongside one another, like plants. We may have other such forms lurking within us. Sometimes a potent fragment is tucked away under other sentences in a book or an article. Sometimes the achievement of an essay lies only in a single sentence, where something is essayed. I once managed to reach such a line: "As our bus neared the village of Mamoni, my destination for now, I was startled by a luminous orb hovering close by, atop a low hill. I had seen it before. Nonetheless, this was the first time the moon chose to reveal itself to me, so blatantly round and brilliant and near. No wonder dogs howl and tides stir. Ours are water bodies too."[1]

Ours are water bodies too. This sentence was given to me by the inspiration, that is to say the inward outward breath of the landscape of Shahabad. Now a four-lane highway runs through that landscape and blocks many of the byway vantage points passing through which I slowly gained this insight. But maybe others will proceed and see differently. At any rate, I remain grateful for having been the vehicle for this insight that grew out of many days and nights and years of labor. Perhaps there are easier ways of being sentenced.

SOME FRIENDS OF MINE later said that I wrote a very "affirmative" book. But these friends either don't know me well enough or they don't know how to read between the lines. Cheerfulness often conceals great loathing. So that is my advice for today, for any unlikely seer or seeker who happens to land on these words: learn to hate well too.

WHAT DO I HATE? So much even in my own neck of the woods that I have to conceal it out of civility and self-preservation. A brief list: bleeding hearts and their moral tartuffery, but also scamster Marxists and pseudomilitants who have nothing left but a way of "talking" about the world that works mostly only to their own social advantage; Saidians whose anger expresses only their desire to be "recognized," who don't realize the rivers they are damming under the guise of so-called orientalism; picking up anthropology journals and reading tepid analyses of current events with a smattering of Foucault thrown in; the commemorative self-congratulation and self-flagellation of *Writing Culture*, as if they discovered the self; almost all invocations of "neoliberalism" and "the good"; I continue at my own risk. In any case, as Deleuze says, nothing is ever gained by books against something: "If you don't admire something, if you don't love it, you have no reason to write a word about it."[2]

BUT ANIMOSITY IS ALSO a kind of anima. What else do I hate? In writing about India, which I marginally inhabit, I hate almost all contemporary nonfiction and fiction writing. Here is what I say in public about this. I am referring in these lines to a genre and to a book that was awarded the Booker Prize: "Most contemporary Indian fiction and nonfiction is about call centers and cities and young men trying to get rich in the new India. These 'new' India books have a very impoverished idea, if any, of what the 'old' was, and of what newness may be. Consider an award-winning 'new' India book, better left unnamed. A supposedly demonic businessman narrates his story of capitalist greed and divides the world into Dark and Light, in the process giving us insufferable chicken-coop metaphors about the horrors of poverty in India. Such an author knows nothing about demons or about poverty."[3]

But why target these Johnny-come-latelys? These problems persist even in the upper ranks. For instance, I hate Naipaul. He is Caliban cursing well. And he is Prospero, magisterially confirming the European tourist-traveler's eye: "Ah, it was not only we who felt like this!" But we can also learn from what we hate. From Naipaul we can learn to write sentences of commanding precision, organized like phalanxes. Consider this, from one of his more egregious texts, *An Area of Darkness*: "Feature by feature, the East one had read about. On the train to Cairo the man across the aisle hawked twice, with an expert tongue rolled the phlegm into a ball, plucked the ball out of his mouth with thumb and forefinger, considered it, and then rubbed it away between his palms."[4]

Hateful, but what a wonderfully, rhythmically composed sentence! And then, in a very classic Naipaul technique, in the next sentence he zooms out from the nitpicking detail within the portrait, suddenly, to a world-historical canvas: "Cairo revealed the meaning of the bazaar: narrow streets encrusted with filth, stinking even on this winter's day; tiny shops full of shoddy goods; crowds; the din, already barely supportable, made worse by the steady blaring of motor-car horns; medieval buildings partly collapsed, others rising on old rubble, with here and there sections of tiles, turquoise and royal blue, hinting at a past of order and beauty, crystal fountains and amorous adventures, as perhaps in the no less disordered past they always had done."[5]

The lines are evocative and masterful, yes, but even when we try to convey a feel for a place, anthropologists do not write like this, with good reason: out of obligation, out of disciplinary prohibition, but also out of love for this world. It is our discipline, our devotion, to go beyond such beautifully painted "writerly" impressions of the world.

SO, IN SUM, in this era of right swipes and social media selfhoods, we might learn again to be attentive to the sentence, just as our predecessors learned to harness the energies latent in the pressure of opposable thumbs.

Notes

An earlier version of this essay appeared online in *Savage Minds: Notes and Queries in Anthropology*, November 30, 2015.

1. Bhrigupati Singh, *Poverty and the Quest for Life: Spiritual and Material Striving in Rural India* (Chicago: University of Chicago Press, 2015), 7.

2. Gilles Deleuze, *Desert Islands and Other Texts, 1953–1974* (New York: Semiotext(e), 2004), 152.

3. Singh, *Poverty and the Quest for Life*, 228.

4. V. S. Naipaul, *An Area of Darkness: A Discovery of India* (London: Picador, 1995), 4.

5. Naipaul, *An Area of Darkness*, 4.

29

PEER REVIEW
What Doesn't Kill You Makes You Stronger
Alan Kaiser

Eleven editors and more than two dozen anonymous reviewers rejected my scholarly article. It documented the scandal I had uncovered that David Robinson, famed excavator of the Greek site of Olynthos, had plagiarized the work of his forgotten graduate student, Mary Ellingson (see figure 29.1). My article clearly made a number of people uncomfortable, for there is an unspoken rule among American archaeologists working in Greece that it is bad form to criticize our intellectual ancestors in print. In the end, however, I did get the story published as a book. Peer review is, of course, an important part of the writing and publishing process, whereas plagiarism is something that should not be part of it at all. My writing on plagiarism had a difficult time making its way through the peer-review system, but this essay is not a case study in the problems with the peer-review system. Instead, I seek to prove that peer review works to sharpen and clarify our writing despite the flaws in the system.

But first the scandal. In 2003, a decade after Ellingson's death, I stumbled across a scrapbook filled with photos, letters, and news clippings that she had gathered recording her archaeological work as a graduate student at Olynthos in 1931. Ellingson was part of the excavation staff working under Johns Hopkins University professor Robinson, a man still famous as one of the first classical archaeologists to devote an excavation almost exclusively to

FIGURE 29.1.
Mary Ellingson in
Athens, June 1931.
Photo courtesy of the
University of Evans-
ville Library Archives.

uncovering houses and understanding ancient Greek domestic life. Robinson
excavated more houses at Olynthos than have been excavated at any other
Greek site. Ellingson supervised Greek workmen in the trenches and cata-
loged terracotta figurines (see figures 29.2 and 29.3). When she returned to
the United States, she wrote her master's thesis on the figurines, producing
not only a chronological catalog but also an analysis of their use. She completed her dissertation in 1939, which was an expansion of her thesis work to
look at figurines from other sites in northern Greece and the Balkans in addition to those from Olynthos. Robinson published her thesis as volume VII

in the *Excavations at Olynthus* series and her dissertation as the first chapter and a half of volume XIV, listing himself as the sole author, not mentioning her contribution, and without asking her permission.[1] Even by the standards of his day, what he did was flagrant plagiarism. A few archaeologists at the time published the work of their nongraduate student research assistants as well as their wives without crediting them, but I have found no other example of someone publishing the thesis or dissertation of another, perhaps because such a transgression leaves a paper trail that would have been easy to trace.

I wrote an article on this subject, assuming that anyone could see the significance of the story to our understanding of the history of archaeology and particularly the place of women in that history. Every major classical archaeology journal in the United States, and even some abroad, rejected it. My frustration and anger mounted with each rejection, particularly as I read the reasons. One editor claimed that her readers would not find it interesting and so did not send it to reviewers. Some editors and reviewers thought it was not plagiarism in Robinson's day even though I documented quite clearly that it was. Some argued that it was an isolated incident, whereas others argued that such behavior was common; either way, their conclusion was that the story was so trivial that it was not worthy of publication. No one doubted my research, and some even praised my "sleuthing" and "detective work," but they remained unconvinced on the ultimate issue of publication. As one anonymous reviewer stated quite bluntly, "What you are dealing with here is part of the unwritten history of classical archaeology. Best to leave it unwritten." This was the final blow. I gave up trying to publish the article and right the wrong Robinson had done to Ellingson.

It was clear that the story made many people very uncomfortable. Classical archaeology in Greece is unlike any other branch of archaeology in that all Americans who want to work there must spend a year or more at the American School for Classical Studies in Athens. The American School has a reputation for conservatism; Stephen Dyson has written that the school's conservative ways produce "an archaeological Confucius devoted to the word of the ancestors rather than a classical Lewis Binford, willing to challenge received tradition."[2] I suspect that this conservatism is what led to the great discomfort many editors and reviewers felt and the eventual death of the article.

Six years passed, and Ellingson remained on my mind despite the fact that I busied myself with other projects. Because the gnawing feeling of unfinished business would not go away, I knew I had to try to publish again. I owed it to Ellingson: I was the last person alive who knew her tale. Upon

FIGURE 29.2. Mary Ellingson (left) standing among the excavated house founda-tions at Olynthos that she helped excavate, spring 1931. Photo courtesy of the University of Evansville Library Archives.

FIGURE 29.3. Terracotta figurines excavated at Olynthos, spring 1931. Photo courtesy of the University of Evansville Library Archives.

rereading all the comments from the reviewers, I was struck by several statements about the need for more context that I had not noticed six years earlier. Her story needed more space than an article permitted; it was time to propose a book. The proposal landed on the desk of a sympathetic editor, and in 2015 I tore open a box from the publisher, lifting out a copy of my book with Ellingson's picture on the cover.[3]

The interesting question that arises from this story is whether or not the peer-review process failed in this instance. I don't think it did. With each rejection I rewrote the article to address concerns that the reviewers raised, which improved it a great deal. Ultimately being forced to tell the story in a book rather than an article allowed me to explore the objections raised by the reviewers in more detail and supply much more context than was possible in an article. Writing a book rather than an article also provided me the opportunity to quote extensively from Ellingson's own letters and writings, allowing her to regain her voice, which was one of my goals. I don't hesitate to say that the book is significantly better than the article. The reviews written to date confirm that publication as a book was the right choice.[4] The many letters that I have received from readers, some of whom had experiences similar to Ellingson's, also demonstrate that this was a story that had to be told. The peer-review process can feel soul crushing, but what doesn't kill a publication-worthy article or book only makes it stronger.

Notes

An earlier version of this essay appeared online in *Savage Minds: Notes and Queries in Anthropology*, February 23, 2015.

1. David Robinson, *Excavations at Olynthus VII: The Terra-Cottas of Olynthus Found in 1931* (Baltimore: Johns Hopkins University Press, 1933); David Robinson, *Excavations at Olynthus XIV: Terracottas, Lamps, and Coins Found in 1934 and 1938* (Baltimore: Johns Hopkins University Press, 1952).

2. Stephen Dyson, *Ancient Marbles to American Shores* (Philadelphia: University of Pennsylvania Press, 1998), 86.

3. Alan Kaiser, *Archaeology, Sexism and Scandal: The Long-Suppressed Story of One Woman's Discoveries and the Man Who Stole Credit for Them* (Lanham, MD: Rowman and Littlefield, 2015).

4. "Archaeology, Sexism and Scandal/Reviews," Rowman and Littlefield, accessed April 28, 2017, https://rowman.com/ISBN/9781442230033.

30

WHEN THEY DON'T LIKE WHAT WE WRITE

Criticism of Anthropology as a Diagnostic of Power

Lara Deeb and Jessica Winegar

"She looks like a chimp to me no offense intended to the apes."
"I hate to stoop this low, but you can tell just by looking at her that her driveway
doesn't go all the way to the road. #justsayin"

Over the course of twenty-four hours in spring 2017, anthropologist after anthropologist—all organizers of the AAA campaign to boycott Israeli academic institutions—were trolled on Twitter after the website Canary Mission launched negative profiles of them. As of May 22, 2017, this website claimed to "document the people and groups that are promoting hatred of the USA, Israel, and Jews on college campuses in North America" but in fact circulates libelous portrayals of respected scholars and student activists who are critical of US and Israeli government policies. The website and Twitter trolls accused us and our colleagues of things like being "sick and mentally disabled," "degenerate," "evil," "ugly," and "anti-Semitic" among other racist, gendered remarks such as those quoted above. Anthropologists have always risked harassment when they write critically about racism, sexism, and state power, but such attacks have increased with the advent of the internet. The infamy of outlets such as Canary Mission (and Campus Watch before it) and cases like that of Nadia Abu El-Haj, who faced a tenure battle because of her scholarship on Israel, has trained anthropologists' attention on the most extreme forms of reprisal. But there is another realm of politicized pushback that may or may not be called harassment but that is critical to analyze if we are to fully understand the relationship between knowledge and power. Here we mean both the structures of power that shape our writing and those that our writing challenges. Less overt forms of resistance to our writing can also serve as a helpful diagnostic that reveals pressure points on our scholarship about which we may be unaware. These often come from within our disciplines but connect to forms of power beyond.

At the final stage of drafting our book *Anthropology's Politics: Disciplining the Middle East* (2016), we received unexpected resistance from some of our interlocutors that revealed both generational forms of sexism and classism that persist in the discipline, as well as an underrecognized dimension of the observer/observed relationship. Before publishing, we decided to check anthropologists' quotations and specific mentions of interview material with them. Numerous colleagues wanted to change their recorded speech to make it more polished, to avoid sounding incoherent or "dumb." We granted these requests, noting how frequently our interlocutors chose to delete precisely those little "uhs" and "ums" that anthropologists have often analyzed. These small deletions show the pressures that scholars experience to shape their speech as "articulate" as they are socialized into academe and away from generational, gendered, and classed speech practices. Even more revealing to us were refusals to include specific interview material and refusals to allow our interpretations of that material to stand. In one case an anthropologist vehemently denied saying sexist things in the interview and patronizingly rejected our interpretation of parts of our exchange. Such challenges came mostly from senior white men, who sometimes reproduced the sexism they wished to erase in the emails requesting the erasure. Although we had of course known that academe was not a realm free of sexist rhetoric and practice, the details of these interactions reminded us of the persistence of sexism in anthropology and revealed the ways in which it is connected to generational and racialized hierarchies.

Analyzing peer review can also be diagnostic of power. As we discuss briefly in our book, reviews of anthropological scholarship on the Middle East sometimes expose anti-Muslim, anti-Arab bias. A few years ago we were invited to contribute an essay for an edited volume, which elicited such a response. Our essay analyzed the stereotyping and generalizing about Middle Eastern Muslims found in feminist anthropology and the racism and sexism that Middle Eastern/Muslim scholars face from their own colleagues.

Peer reviews, while containing some good suggestions for substantiating our claims, were generally hostile to those claims in ways that reveal the nexus in academe of Zionism, second-wave white feminism, the equalizing relativist impulse in anthropology, and liberalism. For example, when we highlighted the specific forms of discrimination perpetrated by academics against their Muslim/Middle Eastern colleagues, we received numerous comments essentially stating that "other minorities face this too," thereby diminishing our analysis of Islamophobia's specificities. Even more revealing were comments suggesting that these colleagues were not "of color," thereby challenging our description of this discrimination as related to the racialization of Muslims/Middle Easterners, about which there is an entire body of scholarly literature. Ironically, some of the feedback reproduced the stereotypes of the Middle East that our essay challenged. We were told that female scholars cannot research men because the region is gender segregated, that authoritarian regimes in the region are "Islamic," and that, in response to our statement that racism against Middle Eastern scholars must be understood in the context of US and Israeli colonialism and imperialism, "Waahabi [sic] funds in the region . . . teach about a very conservative, fundamental Islam [that is also] a form of imperialism." Indeed, it was our analysis of Zionism in anthropology that received the most intense pushback. Reviewers countered our claims by first affirming their bona fides as critics of Israel and then resorting to two well-worn rhetorical strategies: arguing that Zionism should not be "singled out" from other forms of imperialism and falsely accusing us of "conflate[ing] Israel/Zionism with all Jews in the US academy," a subtle insinuation of anti-Semitism. They also ignored our ethnographic data and experience, taking issue with our argument that Zionist assumptions have dominated many sectors of the academy, dismissing our over forty years of combined experience of this and our published book on this topic that is based on empirical data.

These examples of pushback during the process of publishing anthropological writing expose new angles on several aspects of power at the heart of academic knowledge production, including the efforts of external groups to sully scholars' reputations; the power of anthropologists to control the appearance and interpretation of their interlocutors' speech; the self-disciplining of academic speech in relation to gender, generation, and class; the subtle and not-so-subtle persistence of stereotypes about Muslims and Arabs among anthropologists themselves; the persistence of Zionism even among its so-called critics; and the power of some older white men to deny their own biases and dismiss the analyses of junior female scholars. For us, these seemingly inconsequential incidents served as crucial reminders and diagnostics. They are reminders of the work that remains to be done, and they are diagnostics of the spaces where academic critique slips into political barrier. These are the moments when our writing is having the impact of making people uncomfortable in politically productive ways. So take a minute to think about that comment you received that did not quite make sense, or the time a reviewer's tone shifted suddenly or a colleague tried to block you in some way. Those are the moments when we might learn something about the broader politics that our writing is shaking up and when our writing might also become sharper in response.

SECTION VII
ACADEMIC AUTHORS

31

WRITING ARCHAEOLOGY "ALONE," OR A EULOGY FOR A CODIRECTOR

Jane Eva Baxter

For the past couple of years I've been suffering from the condition we know affectionately as "writer's block." This has not been a generic or widespread condition, for much of my writing is progressing as swiftly and smoothly as my job structure allows. This particular writer's block has been confined to the writing associated with several years of archaeological work that I conducted on the island of San Salvador in the Bahamas. The reason for this particular condition is easy to identify: my project codirector simply decided to stop writing.

My codirector and I began planning our research in 2002, and from 2004 to 2012 we conducted archaeological and historical work investigating transitions in the daily life of the island's residents. During this time, we coauthored conference papers, site reports, proceedings volume papers, and articles for the *Journal of the Bahamas Historical Society*. We often coauthored work with our students. We developed curricular materials for the local school; coauthored a popular guide to the historic sites on the island for residents, tourists, and student groups; and created archaeology posters for a small, local museum.

And then, my project codirector stopped writing. At first, this decision to stop writing manifested itself as a waning interest in what had become a rather routinized and comfortable process of coauthorship. Writing plans were disregarded. Deadlines were missed without renegotiation. Discussions about writing ceased. Eventually, he announced that he no longer had an interest in publishing scholarly articles and told me to just go ahead and write everything up on my own. For many, being freed from the bonds of coauthorship might seem liberating, but to me it has been rather paralyzing. It also has given me cause to reflect on the production of archaeological knowledge and left me to wonder exactly what it means to write without him.

A Few Quick, General Thoughts about Fieldwork and Writing

Archaeological research is always a collaborative endeavor. Regardless of the size of the project, an archaeologist never goes into the field alone. Collaboration in archaeology is not a choice or a particular research stance; it is necessary in order for the work to get done. The relationship between a field project comprising many individuals and the writing process, generally undertaken by at most a few individuals, is a complicated one.

A multiplicity of ideas and voices exist in the field as different project participants have their own engagements with the archaeological record. This diversity of experience moves through a variety of social (gendered, status-based) and organizational (personnel hierarchies) mechanisms and generally becomes distilled into a singular narrative: the book, the site report, and/or the article, which is authored by the project director(s) (e.g., Berggen and Hodder 2003; Gero 1996; Roveland 2006). Alternative ideas, different perspectives, and contrasting opinions that existed during fieldwork are rarely part of a final narrative. A rare exception to this practice was some of the publications of the Colorado Coalfield War Project that were written as the Ludlow Collective, with the contents of the writing attributed to the entire project team.[1] The archaeological voice is almost always a singular one, even when the research comes from the collective efforts of many.

Some Specific Reflections on Losing My Codirector and Writing

Losing my codirector as a writing partner made me acutely aware of this particular dynamic in archaeological work and of a certain kind of responsibility that exists in archaeological writing. How is one person writing alone supposed to become the voice for over a decade of collaborative thinking?

On the positive side, I realized my own writing crisis stems from a healthy, open working dynamic cultivated over so many years. It was this positive dynamic of sharing and negotiating knowledge freely that has made it so difficult for me disentangle my voice from my codirector's. I have repeatedly revisited the countless hours deliberately spent in thought together on issues of project design, logistical planning, student evaluation, and archaeological interpretation. Through these interactions we jointly had made every critical decision about how our field project was to be run and how we wanted to approach every aspect of our analysis, teaching, and writing.

More poignant in my reflections were recollections of the casual conversations that peppered our days both in and out of the field. Many of these interactions were fleeting: a few minutes of banter in the truck to or from the site, a moment on an airplane, a scribbled note at a conference, or a quick IM during the course of a workday. Other interactions were much more involved, such as the times that a "nonwork" dinner was hijacked completely by wonderings about one analysis or another, or the evenings when lab work went on hours longer than necessary because ideas were flying back and forth. I don't remember the specific outcomes of any of these interactions, but I am certain that these were the moments when my ideas and my voice became inextricably entwined with his. I have also become acutely aware of similar interactions I had over the years with project staff and my students, and the many ways that their thoughts and voices have become a part of my own.

At the end of the day, it has become my responsibility as the last project director standing to "write it all up" and disseminate the work of this collaborative project as widely and appropriately as possible. Writing in archaeology is always about taking responsibility for the different voices in our narratives. Historical archaeologists have long characterized their work as bringing lost or forgotten voices from the past into contemporary dialogues. Archaeologists are increasingly attentive to the diverse voices of community members who are stakeholders in the places where archaeological work takes place and who often play collaborative roles in archaeological projects. I think, as a generalization, archaeologists are less aware of the voices of those participating in projects as day-to-day coworkers, or maybe we just aren't as sure what to do about them all. It has taken the departure of a codirector for me to recognize the challenges and responsibilities of writing archaeology "alone," and I'm thinking about new ways to write about archaeological fieldwork in the future. For now, these articles need to be written. These stories need to be told. And although my name may be the only one on the marquee, I know I won't be alone on stage.

Acknowledgments

Thank you to my colleagues Rachel Scott and Morag Kersel, who helped me with these ideas over a nice cup of tea. Many thanks to Carole McGranahan for including me in such an exciting and meaningful project. And thanks to my codirector, who, while not a writing partner, is still an amazing colleague and very dear friend.

Notes

An earlier version of this essay appeared online in *Savage Minds: Notes and Queries in Anthropology*, March 16, 2015.

1. "The Colorado Coalfield War Archaeological Project," accessed August 24, 2018, https://www.du.edu/ludlow/project_000.html.

32

COLLABORATION

From Different Throats Intone One Language?

Matt Sponheimer

I've been thinking a lot about collaborative writing of late, but not the internecine conflict it sometimes engenders within US anthropology departments.[1] We are all aware of subdisciplinary differences with regard to multiauthored manuscripts and the occasional contestation that occurs when credit for such undertakings must be meted out.[2] No, I'm talking about something rather different, and I also hope much less charged. I've been contemplating the act of collaborative writing itself, both what it represents from a practical standpoint and as an intellectual exercise. Most of the internal wrangling is captured by the question "How do we make collaboration truly collaborative, rather than additive, in practice?"

Dual-authored pieces can be a joy to write. At their best, they are natural collaborations where two people riff off each other and push one another to deeper insight and synthesis. For such work, it can be quite easy to negotiate the overall structure and one's respective topical coverage. This assumes, of course, that the writers are more or less compatible and bend rather than break when buffeted by intellectual crosswinds. I've been lucky in this area, and my experiences with dual-authored papers are among the most rewarding I've had as a writer.

But what about papers with five, six, or more authors? Such experiences will vary tremendously depending on the nature of the participants, their relative positions of power, and common practices within and between research groups, making it difficult to generalize, and I won't really try to do so here. I've published with biomedical researchers, botanists, philosophers, anatomists, geochemists, veterinarians, engineers, and anthropologists of various stripes, and this has taught me that there are many effective ways to approach multiauthored projects. Yet there are many potential hurdles, such as negotiating the Scylla of coauthor disagreements on matters of interpretation and the Charybdis of radically different ideas about writing style. Such issues are legitimate and occasionally frustrating, but most of us are reasonable most of the time, and my coauthors have always been understanding about sincere, if not entirely effective, attempts at interpretive and stylistic triangulation.[3]

What is rarely discussed about such endeavors, however, is how one makes them truly collaborative intellectual exercises rather than quilt-like products where the efforts of individual contributors are sewn together after the fact. Now, understand I am not arguing that the typical multiauthored paper should be deeply integrative in its bones. It will often make sense for individuals to stick to their scholarly lasts and for papers to be built in an orderly and modular fashion. However, there are also times where one would prefer a true group voice, such as in reviews or other highly synthetic efforts. I've found this easily achieved with one or maybe two collaborators, usually after hours of discussion to frame the paper, followed by a cooperative outline to work through arguments and apportion writing assignments. All of this is certainly possible with more authors but not easy to pull off in practice.

After all, coauthors bring different data and knowledge sets to bear on the questions at hand, and as a result there will typically be sections or data that can be provided only by particular individuals. I do not see any way around that. However, it is the next step that interests me: the confluence of individual efforts where interpretation and synthesis flourish. In my experience, there is often some general understanding among the group, and the interpretation may even appear to be self-evident, but in practice usually one or two people make the requisite decisions for constructing the first draft. It is then typical for others to chime in, usually making small comments here and there, which tend to be focused on matters of fact or small matters of interpretation. What I've rarely seen at this stage is a significant conceptual advance.

I think that this situation is almost inevitable. The act of writing closes doors even as it opens them, especially the sort of academic writing in which many of us regularly engage. Each paragraph is another nail in the project's frame, so what began with unwieldy and limitless possibility soon becomes manageable and canalized, allowing fewer interpretive alternatives from page to page. This is positive insofar as it helps produce writing that is on point and lucid. It is not an unalloyed good, however, because the very process that makes a manuscript highly readable also makes it less subject to emendation. Who has not seen a manuscript that would be best served by immolation and a fresh start, but nevertheless had to struggle to make improvements on its shaky foundation? In short, a draft often curtails a coauthor's ability to contribute.

So what approaches minimize such difficulties? In fields and in research groups where lab meetings are a regular occurrence, the collective can hammer through an outline over the course of one or a few meetings. This should elicit broader input and increase the likelihood that whoever undertakes the initial draft speaks for, or at least understands the positions of, all coauthors. Of course, anthropological collaborations frequently occur across institutional and national boundaries, rendering these in-depth face-to-face discussions impractical.[4] In such circumstances where I am the first author, I sometimes send out a brief outline to perhaps two coauthors. This strikes me as a reasonable balance between improving collective representation and the chaos of processing many (and sometimes contrary) voices at once. Overall, this seems an acceptable approach, although I am sure there are others who find it a bit lazy. After all, isn't it the job of the first author to take care of such things rather than spread the onus across the crew?

A second step that I sometimes undertake is almost certain to invoke criticism and convince people that sloth, rather than any theoretical disposition, is driving my choices. Once the outline is settled, I often write up a draft and do some very basic spelling and grammar checking and nothing more. The manuscript is very rough at this stage, but I nevertheless send it to two or three coauthors, warts and all.[5] My thinking here is that the more polished the manuscript, the less likely I am to get substantive comments, and I hope that the obvious roughness of the text serves as an invitation screaming, "Please improve me!" Now, I do try to warn my colleagues to not worry about grammar and style, and focus instead on the substance of the arguments, but I have to admit that this may be a losing battle. After all, many of us are probably academics because we have a hard time letting such "trifles" go. I send a draft to all coauthors only after these initial comments have been addressed and after I've spent a bit more time sharpening the arguments and polishing the prose.

So what have been my results? I think it is fair to say that these steps ensure that I get more substantive input than I do when I simply produce a polished manuscript and send it out for comments. When I do the latter, I am likely to get two or three small comments from a few people and no input from others. After all, in such instances the manuscript arrives in collaborators' email in-boxes more or less fully formed like Athena from the head of Zeus. Even if people are inclined to take things in a different direction, the manuscript is usually sufficiently coherent that the potential benefits of significant revision are outweighed by the certain costs. As for my coauthors, I suspect the process is not entirely a pleasant one, and it no doubt convinces some that I'm a barely competent layabout—but I think I can live with that.[6] I would never have considered such a strategy when I was a graduate student or postdoc: at that career stage, being labeled inept or slothful would have carried more sting.

In the end, I've been lucky to work with some of the sharpest and most amenable people around, so the above should be considered less a lament than the ramblings of a compulsive worrier. Nonetheless, I think the goal of deeper cooperation for multiauthored projects is a sound one, even if its lack is rarely a salient problem. I close with a few words about my kindred spirit the distracted centipede:

> The centipede was happy quite
> Until a toad in fun
> Said, "Pray, which leg moves after which?"
> This raised his mind to such a pitch,
> He lay distracted in a ditch
> Considering how to run.[7]

Notes

An earlier version of this essay appeared online in *Savage Minds: Notes and Queries in Anthropology*, March 24, 2014.

1. This essay's title, which is from Robinson Jeffers's poem "Natural Music," kept coming to mind as I was writing. I've learned to respect unexpected and unbidden connections, so I thought it might serve as a title.

2. Contributions to multiauthored manuscripts can be of various sorts and need not involve much writing. Indeed, nonwriting contributions can represent much more of the intellectual heavy lifting than writing the manuscript itself. Who does what, and what this means in terms of authorship order, is also likely to vary a good deal across disciplines, research groups, and individual projects. Hence, evaluating an

author's relative contribution can be complex and is beyond the scope of this small contribution.

3. One does hear horror stories about certain multiauthored projects, which is why when choosing collaborators, one must choose wisely! I've been very lucky to work with some remarkable people.

4. It has become easier to get around this constraint with free tools such as Skype and Google Hangouts. Nevertheless, I still find it much easier to engage in meaningful dialogue face-to-face. However, I confess that I can't rule out the possibility that such conversations are enlivened, or appear to be more profound, because of their frequent co-occurrence with the consumption of fermented libations.

5. I write initially in a logorrheic flood. Rather than getting bogged down with the wording, I write quickly so as to capture basic ideas and their underlying logic before they have a chance to evaporate. I've found this approach to be effective, for even though the initial text is far from stellar and littered with fragments that do not entirely capture what I want to convey, it is much easier to fix this after the fact than to struggle with language from the outset. As a result, the first drafts I send out may be rougher than is evident from my description above, even though I do rectify the most egregious problems before the draft is shared.

6. Although I could tolerate this perception, I'd be lying if I said it would not bother me. Moreover, I'm not at all convinced that the benefits of this approach exceed the costs, so it is possible I'll abandon it entirely in the near future. However, it is certain that I will continue to look for better ways to do my job.

7. This poem, attributed to Katherine Craster, apparently first appeared in *Cassell's Weekly* in 1871. I have been unable to find the original, but I have come across it in other texts from the 1880s. For more, see https://en.wikipedia.org/wiki/The_Centipede%27s_Dilemma.

33

WHAT IS AN (ACADEMIC) AUTHOR?

Mary Murrell

Anthropological writing is academic writing in that it adheres to the norms of a disciplinary discourse. However, the social field of academic writing encompasses much more: capitalist enterprise, material networks of circulation, and a complex legal regime, among other social and institutional relations. Publishers have performed a sort of boundary work between the scholar and this broader social field, but as electronic dissemination reconfigures the material infrastructures of academic practice, scholars have to negotiate more of these relations themselves and to actively participate in the rethinking and restructuring of prior settled arrangements. Open-access publishing is one well-known example of such renegotiation. Here I present another, lesser-known example of such renegotiation. It involves academic scholars coming together to deploy the "academic author" as a new and special figure capable of reconfiguring the relations within the social field of academic writing.

Between 2008 and 2011, I conducted fieldwork among advocates for free public digital libraries. Within a fraught legal landscape, they were seeking what the legal scholar James Boyle has called "spaces of freedom" within US copyright law in order to make such libraries possible.[1] A central focus of their concern during this time was Google's mass book-digitization program, which, in partnership with research libraries, sought to digitize "all the world's books." In 2005 author and publisher groups had sued Google, claiming that its book-digitization project committed massive copyright infringement. In 2008, however, the authors and publishers reversed the course of this class-action lawsuit and agreed to end the case, in exchange for which Google would turn its digitized books into a commercial database that would be sold by subscription to libraries. The parties agreed to split the revenue that this new commercial enterprise would generate.

In the secret negotiations that produced the settlement, the New York–based trade group the Authors Guild represented authors, and the Association of American Publishers (AAP) represented publishers. A novelty of US law, class-action lawsuits allow a few plaintiffs to stand in for a much larger class of people who have been similarly harmed by a defendant's action. Although most anthropologists were likely unaware, if you had published a book or even a part of a book before 2000, you were represented in this legal proceeding by these book-industry representatives.

Most of the digital librarians with whom I worked saw the agreement between Google and the book publishing industry as a threat to the creation of future digital libraries. The agreement gave Google a special carve-out from copyright law while other entities would continue to be constrained by it. As such, my informants feared that the deal would keep noncommercial, large-scale alternatives to Google's project from getting off the ground. It also left unaddressed the original, pressing legal question that the Google book-scanning program presented: was it a legal or "fair" use to digitize a copyrighted book? Digital libraries would have stood to gain from a finding of fair use.

Within what was a sprawling debate, both in and outside of courtrooms, I want to bring attention to just one of its subplots, wherein the "academic author" plays a starring role. Copyright law, of course, centrally enshrines the author as the privileged figure upon whom rights and protections are conferred. In the legal proceedings involving Google's book project, the Authors Guild asserted itself as the representative of the "author." But, as became clear, the Authors Guild understood itself as representing a specific type of author. Membership in the guild required an author to have earned writing income "of at least $5,000 in an 18-month period" and to hold book contracts with "meaningful" advances. In other words, the "author" of the Authors Guild was a commercially motivated writer, and in negotiations with Google the guild had the key goal of collecting revenue for its members.

Many of the closest observers of the dispute around Google's digitization project were, unsurprisingly, legal scholars. After reading the settlement agreement, a group of them came to see that their interests, as university-based scholars, were different from those of the Authors Guild. Labeling themselves "academic authors," they contested, in official letters and court testimony, the guild's capacity to represent them to the standard required by law—that is, "fairly and adequately." They insisted that the Authors Guild had failed to represent their interests in the settlement with Google because academic authors are "committed to maximizing access to knowledge," whereas the guild is "institutionally committed to maximizing profits."[2] (Elsewhere, they described the motivation of academic authors as "writing to be read," in implied contrast to commercial writers, who write to be remunerated.) They further pointed out that academic authors had been given no seat at the negotiating table, despite two key facts: (1) that university-based scholars vastly outnumber the Authors Guild membership, and (2) that they were more likely than Author Guild members to have written the books that fill research libraries and thus the books that Google was scanning.

Their strategy to expand or ramify the "author" beyond its institutionalized position within the book trade was effective. When the judge finally ruled on the fairness of the settlement in 2011, he rejected it, in part, because he concluded that the negotiating parties—Google, the Authors Guild, and the AAP—had neglected to fairly represent the "interests and values" of academic authors. Later, the then-head of Google Books singled out those who had presented themselves as "academic authors" as the reason that the settlement met the fate it did.[3] This strategic deployment of the "academic author" not only weakened the power of the Authors Guild to speak for all authors, but it also inserted a conceptual wedge into copyright politics. By positing a new author, one who was not writing for profit but for the broadest possible dissemination, it opened up the animating figure of copyright law—the author—to reconfiguration.

Taking the figure of the "academic author" further, in 2014 some of these same scholars launched a nonprofit organization called the Authors Alliance to "represent authors who want to disseminate knowledge . . . broadly" and to "facilitate widespread access to works of authorship." In more obvious political terms, the Authors Alliance hopes to increase the authority of noncommercial, academic authors—to give them a seat at the table—as Congress considers major revisions to the country's copyright statute. It could become a countervailing force to that of the Authors Guild and other industry groups that have historically spoken most powerfully in the name of the "author."

As the material infrastructure of our writing changes, the settled, habituated relations around academic writing and publishing are slowly being disturbed and rearranged—indeed, quite slowly. The "academic author" I describe here is a figure deployed within a field of power. I do not mean to reify it as an accurate or necessary way to understand ourselves. Rather, I mean for it to show that authorship is a material and discursive terrain open to intervention.

Notes

An earlier version of this essay appeared online in *Savage Minds: Notes and Queries in Anthropology*, October 6, 2014.

1. James Boyle, *The Public Domain: Enclosing the Commons of the Mind* (New Haven, CT: Yale University Press, 2008).

2. See Pamela Samuelson, "Academic Author Objections to the Google Book Search Settlement," *Journal on Telecommunications and High Technology Law* 8 (2010): 491–522.

3. James Somers, "Torching the Modern-Day Library of Alexandria," *Atlantic*, April 20, 2017, https://www.theatlantic.com/technology/archive/2017/04/the-tragedy -of-google-books/523320.

34

THE WRITING BEHIND THE WRITTEN

Noel B. Salazar

As Henry David Thoreau once wrote, "How vain it is to sit down to write when you have not stood up to live!" Indeed, grounded fieldwork, the "having been there," forms the basis of the captivating stories narrated by the most widely read anthropologists. From a historical perspective, the discipline made a big leap forward when it changed from armchair philosophizing to scholarship that is deeply rooted in empirical data gathering. Many people nowadays associate anthropology with ethnography. Even if the referents to the former part of the word have become blurred, the latter part does not seem to have lost any of its significance; it refers literally to the written report of whomever (or whatever) is being studied.

Students become aware of the importance of writing from the moment they enroll in an anthropology program. Through reading exercises, they learn to appreciate various types of anthropological writings, be it peer-reviewed articles, book chapters, or monographs. However, it is the process of writing up fieldwork experiences that confronts anthropologists in the making with the intricacies of writing. The less you have written yourself, the less you realize how much time and energy go into the reiterative process that leads to a finalized text worth reading. Unless you are a prodigy, creating a quality manuscript requires sustained effort (and patience). Hence the frustration, insecurity, and anxiety many feel when returning from the field, not knowing how on earth they will manage the daunting task of converting messy data (not all in written form) and field notes into readable text.

I involve my own graduate students in reading and commenting upon the various drafts of my own manuscripts to give them a sense of the arduous labor involved in writing. Although there are many excellent resources available concerning how anthropologists should write, certain aspects are harder to teach, unless you give people a chance to practice them personally. In my experience, there is always something mysterious about the creative writing process. When or how it happens is impossible to predict, but the moment a new insight dawns and the various parts of the (often complicated) puzzle start coming together, what others have described as the Aha-Erlebnis or Eureka effect is kind of magical. Like the runner's high described by long-distance runners, achieving this feeling is extremely gratifying and part of the reason why writers love writing.

Unfortunately, not all writing endeavors lead to elated feelings, and to be honest, not everything written is worth publishing (just like not everything published is worth reading). It takes courage to abandon a writing project that, for some reason or the other, does not seem to pan out. The ongoing pressure in academia to publish (or perish instead) has led to a noticeable increase in published work, statistically coupled with a marked decrease in the quality of academic output. Because writing is so crucial to our discipline, we should be much more vocal about criticizing this system. Anthropology is a notoriously "slow science" and does not fit the dominant mold of "quick and dirty" scholarship. It takes time to prepare our research carefully, to collect our ethnographic data, and to analyze them properly. We should certainly not try to compromise by reducing the write-up time.

Because there is so much pressure on publishing in academia, many seem to be forgetting an essential aspect of writing, namely the intended audience. For whom do we write, and for whom should we be writing? Apart from some exceptions (e.g., writing as therapy), I sincerely hope that most anthropologists write expecting that someone will read their work. Internal academic dialogue and exchange are important for the discipline to grow intellectually, but far too many precious anthropological insights are lost because the readership does not reach beyond the boundaries of the ivory tower. The blame does not necessarily lie with the author. There is something terribly wrong with academic publishing models that limit free access to scholarly writings, particularly when the underlying research is supported by public funding. Seriously, what is the purpose of writing a text that sits behind a pay wall and is not read by anybody? This situation undermines the credibility of the entire scientific endeavor and is unsustainable in the long run.

Considerations about our audience(s) should also lead us to reflect upon our writing style and the readability of our writings. We should put more effort into making anthropological writings more accessible, including to the people whom we study. Is it not contradictory that academics in countries such as France have a long and reputed history as public intellectuals, participating actively in societal debates, but that most of their scholarly writings are so arcane? We may want to think about more variety in the writing genres we use to disseminate our insights. I am pleased to see an increased presence of anthropologists in newspaper and magazine op-eds and postings on blogs and websites. This is relevant work, and we should continue to do it because it broadens our readership. However, I see this as complementary to our other scholarly work, not as a replacement for it.

In sum, as anthropologists we have a whole array of tools at our disposal to upgrade our writing skills and to increase the impact of our work. With the constructive help of mentors and peers, we need to find our own way of mastering the art of writing. We should not get lost in the plethora of formats and fora available, but focus on those types of writing that suit anthropology best and that matter to the world "out there." To wit, captivating storytelling is only one part of the story. Good ethnographic writers can translate complex anthropological analyses and insights into a language that is understood by broad audiences. Only sustained practice (which includes occasional failures) can make us excel. This involves working on our own texts as well as reading and commenting upon what others have written. After all, a good anthropologist is not only an excellent writer but also a seasoned reader.

Note

An earlier version of this essay appeared online in *Savage Minds: Notes and Queries in Anthropology*, September 15, 2014.

35

IT'S ALL "REAL" WRITING

Daniel M. Goldstein

Like many writers who have to sustain themselves with a paying job—in my case and probably yours, too, an academic job—I spend a lot of my time fretting about not having enough time to write. Many of my friends in the profession are the same way. We have to teach, we complain, which requires time to prepare, deliver, and grade our lessons, while managing students and their many needs. We serve on committees, attend faculty meetings, and hold office hours. We devote countless hours to reviewing the work of our peers: others who seem to find the time to write, which we must review at the cost of our own writing time.

As a result, I think, many of us don't feel like writers. I know I don't. Not a real writer, anyway. A real writer, in my mind, is someone whose principal vocation is writing. I picture someone like Honoré de Balzac, writing through the wee hours of the morning, fueled by endless cups of coffee; Joyce Carol Oates, author of more than fifty novels and countless other works of fiction and nonfiction; or Maya Angelou, who kept a small hotel room as a writing space, which she called "lonely, and . . . marvelous" (in Currey 2013, loc. 1557). These to me are real writers.

Meanwhile, I struggle along through my own daily routine, frustrated at not having enough time to write. I don't feel like a real writer.

On further reflection, however, I am forced to reconsider this self-evaluation. If a writer, by definition, is someone who writes, then I—again, like many others in the academic profession—am a writer through and through. I write constantly, although I fail to appreciate what I do as real writing.

Curiously, much of my writing is joined to those very activities that appear to distract me from writing. Writing a lecture, for example, may not seem like writing—no one, after all, will ever read it. Plus, a lecture is typically written in outline form, on note cards, or even—shudder—as a PowerPoint slide show. But an anthropology lecture delivered to a roomful of undergraduates is a particularly challenging form of writing. It has to convey facts and theories without oversimplifying while also engaging the mind and imagination of a drowsy, possibly hungover adolescent. My technique for accomplishing this is humor: I try to write lectures that amuse and startle and even offend my students (McDonald's hamburgers, Silly Putty, and penis sheaths all feature in my Day One lecture in Intro) in order to grab their attention and reel them in to the concepts. And yes, I use PowerPoint—it requires all my creativity as a writer to condense my message into brief and pithy takeaways that fit the eighty-minute time frame of the class session.

Peer reviewing also demands its own unique forms of writing. If done correctly, a review of a manuscript or grant proposal can contribute to both the advancement of anthropological knowledge and the career of a fellow academic. Done poorly, of course, reviewing can be destructive and devastating to those same things. Writing a peer review requires us to be critical without being nasty, to offer productive suggestions for how to improve a piece of work without being offended when our own work is not cited. Again, this calls on the writer to deploy all of her talents to advance the scholarship without eviscerating the scholar. Not easy work, but vitally important, and another form of writing that we don't recognize as writing.

Even in my personal life, I am constantly writing. When I originally wrote this piece, one of my sons was a junior in college and the other was a seventeen-year-old high school senior, neither of whom seemed capable of verbal communication. But, remarkably, they both were and continue to be quite willing to correspond with me via text. This was especially useful with Ben, who was away at college. We would text several times a week: about his work, his friends, and our shared love of New England sports teams. Eli still lived at home, emerging from his cave for meals and disappearing just as quickly afterward. But he, too, communicated by text. I may have been downstairs and he upstairs, but we wrote back and forth to each other, sometimes about important topics (global climate change was very much on his mind). Although it typically occurs in short bursts and can be dictated rather than typed, texting is writing. Like the other forms of writing I've mentioned, texts can inspire, provoke, and deflate. They can forge relationships or destroy them with a word.

There are many other kinds of writing that form part of our daily lives as academics, anthropologists, and modern humans. With my graduate assistant and immigrant research collaborators, I recently wrote (and performed) a play. I've written op-eds and letters to the editor. Many of us write like this. We tweet, we comment, and we blurb. We write field notes and syllabi and blog entries and writers' workshop contributions. We provide feedback on student papers and craft emails to colleagues and collaborators. Each of these is its own genre, with its own particular rules and styles. We have to master all of them.

No one would ever equate a text message with an ethnographic text, but recognizing both as real writing helps me feel better about things as I go through my daily routine. Writers, they say, write; the best way to improve your writing is through a regular writing practice. Instead of feeling frustrated that I don't have time to write, I now choose to regard all my work as writing, a daily practice alongside, or in advance of, writing other, deeper pieces. I still dream of writing a novel, and perhaps one day I will. But in the meantime I live the writing life, doing the work of a real writer, one text at a time.

Note

An earlier version of this essay appeared online in *Savage Minds: Notes and Queries in Anthropology*, September 21, 2015.

Reference

Currey, Mason. 2013. *Daily Rituals: How Artists Work*. New York: Alfred A. Knopf.

36

DR. FUNDING OR

How I Learned to Stop Worrying
and Love Grant Writing

Robin M. Bernstein

As an anthropologist doing fieldwork on different continents and running a laboratory that needs a full-time technician to operate properly, I am dependent on continuous external funding to keep things going. There was a time when I resented this, and felt utterly exhausted and desperate in the context of the endless application-rejection cycles, waiting on the edge of my seat to find out whether I could continue my projects uninterrupted, keep my employees employed, and offer any resources to my students.

I will admit that "scientific writing" has never come naturally or easily to me. A certain structure and sequence are expected and required, and for some reason I have always found it difficult to wedge my thoughts into the mold that is necessary for positive peer review and publication. As with anything one considers somewhat unpleasant, I generally avoid it until it can be put off no longer. But what good is scientific research if you can't communicate it effectively to an audience of your peers? I have always found it easier to communicate with a wider audience, where I can focus on the ideas, the broader background, and the potential of any results that might otherwise be doomed to insignificance by a p-value of >0.05.

And this, I have realized, is why I rather like grant writing. I understand that many of my colleagues see this process as a necessary evil (perhaps the way I see writing papers?), one that is stymied by not knowing what a given panel on a given cycle will find worthwhile (somewhat like that notorious third reviewer of manuscripts). It is often discussed as a fishing expedition in the dark, putting significant amounts of time and energy into trying to convince people that your ideas are important enough to merit being awarded money to explore them. But, perhaps perversely, this is the very reason that it appeals to me.

When writing a manuscript, I am trying to convince reviewers that my results are worthwhile, important, and of value to the field in a broad sense (no easy task, even with p-values <0.05). When writing a grant proposal, I aim to convince reviewers that my ideas are worthwhile, important, and relevant. This is liberating: it keeps me in a frame of mind where I am constantly looking forward. Although in many cases I do include results from previous research as pilot data (p-values and all), or justification for what I'm proposing, these don't take center stage. Instead, I become deeply involved with the challenge of convincing that anonymous panel (or perhaps just a person or two) that my project is one worth investing in, within a page limit and specific format. I take delight in condensing a page of text that would put me over length into a creative and informative figure to take its place. Reading and rereading drafts of a proposal serves to reaffirm my excitement for the work, and that enthusiasm becomes incorporated into the proposal with each revision. It is possible that I am an anomaly in taking pleasure in this process. But perhaps it is just that it allows me to tap into the optimism, enthusiasm, and excitement that led me to choose a career in research in the first place. I can unreservedly dream about what could be rather than fret about what has come to pass: I can live in a future of my own making while I am writing a grant proposal. When the submission gong sounds and the proposal is out of my hands—then the stress begins.

With that, I offer a few thoughts on the grant-writing process. This is not a how-to; those sorts of guides abound on the internet, can be very specific or broad, and are more or less effective. Instead, these are some lessons I have learned in the time since I submitted my very first proposal, and they may be of some use to someone out there.

Know Thy Funding Agency

This may seem obvious, but if the aims of your proposal do not clearly speak to the overarching goals and priorities of the organization with the money, it will be hard to get that organization to see how funding you makes sense. Familiarize yourself with the organization's mission statement, with its target areas and goals (these can change frequently). Think of ways that what you are proposing to do can speak to these, and be sure to clearly articulate your ideas.

Background

When contextualizing a research question, one frequently runs into the problem of how to tame the "introduction" or "literature review" section. This is the place to show reviewers that you have a thorough and current understanding of research in the area where you are proposing to do your work. Write too much, and your original thoughts and ideas are outweighed by the work that's been done before you. Write too little, and you run the risk of being seen as too selective. I've often found it helpful to, in initial drafts, skip the "introduction" section altogether and instead challenge myself to incorporate specific and succinct literature reviews as part of my "research question" section. This ensures that the background that I present is directly relevant to, and highlights, my own original thoughts and proposal ideas. Then it's easy enough to copy and paste into another section.

Nice to Know vs. Need to Know

This subject piggybacks on the prior section on background, but it also holds relevance for your proposal at large. In today's funding climate, it is often not enough to propose to do something because there is a gap in the literature or because a reanalysis of a previously proposed idea is now possible with new samples or technology. Why do we need to know the results of your research? This "need to know" is sometimes required in a clearly articulated section of a proposal (such as "Broader Impacts" for a National Science Foundation [NSF] proposal). Keeping the question "Why do we need to know this?" instead of "Why would it be nice to know this?" in the forefront of your mind while writing will help you craft a compelling narrative.

Clarity, Clarity, Clarity

Sometimes you will luck out and get a true expert in your domain to review your proposal. Most often, you will have one or two reviewers who are familiar with your area of research, with the remainder being competent nonexperts. These nonexpert reviewers do not delight in sorting through your writing to decipher your meaning from nuanced and flowery prose. They want to know what you want to do, how you plan to do it, why it's important, and how much money you need. Don't make your reviewers go on a treasure hunt: put all these nuggets up front, make them clear, and ensure continuity throughout. Bold, italicize, underline: don't be afraid to use these actions to draw the reader's eye to key points. Use white space to delineate mental pauses between sections. Hand-holding and being overly simplistic are not necessary, but writing as a clear, succinct, and thorough tour guide is helpful.

Never Give Up . . . Ever

I think one common theme tying grant writing together with manuscript writing is that the work is never "done" done. There is always room to improve, to expand, to reorganize, and to match your product to that inaccessible archetype of perfection that we all carry in our heads. In both cases—grant and manuscript writing—there is the "x-factor" of the outsider's perspective. Even if you obsess over every last detail in a proposal and feel supremely confident that it is the best thing you've ever written, it is no guarantee of funding. In fact, you can probably count on not being funded on your first submission. If you can keep this in mind, it may make it easier to let go of the idea of perfection and view the first submission as an opportunity to make room for the reviewer's perspective on what you've written. Cinching your proposal so tightly that there is no flexibility in organization or content will make revisions painful at best. I've lost track of the number of grant, fellowship, and program proposals that I have submitted over the past fifteen years in order to arrive at the handful that have been awarded. What I have held onto is the thrill of the pursuit. Viewed through this lens, grant writing becomes less about reaching for that gold ring and more about reconnecting with the passion that drives us. Renewing that on a regular basis is worthwhile, even if the result doesn't come with a dollar sign in front of it.

Note

An earlier version of this essay appeared online in *Savage Minds: Notes and Queries in Anthropology*, March 10, 2014.

ETHNOGRAPHIC GENRES

37

POETRY AND ANTHROPOLOGY

Nomi Stone

As an anthropologist, I think a great deal about how to render the condition of being in a body and being in time, how to represent the textures of living in the world: its crisscrossing structures, its constrictions and openings. I was a poet first; I've been writing poems since I was six years old and my father began leaving Walt Whitman poems under my pillow. I know and love poetry's tools, and so as soon as I became an anthropologist (thirty years later!), I began to think about what those tools might offer to anthropology. According to the poet Lyn Hejinian, "Writing forms are not merely shapes but forces."[1] And indeed, a poem can animate or unhinge a cosmos by using its unique formal vocabulary: through language and rhythm, through the edge of the line break and its activation of negative space around it, and through the syntax's system of contrasts, between long sentences winding across multiple lines followed by the sudden compression and punch of a short line. Through these tools, it is possible to enact conditions of thought, temporalities, ontologies, and the cadences of both the imagined and the lived. Anthropologists might make use of these tools as they extend how they represent the world.

Last year, I was thinking about how to render loss, both loss and absence in my own life and the losses experienced by Iraqis I had been interviewing during my fieldwork, many of whom had lost loved ones during the war. In particular, an Iraqi friend of mine had lost a lover, and amid the other ravages, this one was especially acute. Around this time, my friend the poet Kaveh Akbar published the poem "Orchids are Sprouting from the Floorboards."[2] The poem answered a question for me about representation, mourning, and longing. The poem begins:

> Orchids are sprouting from the floorboards.
> Orchids are gushing out from the faucets.
> The cat mews orchids from his mouth.
> His whiskers are also orchids.

The poem tumbles the reader into a topsy-turvy dreamscape: orchids rupturing the built world, bursting through and becoming, alternately, animal and mineral, time, space, memory, dream, commodity, image, song, ache. The orchids become the condition of all experience for twenty-four lines, nearly dizzying the reader, depleting the reader: bringing us to a pressure point. And then the poem breaks, pivoting the source of the world's dizzying refiguration. Here is the final turn in the poem:

> The walls are orchids,
> the teapot is an orchid,
> the blank easel is an orchid
> and this cold is an orchid. Oh,
> Lydia, we miss you terribly.

What Kaveh conjures here is a world turned upside down after grief: its ferocious, glinting dazzle compounding every direction you look. Or as Rosebud Ben-Oni offers in her blog about the poem on the *Kenyon Review*, "The speaker's longing transfigures everything he sees into orchids."[3] This is accomplished mimetically, with the unique tools of poetry: first, most obviously, extravagant repetition—of the word orchid, yes, but also with other secret sonic echoes: consider, for example, the abundance of o-like sounds in the first few lines of the poem: "Orchids are sprouting from the floorboards. / Orchids are gushing out from the faucets. / The cat mews orchids from his mouth." This dark whimsy turns the vowels themselves into opening blooms, doubling the effect of the recomposed world. This is not all: the poem's syntax—the relationship between the sentence and the line—has crucial effects. The first eleven lines of the poem are end-stopped, creating the effect, with their self-enclosure, of something like a series of theorems about the world. The next three lines are enjambed (the sentence is broken by the line): "Teenagers are texting each other pictures / of orchids on their phones, which are also orchids. / Old men in orchid pennyloafers / furiously trade orchids." This shift dashes us forward. The orchid world increasingly takes us over. Then consider how syntax is used in this final turn in the poem: "The walls are all orchids, / the teapot is an orchid, / the blank easel is an orchid / and this cold is an orchid. Oh, / Lydia, we miss you terribly." That is, through the longer sentence winding over multiple lines, the orchids rain down finally toward their source, Lydia.

What I mean here is that the poem recruits secret tools, its own embodied laboratory, to amplify sensation, to make a lived world. As anthropologists, we might extend our inquiries into these zones—writing poems from the surfeit of our fieldwork—or perhaps we might borrow poetry's tools, attuning closely to the effects of sound and repetition, image, metaphor, sentence length, and the like, allowing for a more mimetic experience for the reader. To close, I'll offer one of my own poems, "Drone: An Exercise in Awe-Terror," recently published in *Best American Poetry 2016*, which brings together my readings of theory and interviews of drone pilots (not my own, but rather those of a close friend who was making a documentary for *Frontline*). The poem is a thinking through of the drone pilot's sensory and affective experience as his or her hands render the fate of a faraway landscape, and alternating expressions of certainty around the mission and uneasiness. In order to think with these interviews, I was reading a great deal about both empire and terror. The first poem in the sequence was influenced by Immanuel Kant's theory of the "sublime," wherein awe and terror are almost domesticated as the Imagination and Reason meet their trembling interface. The second poem draws on Theodor Adorno, who capsizes an Enlightenment myth wherein humans might tame the tremendous: mountain, or ocean, or nuclear fission. Brought into a contemporary warscape, the unfathomable object is an adversary, imagined by the US military as a relentlessly mobile entity that must be pinned down.

To represent the drone pilot's encounter, the poem begins with two stabs at interrupted metaphor: "A sea of, a drowning of." Indeed, Kant's theory of the "sublime" presupposes the incapacity of the Imagination from the outset, and thus metaphor flails, not allowing the approach to the object. The pilot thereafter tries to conjure (a remote) place through the Imagination, via absent sensations, textures, and aromas: "Prickling of dust and salt. / Seething, the sun between / the shrubs," thereafter shifting from the exterior landscape to that which is truly inscrutable by the Imagination: the subterranean. The poem's second stanza lurches us into a space that resists entry: "Rocks are pocked with / gorges to the core. Something / bad in there, in each / one, every cave caves into / more caves than seconds / in which a man can yes / can die. . . ." The first couplet, with its internal rhyming, suggests that the Imagination has almost domesticated the phenomenon in language—for a moment. Yet that sense of control immediately gives way to "Something / bad in there": the cave's extension into the earth's core, the Imagination's attempted progress towards infinity. As "every cave caves into / more caves than seconds / in which a man can yes / can die," seconds turn into punctures, dropping the body through. The pilot can only re-tether himself through the voice of authority and via Reason's slipping grip: "They / told me there's a place like / that, and I am actually in it. . . ."

In the final poem, I sought to represent the texture of the life of the drone pilot. The interviews I drew from showed the pilots in their daily trajectories, from the control room to returning home to their families around the dinner table. The poem sends us into that space, all absent pronouns, a floating between space-times. We seem to be situated in Nevada: "Walking through the park in Indian Springs. Watching / TV about what they did." The next movement is enclosed in parentheses: "When the rocks turn black: it has happened." The imagined aftermath of an event haunts: the rocks have already turned black; there is a missed encounter. Meanwhile, dissolution: "Watching reflections / in the cloudy glass Liquefying / completely." The two space-times begin to merge, as the cave encroaches: "(The heart's cavity held stone and clear, cold lakes)." The pilot has been in the control room the whole time. He locks up the target and spins up the weapons. An encounter (Has it been assimilated into the psyche of the pilot? Or into the psyches of the Americans in whose names the act is done?) is already a scar upon the land. Language breaks down in that instant: "Blacken did / the shrubs, the ridged / rock." We are forever implicated, and it is only through a rupture in the typical form of ethnographic writing that language can collapse upon itself thus: "Black go / Nevada."

DRONES: AN EXERCISE IN AWE-TERROR
Pilot, Creech Air Force Base, Nevada

I. The Imagination Cannot

A sea of, a drowning of—everything seems
to be red rock. Prickling of dust and salt.
Seething, the sun between
the shrubs.

Rocks are pocked with
gorges to the core. Something

bad in there, in each
one, every cave caves into
more caves than seconds
in which a man can yes
can die. They

told me there's a place like
that, and I am actually in
it (changing
it) (right now)

II. When Reason Came

Across this gray terrain: North
South East West. "Your enemy
doesn't wear a uniform. Find him. Find
his patterns of life. There's no place

in this country where we cannot see him."
There are two men, carrying
guns. Adjust the crosshair above
the bodies. Fifteen seconds. Five

four three two one
zero. White fire
opens a seam in the map.
We nicknamed our eye in the sky

the Gorgon stare. I stare there,
right there: It turns
to a perfect not-
there.

III. Black

   Walking through the park in Indian Springs. Watching
TV about what they did.

   (When the rocks turn black: it has happened.)

   Watching reflections
in the cloudy glass   Liquefying
              completely, like spring

snow like expiring
during sex.

(Rocks turning black: it has happened.)

Dreaming of those who hide
in caves. Watching TV about what they
did.
    (The heart's cavity held stone and clear, cold lakes)

      Surely, the people wanted

(Lock up the target. Spin up
the weapon)

               Blacken did
               the shrubs, the ridged
               rock. Black go
               Nevada.

—Nomi Stone

Notes

1. Lyn Hejinian, "The Rejection of Closure," *Poetry Foundation*, accessed October 1, 2018, http://www.poetryfoundation.org/learning/essay/237870.

2. Kaveh Akbar, "Orchids are Sprouting from the Floorboards," *Linebreak* 40, no. 2 (spring 2016), http://thejournalmag.org/archives/11342.

3. Rosebud Ben Oni, "Orchids We Have Been: On the Transformative Power of Longing," *Kenyon Review Online*, August 19, 2016, http://www.kenyonreview.org/2016/08/orchids-transformative-power-longing.

38

"SEA" STORIES

Anthropologies and Poetries beyond the Human

Stuart McLean

Why might an anthropologist turn to poetry? Although a number of anthropologists have published works of poetry (Edward Sapir, Ruth Benedict, Paul Friedrich, Dell Hymes, Stanley Diamond, to name but a few), such works have usually remained distinct from their authors' scholarly output as anthropologists. Recently, however, some anthropologists have begun to explore poetry not as a supplement to but as an integral part of their academic research and writing. What is it that anthropology and poetry have in common—or what might they impart to one another? Is poetry a means of extending and deepening anthropology's remit as a "humanistic" discipline, or might it offer something else?

For many poetically inclined anthropologists writing today, it is the former possibility that matters most. Renato Rosaldo, in a recent essay, coins the term antropoesía or "anthropoetry" to refer to "poetry that situates itself in a social and cultural world; poetry that is centrally about the human condition."[1] Rosaldo's essay appears as the afterword to a collection of his own poetry, published by a leading academic press. The poems, written over a period of more than a decade, reflect upon the loss of Rosaldo's partner, Michelle ("Shelly") Zimbalist Rosaldo, who on October 11, 1981, fell sixty-five feet to her death from a cliff path into a river in a remote region of the island of Luzon in the Philippines. Rosaldo finds in poetry a means of attending to that which risks being lost through too strident an insistence on facts, evidence, and sequences of cause and effect: "My verse does not try to transform the ill-defined into the well-defined. My task, as a poet, is to render intelligible what is complex and to bring home to the reader the uneven and contradictory shape of that moment."[2] Poetry, like ethnography, is for Rosaldo a way of slowing things down: "a place to dwell and savor more than a space for quick assessment."[3] Antropoesía allows him to explore not only his own response to the traumatic event of Shelly's death and its aftermath but also the subjectivities of others encountered on that day and subsequent days. The latter include Conchita, a friend who was standing beside Shelly when she fell, a soldier assigned to investigate the death, a tricycle taxi driver in the regional capital of Lagawe who offers a free ride to Rosaldo and his two sons, and a Catholic priest ("Father George") who finds them overnight accommodation in a nearby convent. Yet, curiously, not all of the other voices that speak in these verses are human. In one remarkable poem it is the cliff from which Shelly fell that speaks for itself:

but I
am blamed
though I
never wanted
this day
of lamentation[4]

What is it then that speaks through the language of poetry? Does poetry operate predominantly in the register of subjectivity (or intersubjectivity), giving expression to shifting and inchoate states of feeling that are too easily falsified and flattened by the linearity of scholarly prose? Or does poetry's capacity to delineate subjectival states depend upon the fact that its language furnishes access to something beyond or beneath subjectivity? Ezra Pound once defined literature as "language charged with meaning to the utmost possible degree."[5] Yet literature, and most conspicuously poetry, also reminds us continuously of the materiality of language: of the sounds, rhythms, and shapes of words, including their appearance on the page and their relationship to the empty spaces or silences that surround them. Could we say then that the language of poetry is inescapably evocative of the openness of human worlds to the other-than-human presences (both material and intangible) by which they are at once constituted and carried beyond themselves?

Four years ago I found myself turning to poetry for the first time in many years. The occasion was an advanced seminar (titled "Literary Anthropology") at the School for Advanced Research, Santa Fe, New Mexico, that I convened with Anand Pandian and that was subsequently published under a different title as an edited volume. My own contribution to the seminar and to the volume took the form of a long poem, "SEA," arranged in one hundred sections, numbered with Roman numerals, culminating (punningly) in "C." The poem combined "original" writing (whatever that can be taken to mean in this context) with collaged fragments of other texts, most of them encountered in the course of my ongoing research on art, storytelling, and perceptions of long-term environmental change in the Orkney Islands, off the northernmost tip of Scotland. These found texts included historical sources, folklore, oral histories, and the work of other writers such as T. S. Eliot, James Joyce, Clarice Lispector, H. P. Lovecraft, Alice Notley, and the Orcadian poet and novelist George Mackay Brown. On first visiting Orkney ten years ago (and, indeed, on subsequent visits), I had been struck overwhelmingly by the presence of the dead. Their presence took many forms: the Neolithic stone burial cairns that dot the Orcadian landscape; traces of the era of Viking settlement (when the islands were part of the kingdom of Norway); memorials to the fallen of the world wars (when the islands were a major British naval base); and the shipwrecked and the drowned, resting invisibly beneath the waves; along with the oil, composed of the compacted, geothermally heated remains of long-extinct prehistoric marine organisms, that is now pumped so profitably from beneath the North Sea to a terminal of the southern island of Flotta. At the same time, the islands of Orkney and of its northerly neighbor Shetland are being continuously eroded by the sea, a process that will eventually cause them to disappear beneath the waters from which they first emerged. Orkney seemed to me, in other words, to be a setting in which the dead and the material record of their passing merged into a more expansive evolutionary and planetary chronology. I was drawn to poetry as a medium that might register the presence of these multifarious dead as a real and tangible one, a medium through which the dead might speak. My aim in the poem was to evoke through writing a time-space of virtual simultaneity and coexistence in which pasts and presents, history and mythology, the human and the other than human might interact and reciprocally transform one another, and to make manifest at the same time the embeddedness of human histories within the planetary longue durée of geological processes. Some of the dead who return here are identifiable historical figures, such as Earl Sigurd of Orkney, killed at the Battle of Clontarf in Ireland in 1014, or the British secretary of state for war, Lord Horatio Herbert Kitchener, presumed lost with the sinking of the HMS Hampshire by a

German mine in 1916, whose stories, separated by nine centuries, intersect in the lines:

> Dazed, in pitch-darkness
> > The starboard portholes submerged
> > > No one would carry the raven banner[6]

Others of the dead are less immediately recognizable, their voices fading into a mass of other voices and into the vastly more than human time span of geologic prehistory and post-history:

> The multiplicity of every person's possible identifications
> The best wave resources in Europe
> Its hints of earlier and other creation
> Scrape them down, marl, parcel and serve them[7]

I consider the poem anthropological because it sets out to explore not individual subjectivities but the thresholds of dissolution and emergence of the human. Poetry's engagements with the dead are not simply a matter of making reference to them. Such engagements involve also the shapes, sounds, and rhythmic pulsions of words as they carry us beyond human-centered meaning and into the anonymous, impersonal life of the material universe:

> Deadalive languages
> Beforeafter
> Word stuff
> Sea stuff
> > The ghouls are always coming[8]

As new-media theorist Jussi Parikka writes, "The world of thought, senses, sensation, perception, customs, practices, habits and human embodiment is not unrelated to the world of geological strata, climates, the earth, and the massive durations of change that seem to mock the timescales of our petty affairs."[9] If Parikka's focus is on the geologic underpinnings of contemporary digital media (for example, the chemicals, metals, and minerals used in the manufacture of computer batteries, hard drives, screens, liquid crystal displays, and miniaturized circuits), verbal art, as old perhaps as the human species, has been no less a conduit for such other than human, chthonic, and cosmic powers and presences. Perhaps indeed one of the most urgent lessons that poetry can impart to anthropology concerns the immanence of human thought and imagination to a universe that both preexists and surpasses them:

Almost every marine plant and animal brine goes more bitter petro-
leum is the result of fundamental earth processes paleozoic the living
and dying

Of creatures at once completely changed those first voyagers everflow-
ing stream of time pumped through subsea pipelines to the

Terminals at Sullom Voe and Flotta

And now worshipped heathen fiends[10]

Poetry matters (and should matter to anthropology) not only as a medium
for the expression of elusive subjectival states but also because it manifests
an engagement in the world that is prior to both meaning and subjectivity, that is indeed at once their precondition and their limit. The vibrational
intensities, sounds, shapes, and rhythms of words affirm that language does
not simply represent a world external to itself. Rather, language is the world
speaking. If a human-centered preoccupation with meaning has sometimes
rendered us (anthropologists and others) forgetful of this fundamental fact,
then the overwhelming importance of poetry surely lies in its capacity to
remind us of it, endlessly but always differently.

Notes

1. Renato Rosaldo, *The Day of Shelly's Death: The Poetry and Ethnography of Grief*
(Durham, NC: Duke University Press, 2014), 101.

2. Rosaldo, *The Day of Shelly's Death*, 107.

3. Rosaldo, *The Day of Shelly's Death*, 105.

4. Rosaldo, *The Day of Shelly's Death*, 84.

5. Ezra Pound, *ABC of Reading* (London: Faber and Faber, 1936), 36.

6. Stuart McLean, "SEA," in *Crumpled Paper Boat: Experiments in Ethnographic
Writing*, edited by Anand Pandian and Stuart McLean (Durham, NC: Duke University
Press, 2017), 160.

7. McLean, "SEA," 149.

8. McLean, "SEA," 157.

9. Jussi Parikka, *A Geology of Media* (Minneapolis: University of Minnesota Press,
2015), vii.

10. McLean, "SEA," 153.

39

DILATIONS

Kathleen Stewart and Lauren Berlant

The Hundreds is an experiment in keeping up with what's going on. We tell ourselves that we are sensing a new ordinary made through encounters with the force of the world. The encounter is not an event, though, a self-evident staging of shattering intensity or disavowal. *The Hundreds* values interest over assurance and objectivity. It induces form without relieving the pressure of form. It puts thought under the pressure of words. But if our job is to notice the presence of things measured in impacts, the impact is not a unit of anything: it's resonance registered, not just duly noted. (100)

Swells

We write to what's becoming palpable in a sidelong look or a consistency of rhythm or tone. Not to drag things back to the land of the little judges but to push the slow-mo button, wait for what's starting up, what's wearing out. We want to be there for the swell in realism of a tendency dilating or an overblown endurance. Words make a pass at what's all loss and allure. We back up at the hint of something. We butt in. We try to describe the smell; we trim the fat to get to the this-ness of what's happening.

Words sediment next to what's bowled over or detour with a crazed pragmatic thought cell. I saw a woman standing on a sidewalk, chain-smoking while she talked to a buff younger man. She was trying to get him to give someone else a break because he means well or he didn't mean it. Maybe her son. "He don't know no better." She was hanging in there, but the whole top half of her black hair was a helmet of white roots. She was using her fast-thinking superpowers to run a gauntlet of phrases and get out quick even though everyone knew she was just buying time.

A thought hits at an angle. Subjects are surprised by their own acts. But everyone knows a composition when they see one. Scenes can become a thing after only a few repetitions. At the Walmart in New Hampshire, scruffy middle-aged men hang back at the register, letting their elderly mothers pay. The men, in this, are a sour abject; their mothers are a worn autopilot. Women talk in the aisles about the local hospital; it's incapable; it misreads people, handing out exactly the wrong, killer drug.

The new ordinary is a collective search engine, not a grammar. A table of elements flashes up erratically, maybe adding up to a mood or a practice you may or may not take to. Things cross your path like the fireflies you once dreamed of collecting in a jar. Memories come at you like space junk. My sister, Peg, remembers that our mother made us get short haircuts when we were kids because it was easier to take care of. All I know is that when my hair is cut short, it's chaotic. What I remember is the humiliation of the high school yearbook picture with the parted hair poofed up on one side. And I remember that only because the picture showed up at the bottom of a box forty years later.

Anything can start to act like a hinge, activating something suddenly somehow at hand.

Living can be a claustrophobic accrual of direct hits. Contact can be a problem, especially at any sign of a downturn. This year, the holiday mall brawls broke out in twelve different states in an instagram of contagion. A dropped chair mistaken for a gunshot set off a stampede, people running over the tops of one another.

The social is too much and too little: a charge of free radicals. Sometimes it's carefully selected, like the guests at a dinner party, or pointedly scheduled, like the ten-minute mandatory time-outs every hour at the swimming pool just to be safe. In the corporate key, a punishing realism gestures at best practices, as if that's all it takes. Meanwhile, orders of a different kind drift around like gases looking for places to solidify: a change in the social temperature, the trouble brewing in an atmosphere.

The weak links go off; we're all weak links sometimes. I was walking my dog when a man screamed at me not to let her pee on his yard, which we had already passed uneventfully, but as I was fending him off, she peed in his neighbor's yard, triggering his full-throttle abuse popping on all cylinders. Another dog walker had paused to be witness. She said don't let him get your blood boiling; he's a nut case; at least we use our doggie bags. She was trying to pull me back to the good; we were good enough and somehow together although a little agitated. His words were spitballs; hers were gently bouncing tennis balls. He was a rage machine; she was a sympathy machine, but she seemed tired, too, and I could only imagine why. The phrase "people are idiots" is the lingua franca of the moment, and OK, enough said, but there's also a lot of work going on here. A pressure point is an actual tendon stretched by the torque of things. A change of state is a directional shift. We're down to the bone of attention and response.

The now is a groundswell of provocations and problematics. A life ecology bloats with remedial labors: the constant straightening up, the compulsion to grasp at straws, the manic need to retreat. Matter has a heartbeat. Jokes and denial-distractions well up the nested troubles just under the skin. Thought is an afterthought.

There are ways of being up for all this that no one really wants: splintering tunnels of "how-to" advice, ways of regulating yourself with mindfulness or drugs, the unwitting rhythm of a day's push and collapse, all the speed shifts to keep up a tempo participation. A precision nudges through on a side-glance; there's a mooning over things. Like it or not, we're the backup singers to a world in composition and decomp. (900)

Office Hours, 2015

It is not as though we are reaching toward the ontology of a thing: we try not to presuppose. What we perceive is active pattern at a distance. The image that comes to mind when you read that (if images come to mind when you read) might not be what we're imagining, though, and we might not be imagining the same thing either. What draws affect into form is the matter of concern. Amplifying description as we do tries to get at some quality that might stick in your head like a primary object or a bomb, unsettling your trust in what's continuous but anchoring you enough in the scene to pull in other things as you go. Then relation is rebooted, signally extended. Punctum ought to mean whatever grabs you into an elsewhere of form. There ought also to be a word like animum, meaning what makes an impact so live that it shifts around the qualities of things that have and haven't yet been encountered. Of course you can never distinguish what's forgotten and what's remembered.

One day I was late for office hours, despite a New Year's resolution to aim for the early always. I admit I was irritated that this student had insisted on an inconvenient time, so when I say that my lateness was unintentional, I have no ground from which to speak. As I type this, I remember four references that I need to write for other semi-strangers with bright faces gazing intently through me to a happy future. So I come to the café with the silver light where I like to hold an hour because it's public and no-one can feel more trapped. It is a white room with a high glass ceiling whose purpose, I've been told, is to show that the sky is no limit. We sit at a white table on white chairs made of a metal infrastructural grid. The inadequate cushions are black. I am ashamed that I am writing now rather than doing more tasks like this.

It is hard to focus on her because she's a blur to herself. Her language moves rapidly sideways then trips into hesitation. Students all around us are hugging and bumping fists. She looks tired, and there is a cake-makeup layer that points to what it isn't hiding.

Her idea is that celebrities want to be famous but not to be known. We try to convert her interest into a research question. On interrogation it appears that she hates people who have pushy curiosity and also people who don't.

You can decide not to be known or to be disappointed mostly in the way you are known, I said.

While we were talking, my next office hour walked in. The hair on this specific vector of warmth is shiny, made brittle by too much product. She is very thin, in tights and a roving sweater. When she came over to let us know it was time, I saw that her teeth were worn to fine china discs, and my nerves jump cut to the big frightened smile of the bulimic mouth and the meth mouth's jagged teeth: and my already wrung heart really, not metaphorically, ached into the generosity of the impersonal silence that allows us to focus on what *can* be done.

One time a student asked me to "rip to shreds" their overworked yet dormant object. "Is that what I do?" I asked. "I know that's real," they said. Deadline derives from the line drawn around a prison that permits a police sniper to shoot if a prisoner crosses over it without permission. Survival of the fittest always means a different thing, not all of it bad or good, and not all of it something that has an opposite.

Another time a student got smaller and smaller as a project about houses in literature was offered. Another time someone confessed they were poor and that their mother was a hairdresser. Another time a student was condescending, so I gave them their own echo to play with, disappointing. Another time we were watching a movie, and the students rebelled because I watched the credits in the dark till the end. (700)

Some Things We Thought With

Barad, Karen. "Posthumanist Performativity: Toward an Understanding of How Matter Comes to Matter." *Signs* 28, no. 3 (2003): 801–31.

Barthes, Roland. *Camera Lucida: Reflections on Photography*. Translated by Richard Howard. New York: Hill and Wang, 1981.

Benjamin, Jessica. "What Angel Would Hear Me? The Erotics of Transference." In *Like Subjects, Love Objects: Essays on Recognition and Sexual Difference*, 143–74. New Haven, CT: Yale University Press, 1998.

Blue glass vases

Bollas, Christopher. *Being a Character: Psychoanalysis and Self-Experience*. New York: Hill and Wang, 1992.

Breakfasts

Cain, James M. *Mildred Pierce*. New York: Vintage, 1941.

Deleuze, Gilles, and Félix Guattari. "Percept, Affect, and Concept." In *What Is Philosophy?*, translated by Hugh Tomlinson and Graham Burchell, 163–99. New York: Columbia University Press, 1996.

François, Anne-Lise. *Open Secrets: The Literature of Uncounted Experience*. Palo Alto, CA: Stanford University Press, 2008.

Harman, Graham. "DeLanda's Ontology: Assemblage and Realism." *Continental Philosophical Review* 41, no. 3 (2008): 367–83.

Harman, Graham. "Realism without Materialism." *SubStance* 40, no. 2 (2011): 52–72.

Hints (as in a hint of sour or vanilla, glances)

Ingold, Tim. *The Life of Lines*. London: Routledge, 2015.

Lacan, Jacques. *The Seminar of Jacques Lacan*. Book 1, *Freud's Papers on Technique, 1953–1954*, edited by Jacques-Alain Miller, translated by John Forrester. New York: W. W. Norton, 1991.

Latour, Bruno. "A Few Steps toward an Anthropology of the Iconoclastic Gesture." *Science in Context* 10, no. 1 (1997): 63–84.

Manning, Erin. *Relationscapes: Movement, Art, Philosophy*. Boston: Cambridge, MA: MIT Press, 2009.

Manning, Erin, and Brian Massumi. *Thought in the Act: Passages in the Ecology of Experience*. Minneapolis: University of Minnesota Press, 2014.

Meanwhile

Moten, Fred. "Fugitivity Is Immanent to the Thing but Is Manifest Transversally." In *Hughson's Tavern*, 57. Providence, RI: Leon Works, 2008. https://www.poetryfoundation.org/poems-and-poets/poems/detail/53479.

Ordinary registers—skittish, speculative, sedimenting, funny, overworked, saturated, with or without traction

Pine, Jason. *The Art of Making-Do in Naples*. Minneapolis: University of Minnesota Press, 2012.

Pita Bread

Poe, Edgar Allan. "Cask of Amontillado." 1846. http://xroads.virginia.edu/hyper-/poe
/cask.html.

Rose, Jacqueline. "Where Does the Misery Come From? Psychoanalysis, Feminism,
and the Event." In *Feminism and Psychoanalysis*, edited by Richard Feldstein and
Judith Roof, 25–39. Ithaca, NY: Cornell University Press, 1989.

Sedgwick, Eve Kosofsky. "Paranoid Reading and Reparative Reading: Or, You're So
Paranoid, You Probably Think This Introduction Is about You." In *Novel Gazing:
Queer Readings in Fiction*, edited by Eve Kosofsky Sedgwick, 1–40. Durham, NC:
Duke University Press, 1997.

Stengers, Isabella, Brian Massumi, and Erin Manning. "History through the Middle:
Between Macro and Mesopolitics—an Interview with Isabella Stengers." *In-
flexions: A Journal of Research Creation* 3 (2009). http://www.inflexions.org/n3
_stengershtml.html.

Stillinger, Thomas C. Personal Communication, 1991.

Winnicott, D. W. *Playing and Reality*. New York: Basic, 1981.

40

GENRE BENDING, OR THE LOVE OF ETHNOGRAPHIC FICTION

Jessica Marie Falcone

Open your eyes; listen, listen. That is what the novelists say. But they don't tell you what you will see and hear. All they can tell you is what they have seen and heard, in their time in this world, a third of it spent in sleep and dreaming, another third of it spent in telling lies. —Ursula K. Le Guin, *The Left Hand of Darkness*, 1969

Ursula K. Le Guin was best known as a celebrated science fiction writer, but she also wrote essays, realistic fiction, experimental ethnographic fiction, children's literature, anarchist social theory, and more. I like to slip Le Guin's work into my syllabi as often as possible. I have assigned her writing in several of my courses: Anthropology of Futurity, Utopias, Anthropology and Literature, and Ethnographic Methods. Even when weaving fantastic yarns about aliens on other planets, she was always writing about us, about humanity, about power, gender, identity, and contemporary cultural mores. For an anthropologist attentive to the beating art of ethnography, Ursula K. Le Guin's work is a softly uttered challenge about the complex nature of truth and a whispered promise about the potential of fiction as a means of approaching it. Ever wonder what the "K" stands for? Kroeber. The "K" stands for Kroeber.

Appreciating Ethnographic Fiction

Distrust everything I say. I am telling the truth.
—Ursula K. Le Guin, The Left Hand of Darkness, 1969

Alfred Kroeber, an esteemed early American anthropologist (and Ursula K. Le Guin's father), considered the first ethnographic novel to be Adolph Bandelier's *The Delight Makers*, deeming it a successful and faithful representation of the Pueblo culture.[1] Kroeber called the novel "a more comprehensive and coherent view of native Pueblo life than any scientific volume on the Southwest."[2] Although some of our discipline's most illustrious progenitors embraced and celebrated ethnographic fiction,[3] for a long time it remained a marginalized, perhaps even stigmatized, genre. The broadest definitions of ethnographic fiction tend to delineate the following criteria: (1) it is a narrative nurtured or inspired by lived experience (or "being there"), and (2) it is unfettered from the bonds of the precisely observed. Unfettered. I linger on that word. Unshackled, open, free.

I see myself as an ambassador for ethnographic fiction, albeit a poor one, perhaps. While it has long been a nigh-endangered species within anthropology's literary ecosystem,[4] I have done precious little to slow its attenuation. I have published just one book chapter with pretensions to ethnographic fiction. Although it will probably only ever be read by about a dozen people, it is my most beloved text baby.[5] It is the true story of a particular iteration of a giant statue plan in Bodh Gaya, India, which was canceled, moved, or soundly defeated (depending on who you ask and when). My narrative tacked back and forth between straight ethnography and (crooked?) ethnographic fiction. Because the piece was quite deliberately modeled upon Bruno Latour's *Aramis, or the Love of Technology*, I titled it "Maitreya, or the Love of Buddhism" and called it a work of "social scientifiction." I would argue that my creative licenses made my product more compelling and more achingly true. In my view, insofar as the piece succeeded at all, it was because of the fictions, not despite them.

In genre-normative ethnography, one cannot invent dialogue or scenarios that never were; one can frame but not fashion. In our genre-normative writing culture, conventions require that we are diligently attentive to our field notes and interview transcripts. For example, if I were writing up a narrative of my interview with Sushila, I would not write that "Sushila had tied her silk sari in the Gujarati style, with the gold-tone-embroidered pallu detail arrayed across her chest like a fan," if, in fact, I have no recollection of what she was actually wearing (nor notes referencing her apparel). Nor can

I definitively say how someone else was feeling unless to relate what I had been told: "Sushila told me that she was anxious about our interview, as few people knew the truth of her family's dire financial situation."

While writing ethnographic fiction, however, one can brazenly transgress those disciplinary conventions. In a piece of ethnographic fiction, I can flagrantly put real people in an imaginary situation to get to the heart of the matter. Or I can construct hybrid people out of a multiplicity of known entities without batting an eyelash. Or I can describe interlocutors deep in the midst of a significant conversation that I heard about but did not witness. I can invent feelings, details, and sari colors. I acknowledge that there can be something deeply unsettling about the liberties taken with ethnographic fiction, but it can be profoundly emancipating at the same time. And the release from norms does not just feel good; it can do good. It can be valuable. It can achieve things. Through creative framing, literary flare, poetry, inventive mash-ups, and other flexible techniques of representation, genre-bending writing has the power to manufacture new avatars of the truth, ones that may help readers understand subjects differently, and perhaps more completely, than they would have otherwise. Even some of my most stubbornly hard-science-minded students have sheepishly admitted in class that the ethnographic fiction interludes of Karen McCarthy Brown's *Mama Lola* enhance, rather than detract from, the value and integrity of her ethnography.

The Faction Spectrum

Fiction results from imagination working on experience. We shape experience in our minds so that it makes sense. We force the world to be coherent—to tell us a story. Not only do fiction writers do this; we all do it; we do it constantly, continually, in order to survive. People who can't make the world into a story go mad.
—Ursula K. Le Guin, *The Wave in the Mind*, 2004

Our post-1980s anthropological writing culture is willing and able to embrace our conventional ethnography as "partial fictions"[6] and "faction,"[7] but there is a very clear implicit boundary between "making" and "making up" (both Clifford and Geertz referred to those terms in their work as reflections upon the former as opposed to the latter). But is the difference really so clear-cut? If all of our writing actually sits somewhere between the poles of fact and fiction, then why not massage the portmanteau faction to stretch from one end to the other? Under this framing, all writing is just a particular vintage of faction across a fact-fiction continuum. And that midpoint—that all important churning halfway point that separates "making" from "making up"—is elusive, impossible, and humming with movement. Somewhere in that nebulous center lies the kind of careful inventions that even the most dogmatic genre-normative ethnographer may engage in: the self-conscious, ethical veiling or massaging of details to protect the confidentiality of informants. Isn't even the straightest ethnography always at least a little sinuous? And as for the extreme ends of our faction spectrum, I doubt that it would be controversial to suggest that there is little (if any) writing on the extreme of either end: facts are always still fashioned,[8] and fictions are always still cultural.[9]

I welcome anthropological writing across the faction spectrum, including genre-bending pieces that drift towards more creative, inventive representations of truth, but I do have a stodgy streak. I may revel in a beautifully crafted lie as much as anyone, but as a reader I like to know when I am being lied to. In an article in *Anthropology and Humanism*, Kirin Narayan used various frames through which to discern a border between fiction and ethnography, but of those she elaborates upon—(1) disclosure of process, (2) generalization, (3) the uses of subjectivity, and (4) accountability—I am particularly interested in the first and last of these, as they most directly address both the variability in how authors approach the task of representing the "truth" and the importance of reflection upon it.[10] Ethnographic genre bending ought to be clear about what it is; whether in the title, preface, introduction, footnotes, or the main text itself, anthropological writers should be explicit about their process and products. As a reader, I do not want ethnographic fiction to sneak up on me.

As a writer, I see it as my responsibility to ensure that my compositions are located along the faction spectrum. Genre-normative anthropological writing is most often methodologically explicit. Genre-bending writing can be no less transparent. For example, in "Maitreya, or The Love of Buddhism," I gave my readers a road map; if a section was prefaced with "And thus have I heard . . ." (a Buddhist literary trope), then (and only then) readers knew the forthcoming section was ethnographic fiction. Therefore, my readers could easily determine precisely which sections were genre normative and which sections were genre bending.

Ethnographic fiction ought not to try to hide in the guise of conventional ethnography, for therein lies madness. Therein lies the rupture of a sacred trust. Therein lies the specter of Carlos Castaneda. If you think I am flogging a straw man (or a solitary ghost) here, think again. In AAA sessions, as well as in the context of judging an ethnographic fiction competition for an AAA section, I have heard some contemporary genre benders complain that any sort of explanation could compromise their artistry. However, a commitment to radical honesty with our readers is anthropology's only surefire way to avoid a gradual decline into a post-truth chasm and, ultimately, irrelevance. Today, in Trump's America—where meticulously researched knowledge can be dismissed as "fake news," where news-like, partisan echo chambers (that is, actual fake news) sell willing readers only the "alternative facts" they want to consume, and where expertise and scholarship are being systematically derided and undermined—anthropologists, like many other writers, must be especially thoughtful and deliberate when we color outside the lines.

Querying Ethnographic Fiction

Fiction writers, at least in their braver moments, do desire the truth: to know it, speak it, serve it. But they go about it in a peculiar and devious way, which consists in inventing persons, places, and events which never did and never will exist or occur, and telling about these fictions in detail and at length and with a great deal of emotion, and then when they are done writing down this pack of lies, they say, There! That's the truth! —Ursula K. Le Guin, *The Left Hand of Darkness*, 1969

My deep appreciation for ethnographic fiction notwithstanding, I do not pretend to have a perfect definition of precisely what it is. Is not ethnographic fiction just research-based creative writing by a trained anthropologist? Yes, but is it not also an inventive form of experience-based writing that arguably transcends disciplinary borders? And if yes, then what is the difference between ethnographic fiction and very thickly described fiction (think Orhan Pamuk or Edith Wharton)? In their respective treatises on ethnographic fiction, both Langness and Frank[11] and Schmidt[12] included the novelist (and nonanthropologist) Chinua Achebe in their broad surveys of what counts as ethnographic fiction. In fact, Nancy Schmidt writes that "ethnographic fiction was written before the development of anthropology as a discipline and is still being written by creative writers unacquainted with anthropology."[13] Ursula K. Le Guin's own reflections upon fiction are not unlike conventional descriptions of ethnographic fiction: "Experience is where the ideas come from. But a story isn't a mirror of what happened. Fiction is experience translated by, transformed by, transfigured by imagination. Truth includes but is not coextensive with fact. Truth in art is not imitation, but reincarnation. . . ."[14] To further blur the matter, in a question-and-answer session for an "Ethnography and Fiction" panel that I helped organize at the American Anthropological Association in 2015, an anthropologist known for writing some famously successful pieces of "ethnographic fiction" said that he strongly preferred to just call those works "fiction" full stop.

And then there is the related question of what differentiates some kinds of ethnographic fiction from the genre of creative nonfiction (think Susan Orlean), "new journalism" (think Hunter S. Thompson), or the nonfiction novel (think Truman Capote). That particular hue upon the faction spectrum is crowded and complex indeed.

I was a judge for the Society for Humanistic Anthropology's Ethnographic Fiction award for several years. At a SHA member forum at the American Anthropological Association annual meeting in 2014, I led a discussion about a new dilemma facing the ethnographic fiction award's selection committee: we had started getting an increasing number of submissions from nonanthropologists. More submissions had improved our (still modest) applicant yield, but we had to ask our peers, "For an anthropological subsection award, is an increasingly interdisciplinary pool of academic, professional, and amateur fiction writers good, bad, neither, or both?" Some members suggested closing the contest to all but professional anthropologists (or even just to SHA members), but others fought for more inclusivity.

Even limiting the pool to "anthropologists writing fiction" would have itself been an intractable task. At the time, many of us balked at a process that would require us to establish a definition of who counts as an anthropologist (or as someone anthropologically affiliated), so we decided to leave the pool wide-open. But if ethnographic fiction is not just imaginative writing by anthropologists, then should the genre be inclusive of almost any experience-rooted prose (written by anyone) to the creative side of genre-normative ethnography?

We settled on a compromise of sorts: anyone could submit a piece of "ethnographic fiction" to SHA, but they had to be willing to join us in the exercise of thinking through the enigmatic nature of the genre. For the 2015 prize, SHA asked applicants to submit a short essay accompanying their ethnographic fiction that theorized what ethnographic fiction is and how their submission fit into the genre. Essentially, recognizing that ethnographic fiction is messy indeed, we invited others to get down and dirty in the mud to rassle the vagaries of genre bending along with us. For my part, I do not care if a piece of ethnographic fiction is written by Stephen King or Stephen Tyler, as long as the author is willing to take his or her wobbly seat at the Mad Tea Party and work the riddle that may have no answer.

Notes

An earlier version of this essay appeared online in *Savage Minds: Notes and Queries in Anthropology*, April 13, 2015.

1. Alfred L. Kroeber, "Introduction," in *American Indian Life*, ed. Elsie Clews Parsons (New York: B. W. Huebsch, 1922), 13.

2. Kroeber, "Introduction," 13.

3. Kirin Narayan, "Ethnography and Fiction: Where Is the Border?" *Anthropology and Humanism* 24, no. 2 (1999): 136.

4. As I edited this piece for publication, I came across a few new engagements with ethnographic fiction, such as *Crumpled Paper Boats* and *Fictionalizing Anthropology*, that may indicate fresh momentum for the genre. Only time will tell if this portends a mainstreaming of fiction in anthropology or a momentary softening toward experimentation. See Anand Pandian and Stuart McLean, eds., *Crumpled Paper Boat*, School of American Research Advanced Seminar Series (Durham, NC: Duke University Press Books, 2017). See also Stuart McLean, *Fictionalizing Anthropology* (Minneapolis: University of Minnesota Press, 2017).

5. Text babies, or what Signithia Fordham has called "paper babies." See Signithia Fordham, "Write-ous Indignation: Black Girls, Dilemmas of Cultural Domination and the Struggle to Speak the Skin We Are In," in *Anthropology off the Shelf: Anthropologists on Writing*, ed. Alisse Waterston and Maria D. Vesperi (West Sussex: Wiley-Blackwell, 2009), 79.

6. James Clifford, "Introduction: Partial Truths," in *Writing Culture: The Poetics and Politics of Ethnography*, ed. James Clifford and George E. Marcus (Berkeley: University of California Press, 1986), 1.

7. When Geertz used the word *faction*, he deployed it in service of exploring the inventive work of "making stuff," as opposed to "making stuff up." As he wrote, "It is not clear just what 'faction,' imaginative writing about real people in real places, exactly comes to beyond a clever coinage; but anthropology is going to have to find out if it is to continue as an intellectual force in contemporary culture—if its mule condition (trumpeted scientific mother's brother, disowned literary father) is not to lead to mule sterility." See Clifford Geertz, *Works and Lives: The Anthropologist as Author* (Stanford, CA: Stanford University Press, 1988), 141. It should be noted that although some writers, such as Packer and Horgan, have credited Geertz with coining the term *faction*, there is evidence to the contrary, as I have found it in texts before Geertz's famous mention of it in 1988. For example, Zander Horst's research shows the term in use at least as far back to Dietmar Haack's use of it in 1971 to discuss nonfiction novels. While perusing the literature, I found at least a half-dozen writers claiming that someone or other, not Geertz, first used the term. For example, Demastes wrote that playwright Tom Stoppard invented the term: "Stoppard coined the term 'faction'—a blend of fact and fiction. . . ." See William W. Demastes, *The Cambridge Introduction to Tom Stoppard* (Cambridge: Cambridge University Press, 2013), 40. See also John Horgan, "Stream of Thought Description of Teaching James's 'Stream of Thought': A Work of Faction," *Scientific American* Blog, December 7, 2013, https://blogs.scientificamerican.com/cross-check/stream-of-thought-description-of-teaching

-jamese28099s-e2809cstream-of-thoughte2809d-a-work-of-faction; Zander Horst, *Fact, Fiction, "Faction": A Study of Black South African Literature in English* (Tübingen: Narr, 1999), 403; Martin Packer, *The Science of Qualitative Research* (Cambridge: Cambridge University Press, 2011), 229.

8. Bruno Latour and Steve Woolgar, *Laboratory Life: The Construction of Scientific Facts* (Princeton, NJ: Princeton University Press, 1986), 40.

9. This assertion is supported by Le Guin's recognition that "there's no such thing as pure invention. It all starts with experience. Invention is recombination. We can work only with what we have." Ursula K. Le Guin, *The Wave in the Mind: Talks and Essays on the Writer, the Reader, and the Imagination* (Boston: Shambhala, 2004), 268.

10. Narayan, "Ethnography and Fiction," 139–43.

11. L. L. Langness and Gelya Frank, "Fact, Fiction and the Ethnographic Novel," *Anthropology and Humanism Quarterly* 3 (1978): 20.

12. Nancy Schmidt, "The Nature of Ethnographic Fiction: A Further Inquiry," *Anthropology and Humanism Quarterly* 6 (1981): 8–9, 12.

13. Schmidt, "The Nature of Ethnographic Fiction," 11.

14. Le Guin, *The Wave in the Mind*, 268.

41

ETHNOGRAPHIC FICTION

The Space Between

Roxanne Varzi

Fiction, for me, like ethnography, has always melded with a deep desire to understand and explain the world around me. As an eight-year-old in Iran, I wrote stories to either escape or explain the revolution that had turned my country into an Islamic Republic and had turned my single identity as a dorageh, or two-veined Iranian, into half-American, half-Iranian, forcing me either to choose one identity or to stay in between. Writing helped me to make sense of the in-between, to make sense of my new life while holding on to the one that was already becoming a dream—unreal.

The past was a place where "bombs were flying through the air, the sky was ablaze, there was no night." My American high school teacher read this opening of one of my stories and said, "Write what you know." She smiled at me and told me to try again. I explained that I had seen bombs and that the sky was ablaze and, night or not, I couldn't sleep for days as a child because I was so scared about what was happening in the streets. At least that's how I remembered it. I came to see early on that we cannot fully replicate reality—even and especially in ethnography—in film, text, or sound (the mediums I work in), nor is fiction purely a figment of its writer's imagination. Was I writing fiction or ethnography, and did the distinction really matter?

After college I returned to Iran for a year and then spent the following year back in the States writing about it. To live meant to write about it.

Sometimes if I didn't write about it, it was as if the event had not happened or was somehow unreal and unbelievable, like ethnographic notes jotted down a few hours too late. I thought I was writing a memoir, but it was really something in between fiction and ethnography (which I knew little about but gravitated toward instinctively). It was 1994, and the onslaught of memoirs of Iranian returnees, and of Iranian women in particular, had not yet arrived. There were few publishers interested in nondramatic narratives from Iran, especially one like mine that had no near escapes, imprisonments, or beatings. My account concentrated on the quotidian, which I thought offered a downright exotic view of Iran compared to the American news coverage: angry raised fists and anti-American slogans.

A Booker Prize novelist who read some of my work told me I was shifting between literary nonfiction and fiction, and suggested that I choose a genre and stick with it. Had I listened to her, that book may have been published as a whole rather than as essays in some venues, short stories in others (including *Anthropology and Humanism*, which gave it a prize), and parts of my ethnography *Warring Souls*.

After the ultimately fragmented memoir, my next project was my dissertation on Iran, where I experienced a very new and intense form of writer's block, which was really self-censorship in disguise. The writing was no longer about me, which meant I had the enormous responsibility all anthropologists have of faithfully and respectfully writing the intimate lives we are privy to. This was coupled by the responsibility of being the first anthropologist of my generation to do fieldwork in Iran, a state with all sorts of rules about what one can and cannot talk about. If I messed this up, the door would close for others. I wanted to continue to work in Iran and to protect my family and my anonymous interlocutors and future researchers. The parts of my work that I found the most difficult to write about were the lives of people whose worldview was so different than my own and so contested, especially those men who wanted to martyr themselves for the state.

I was advised to "just write," which I was attempting to do in my little carrel on the roof of Butler Library at Columbia University on September 11, 2001, when further downtown two planes flew into the World Trade Center. The world again felt unreal, and so I turned to fiction. Fiction allowed me to bring the tone, the feelings, the atmosphere of the Iran-Iraq war and what it was like for those who fought it to the fore without making any judgments about their project or what it meant in light of my current situation as a Middle Eastern American living and writing in New York City. In the end, one of my mentors encouraged me to leave the fiction in the dissertation, which I did while secretly bemoaning the destruction of my budding war novel. Next time, I promised myself, I'll write a novel.

As I found out, the choice wasn't mine. My ethnographic material demanded particular genres: film for my work on visual war culture in Iran and a sound project for my work on international war photography. Despite the change in mediums, what remained the same were the hours of research and even more hours of writing. As my five-year-old child would let you know, without research I wouldn't have a story to tell because I'm just not any good at making them up (or at refraining from analyzing and educating alongside narrating). In my latest eight-year long attempt at writing a novel based on fieldwork on underground theater, I couldn't bear not to throw in my analysis and theorize or to stick to an omniscient narrative. I finally broke down at year six and explicitly added the ethnographic back into the novel through the addition of a first-person voice that analyzes and theorizes the ethnographic material. I simply stopped trying to choose between a novel and ethnography and embraced the in-between: a novel or neo-ethnography.

This latest ethnography on Iranian theater is akin to Italian neorealism, in which real people played themselves with lines scripted by a writer toward the goal of creating social change, a new reality. Whether I'm writing the script or writing about the play, what I'm doing or trying to do is to play with ethnography in a very serious way. I believe that ethnography is the genre that is most malleable, most inspiring, most in-between. It gives my loose meanderings a purpose; it gives just living a vocation; it gives gossip and nosiness legitimacy. Ethnography makes me feel twice alive, in person and then on the page. It allows me to analyze, to overthink, to take refuge in that place where I feel that everything is explainable and controllable . . . and then it explodes. My ethnographic notes are a dictionary, a book of short stories, a litany of mistakes and misunderstandings. My ethnographic writings are soon filled with the opposite of ethnography yet are still filled with life, and then when life needs protection, needs cover, needs space to breathe and to change, there is fiction. Fiction allows me to write about Iran uncensored, allows me to play and to change the ending. The thing about ethnography is there isn't an ending. No one writes "The End" at the close of an ethnography. Instead, it's the beginning of discussion, of thought, of change, and it's where as a writer I've found my home, my identity.

Note

An earlier version of this essay appeared online in *Savage Minds: Notes and Queries in Anthropology*, October 13, 2014.

42

FROM REAL LIFE TO THE MAGIC OF FICTION

Ruth Behar

I've spent most of my life writing nonfiction. But I always dreamed of being a fiction writer. Now, at the age of sixty, I am making my debut as a fiction writer. My first novel is a book for middle-grade readers, and it is based on a true experience from my childhood.

Why did it take so long?

As a young woman, I read fiction voraciously. I loved it when a story or a novel cast a spell on me and I had to drop everything and read breathlessly to the end. Whether it's *The Velveteen Rabbit*, *A Tree Grows in Brooklyn*, or the Elena Ferrante novels, the magic of fiction is still hard for me to describe, but the grip it has on my body and soul is undeniable.

The problem I had was that I held fiction in very high regard. It was the genre I placed on a pedestal. Much as I wanted to write it, I couldn't. Not well, anyway. Every time I tried my hand at writing a work of fiction, it felt inadequate to me. I seemed to lack faith in my imagination. I didn't understand back then that the imagination has to be given sun and water and be sung to by the sparrows, like a delicate flower.

My last year of college I wandered into a class in cultural anthropology, and before I knew it I had chosen a career that forced me to pay close attention to real life, nothing but real life. I don't regret my decision. I got to travel. I made friends among strangers. My house is filled with art, pottery, rugs, and tablecloths from all the places I have been. Most important, I learned to listen to diverse people's stories and learned how to pass on those stories in all their cultural complexity in my writing.

But like an addict, I couldn't help myself: I kept coming back to this crazy desire to write fiction. Late at night, or in the summer, I wrote stories and worked endlessly on an adult novel. I don't think that writing was in vain. I was exercising my writing muscles. But it wasn't until I sat down and began writing in the unpretentious voice of a ten-year-old girl that I felt myself swept away by the magic of fiction. Magic that I was creating!

It was a story I had told before, in the form of a personal essay, as an adult woman looking back on a childhood experience, trying to explain and analyze it. I had spent a year confined to my bed in a body cast after a terrible car accident that took place shortly after my family and I immigrated to the United States from Cuba in the 1960s.

In the nonfiction version, the story focused on the psychological and physical effects that this period of forced immobility had on me. In retelling the story as fiction for young readers, I did something completely different: Ruthie, the child, lives the experience a day at a time, not knowing how things will end up. Her fears, her uncertainties, her loneliness, her sorrows, her desperation, her humiliation, her pride, her efforts not to seem pathetic and a freak—the riptide of emotions unleashed by the change in her fate—are at the core of the novel.

As soon as it was Ruthie's story, rather than mine, I happily surrendered control to my protagonist. She'd been a Hopscotch Queen, and now she is immobile and everyone pities her. She'd learned English faster than her mother and felt very grown-up translating for her at the grocery store, and now she is like a baby and her mother has to bring her the bedpan whenever she has to pee or poop. But her bad luck also brings her good luck. Her school sends a tutor to the house so she won't fall behind in school, and that's how she becomes a girl who loves books and loves being smart. And she becomes smart in other ways, learning to feel sympathy for the boy who caused the car accident, learning to give thanks to all the people who try to help her heal: her family, her friends, her neighbors.

The magic of fiction is that it all seems real, although in fact it's a heightened version of the real. Real life is inchoate. We can give it meaning only in retrospect. But in a novel, everything must be meaningful in the present tense.

When creating the imaginary world of a novel, you write not simply about what happened but what you wished had happened. Throughout the year I was immobile, my bed was never moved, and years later I wondered why my parents hadn't noticed that I was always staring at the same wall. But in the novel, a caring neighbor arranges for the ambulance attendants to take Ruthie out to see the snow. That same neighbor has piñatas hanging from the ceiling of his apartment, which utterly delights Ruthie. Or, to use another example, in real life I had a friend who accompanied me to school, carrying my books for me while I was on crutches. In the fictional recreation, she also gives Ruthie her go-go boots, an act of kindness that helps Ruthie to trust her legs again. She was a lovely friend; the novel makes her lovelier.

As Isadora Duncan once said, "If I could tell you what it meant, there would be no point in dancing it."[1] I think the magic of fiction happens in the doing. Once you are deep inside the world of your characters, you let them take the lead and you follow. You trust. You allow yourself to be surprised. You close your eyes. You slip into a dream.

Things happened one way in real life, but in the fictional recreation they can happen another way. The magic of fiction is you can forgive everyone who hurt you and reward everyone who loved you. And it's never too late to start.

Note

1. As quoted in Gregory Bateson, *Steps to an Ecology of Mind* (Chicago: University of Chicago Press, 1972), 137.

SECTION IX

BECOMING AND BELONGING

43

ON WRITING FROM ELSEWHERE

Uzma Z. Rizvi

My childhood imagination enhanced stories told to me by my elders of where we were from, and my history embraced the possibility of exciting seafarers, noble learned men and women, poor housekeepers, exiled princesses, wandering mystics, Marxists fighting the good fight, and revolutionaries standing up against the British. Some of this might very well be true, but when I was age five or six, sitting in New Jersey, truth was a far-fetched notion and irrelevant. As we do, I have carried these stories with me through my life and into my practice, and I revisit them now as I consider the topography of text. I am curious about what it means to write about others from a position of otherness as the cartography of elsewhere informs my writing from within, while positioned somewhere else.

Where are you from?
But where are you really *from?*

Along with the fantastical stories of being from somewhere else, this all-too-familiar pair of questions has followed me throughout my life. From all levels of schooling (and life) in the United States to checkpoints in Iraq: when one is from elsewhere, where that else is, is always in question.[1] When I am asked this question within the context of my practice, there is often an assessment of trust, suspicion, and a baseline assumption that all anthropologists are spies—and guilty of that until proven innocent.[2] As it has been laid out for me countless times, how can one trust someone with such mobility, with no grounding, with no place, and/or with the ability to move into a new sociocultural world *just* for research? Of all of these, the last stings the most because it simultaneously devalues our profession of choice while underlining the privilege that anthropologists carry in our disciplinary bodies. It is that discomfort of privilege that makes me want to pause here for a moment to situate such a question before moving on to what it means to write from such a place.

Given that my own practice has existed within the ambit of the colonial world, writing from landscapes of settler colonialism, in the spaces of colonial transit, or in former colonies, I have wondered about the relationship between land and trust as a colonial by-product. That seems to be the tip of the iceberg. Why is trust, in the few geographies I have encountered (thus not a universal), based upon placedness? *Where* are you from? I used to think it was because part of the human condition was to always place people within sociocultural structures that made sense to us, but as I have grown, I have experienced a different depth to that question. *Where* you are from is not about fitting into the social schema but rather that the where-ness of it all eerily exudes some sort of ontological certainty to belonging.

If you sense some hesitation on my part as I write about this, it is because I bring this up with much trepidation and with a desire (that I am foolishly ignoring) to hedge my bets. This is (at best) a very complicated issue because it is deeply and irrevocably entangled with histories of displacement and land claims, issues of class mobility, and, in my mind, a hegemony of agricultural (read: settled) societies that emerges as far back as the third millennium BCE. (Of course, agriculture starts earlier: I am linking the millennium to a certain hegemonic form of power related to institutions, infrastructure, and agriculture.) At the core of my query is a very contemporary question: Why the mistrust of immigrants? And what relationship does immigration have with a sense of authentic belonging? As one who has never had the ability to transition into a body of authentic belonging, for me this will always loom as an uneasy query and most likely one without any answer.

In my own intellectual upbringing I first tried to wrap my head around questions of citizenship and transcultural and transnational identities, which can be dated to the late 1990s and early 2000s based on some of my touchstone texts, such as May Joseph's *Nomadic Identities* (1999), Pico Iyer's *The Global Soul* (2000), and Aihwa Ong's *Flexible Citizenship* (1999). Simultaneously, I was ensconced in US minority politics, finding my own understanding of a certain type of white ignorance through edited volumes such as Sullivan and Tuana's *Race and Epistemologies of Ignorance* (2007). Thus, having been nurtured in the political efficacy of epistemological critique, when I found myself wrestling with a conflicted sense of deep meaning in the ontological turn, I was worried but curious. It worked brilliantly with archaeology, with some archaeologists claiming that we had been doing this all along. Before you roll your eyes at these claims, I would think about the colonial baggage that archaeology continues to carry in its current neocolonial avatar: perhaps what is being tapped into here is some relationship between coloniality, placedness (that can be excavated), and some ontological certainty of belonging.

A few years ago (in 2013) I co-organized an AAA session titled "Once You See It, You Can't Un-see It (A. Roy): Negotiating Inequality and Coloniality in Anthropological Epistemology and Archaeological Practice" with Sonya Atalay, Whitney Battle-Baptiste, and Jane Anderson. Part of my impetus for the paper I presented (and subsequently published in 2015 with a different title in a reader for the Cyprus Pavilion at the Venice Bienniale), "En Route to a Manifesto: Some Thoughts concerning Epistemic Inequality and Injustice," was to contend with such issues, in particular, the tension between the ontological and the epistemic.[3] What were we doing with this bitter colonial aftertaste that the ontological blue pill was forcing (or maybe enforcing)? Yet there was something very important happening in the recognition of a sort of vitality for things, most commonly heard at the AAAs that year as "the thinginess of things." My only solace was that I could trace my pedagogical tendencies to think about entanglement, my body, and issues of labor to feminist/queer scholarship, and I became that crazy lady at archaeology conferences who kept muttering under her breath, "Well, it would be nice if you cited or read Karen Barad, who actually wrote about this in 2007. . . ."[4]

But there continued to be a nagging epistemic problem—specific to my body and belonging—a problem of deep-set coloniality in archaeology specifically and anthropology more broadly.[5] In some manner of speaking, the issue is not so much about the discipline itself but how my practice was now part of the discipline of anthropology and yet from elsewhere because of its desire to decolonize and dismantle. What sorts of epistemological frameworks was I reigniting that maintained a distinct colonial flavor that I might be able to remove, change, reevaluate? And how might I do this while acknowledging the vitality of every*thing* around me? To be honest, I'm not sure I've figured much of this out (although I am still working on it), except to say that now the Earth has more vitality, I am read as belonging elsewhere, and racism continues to create murky epistemic problems in the academy.

Putting the Earth and the academy aside, what's going on here? Do we or can we belong to a place or not? If we are from elsewhere, can we belong to here?

This sets up an all-too-easy critique of the failure of the modern nation-state, so I am not even going to bother with that. What is more interesting to me is how, in spite of the trickery of citizenship and the bareness of life, there is still a sense of belonging that permeates our discourses. This authentic belonging is constructed and saturated with the politics of everything and the deep privilege of ascribing or prescribing identity to others. And those of us who continue to embody multiple prescriptions (which I would argue is most of us, though some more than others) learn how to switch. But this is not about code switching and identity. This is about always belonging to somewhere else.

It is not a coincidence that I write this while I live in the UAE. It is also not merely a turn of phrase that I have chosen to write about "living" here rather than saying I am "doing research" or that I am "in the field." It is precisely because I live here that I now have a different stake in the cultural work, including archaeology, that happens around me. It is because I live here that I work with collaborators and colleagues as we coconstruct some understanding of the ancient and contemporary.

Yet I still do not belong. When I write about here, I am writing from elsewhere. For so many others here, who also may not belong, I cannot help but wonder where they are writing from. Perhaps what we all have in common are our exciting seafaring grandmothers, housekeeper aunts, roaming mystic sisters, and raging Marxist mothers. Or perhaps there is something about seeing the color of your soil on another body that holds us in place for a moment as we recognize something familiar and dangerous.

Notes

An earlier version of this essay appeared online in *Savage Minds: Notes and Queries in Anthropology*, January 4, 2017.

1. Uzma Z. Rizvi, "Checkpoints as Gendered Spaces: An Autoarchaeology of War, Heritage and the City," in *The Oxford Handbook of the Archaeology of the Contemporary World*, ed. Paul Graves-Brown, Rodney Harrison, and Angela Piccini (Oxford: Oxford University Press, 2013), 497.

2. Uzma Z. Rizvi, "Accounting for Multiple Desires: Decolonizing Methodologies, Archaeology and the Public Interest," *India Review* 5, nos. 3-4 (2006): 407.

3. Uzma Z. Rizvi, "Decolonizing Archaeology: On the Global Heritage of Epistemic Laziness," in *Two Days after Forever: A Reader on the Choreography of Time*, ed. Omar Kholeif (Berlin: Sternberg, 2015), 154–63.

4. Sara Ahmed, *Queer Phenomenology: Orientations, Objects, Others* (Durham, NC: Duke University Press, 2006); Karen Barad, *Meeting the Universe Halfway: Quantum Physics and the Entanglement of Matter and Meaning* (Durham, NC: Duke University Press, 2007); Jane Bennett, *Vibrant Matter: A Political Ecology of Things* (Durham, NC: Duke University Press, 2010).

5. It is important to note that decolonial concerns linked to indigeneity and land are different, and this essay was not written as a way to decenter those, but perhaps even to try to think through how to make a space for the relationship between immigrant politics and indigenous politics as a point of solidarity rather than opposition. For place-based pedagogies from indigenous perspectives, see Eve Tuck, Marcia McKenzie, and Kate McCoy, "Land Education: Indigenous, Post-colonial, and Decolonizing Perspectives on Place and Environmental Education Research," *Environmental Education Research* 20, no. 1 (2014): 1–23.

44

WRITING TO BECOME . . .

Sita Venkateswar

Through writing, I accumulate more being. As I write, I materialize the ephemeral and in so doing become more than I was. Writing grows us. But how exactly does it do this?

I wear the traces of various Englishes, strung like so many iridescent pearls within the necklace of language adorning me. The lilting singsong of Anglo-Indian first granted me tongue, irrepressible, undaunted by the pristine elegance of Queen's English. In studying anthropology, I collided with the unabashed assertiveness of American idiom. But it was in the antipodes that I discovered my place in the world in encounters with the laconic, self-deprecating humor of New Zealand vernacular. A clamor of tongues finds expression through me to constitute the anthropologist I have become.[1]

Writing requires an act of will or a leap of faith. It requires trust that I will find what I need to reach where I want to be. Yet no direct route exists from thinking to writing; it is a spiraling path often littered with impediments. I am sometimes tempted to linger on the path unless an externally imposed imperative channels the steady stream of words to a medium that will be read by others. The yawning pit of terror triggered by such a prospect requires considerable effort to evade no matter how habituated I am to its presence. Despite the testimony of earlier publications, the act of writing exposes an unvoiced vulnerability that I, like others, prefer to mask. To be judged and found wanting: to not find the right words, to not render intelligible or offer something original, to not be considered valuable by academe.

My entry into the world of words is primarily as a reader. I remain enraptured by others' writings, the magic and precision of their words a lure to escape the exigencies of the present. Yet anthropology compels confrontation with those very same exigencies! Anthropology engenders a mode of being, a crafting of sense and sensibility, that is inseparable from writing.

Writing and conducting anthropology are entwined processes; they feed each other yet can reach a standoff when the immediacy of extended fieldwork drives writing underground. Eventually, the accumulated weight of words becomes an unstoppable and urgent torrent as insights reached through fieldwork compel communication catalyzed by "intelligent rage," commitment to research participants and field site, or both.[2]

Not all writing takes the form of a breach. Some modes of writing emerge untethered from the intensities provoked by fieldwork. What contingent conditions enable the alchemy of anthropology as writing, without the boost of fieldwork to unleash its potential?[3] I pose these queries to address my own current predicament, in which a combination of factors curbs my ability to transport myself "elsewhere" at will. When Tim Ingold distinguishes between ethnography and anthropology, he suggests crossing a threshold not necessarily reached via embodied fieldwork.[4] Instead, we enter that threshold through harnessing a more comparative, reflective, and hence more distanced mode of labor. By shifting focus to encompass the spectrum of human and (more recently) nonhuman condition, we enter a calmer, more measured space concurrent with anthropological labor. Instead of fieldwork then, I engage in "memorywork" nourished by imagination to the shifting sands of times past and lives lived. Such writing up occurs in the absence of documentary artifacts and hence is fabricated entirely from "headnotes" to be summoned as I do in the segment below:

> Tangled skeins of narrative possibilities plunge me into Ammam's stories during long, hot afternoons in Calcutta spent lying beside her in the shaded cool of her bedroom. The whirring ceiling fan picks up the occasional gust of warm breeze from the shuttered windows to settle on my increasingly heavy eyelids. I listen to her reveries of a distant village in Kerala, her reminiscent voice casting a dream-like spell, sowing the seeds that have remained buried for decades to finally find fertile ground and germinate at this conjuncture in the antipodes. I recall two stories in particular, both sending a sharp thrill through me

at the time, reverberating through the marrows of memories haunting me ever since.

The first is an incident from the pioneering journeys of my great-grandfather through the dense jungles of Palaghat during the last quarter of the nineteenth century. A player in the futures market of that conjuncture, my great-grandfather's mission entailed identifying and marking jungle tracts rich in spices for auction. It was a dangerous venture through a wilderness teeming with predators. On one of these trips, his path through the jungle intersected with that of a leopard, indolently stretched across a rocky outcrop of the Western Ghats. His eyes locked with the amber, unblinking gaze of the magnificent feline, camouflaged by the dappled shadows cast by the sylvan surroundings. My great-grandfather stood stock-still, then bowing his head and drawing his palms together, he intoned: "Revered elder, if it pleases you, grant me permission to cross your path." The leopard's amber gaze burnished his face; then, in a fluid movement, the animal stretched, yawned, and disappeared into the surrounding jungle. My great-grandfather went on to make a fortune trading in spices but never forgot to give homage to the leopard that permitted him to grow old to tell his tale.

The second story emerges from the context of Ammam's household responsibilities as a daughter and the daily round of chores allocated to her. At the center of the courtyard, the household well provided for the family's day-to-day water needs. Ammam's morning routine began with replenishing the water for the family kitchen. At daybreak, as she drew water from the well, she thought she heard a hissing sound. Ammam's mother also noted the same susurration as she drew water for her morning ablutions. As the murmurs of apprehension among the women in the household grew louder to reach the ears of my great-grandfather, he took it upon himself to investigate the matter. Peering carefully into the crevices of the large well, he spotted a king cobra hidden in the mossy gloom of the walls. Drawing his hands together and bowing his head low, he addressed the cobra. He said, "Revered elder, I live in this household with many children. Why have you come here to live among us? This is not a suitable home for you." He filled a cup of milk and left it by the well, then ordered everyone indoors. The cobra uncoiled itself to slither sinuously away from the well, never to be seen again; the well was emptied and then left to replenish itself from the aquifer that fed it.

I tap into the "black milk" of memories and return to the scene of encounters with predators in Malabar.[5] Whether in the "wild" spaces of the jungle or the "domestic" space of his house, in those contact zones my great-grandfather's mode of address to the two creatures is striking.[6] He displays respect and an unwavering assumption regarding the possibilities for communication. Ammam's narratives confront the predators' ability to take human life head-on. Yet the mutuality of humans and animals, their entitlement to survive, thrive, and cohabit the spaces where both humans and animals range, is never in any doubt.

I fashioned a narrative to conjure alter worlds that were precursors to my own.

I drew on ethnographic memory to foreground my trail of connections to contemporary anthropological discourses.

I write to enter a world where I stand tall among others of my ilk, and know I keep good company.

Notes

An earlier version of this essay appeared online in *Savage Minds: Notes and Queries in Anthropology*, November 3, 2014.

1. Te Ahukaramū Charles Royal, *Te Ara: The Encyclopedia of New Zealand*, Government of New Zealand, September 24, 2007, http://www.teara.govt.nz/en/papatuanuku -the-land/page-5.

2. I have borrowed "intelligent rage" from writer and poet Ben Okri's final phrase in his tribute poem to executed activist Ken Saro-Wiwa, also included in Andrew Rowell, *Green Backlash* (New York: Routledge, 1996), xiv–xv, available from the excerpt in this link: https://content.taylorfrancis.com/books/download? dac=C2004-0-20990-4&isb n=9781351565004&format=googlePreviewPdf, accessed September 18, 2018.

3. Here I have substituted contingent in place of felicity, which is drawn from Bruno Latour's usage of felicity conditions in his recent massive project and book known as AIMES. See Bruno Latour, *An Inquiry into Modes of Existence: An Anthropology of the Moderns*, trans. Catherine Porter (Cambridge, MA: Harvard University Press, 2013), http://modesofexistence.org. Latour, in turn, draws extensively on J. L. Austin's speech act theory and performative utterances. Wikipedia is useful here for a preliminary sense of the contingency of meaning and interpretation that I have attempted to mobilize in replacing felicity with contingency in this narrative: https://en.wikipedia .org/wiki/Felicity_conditions, accessed September 18, 2018. Another substitution applied here, from instauration to alchemy, which works well with the dictionary meaning for instaure. It simultaneously combines the duality of decay and renewal, and can aptly extend to alchemy and its catalytic, transformative potential. Instauration is another term used extensively by Latour in AIMES. Val Dusek's review offers the following interpretation: "Instauration emphasizes that the production of something also

depends on the nature of the object and is contingent. The end result is unknown and involves taking risks." Val Dusek, "An Inquiry into Modes of Existence: An Anthropology of the Moderns," *Notre Dame Philosophical Journal* (2014), http://ndpr.nd .edu/news/an-inquiry-into-modes-of-existence-an-anthropology-of-the-moderns/# _ednref1.

4. Tim Ingold, "That's Enough about Ethnography!" *HAU: Journal of Ethnographic Theory* 4, no. 1 (2014): 383–95, doi: https://doi.org/10.14318/hau4.1.021.

5. Paul Celan's potent imagery from his poem "Death Fugue" leaves its lyrical trail in Karen Bolender's "R.A.W. Assmilk Soap," in *The Multispecies Salon*, ed. Eben Kirksey (Durham, NC: Duke University Press, 2014), 64–86. See this link to Celan's poem online: https://www.poets.org/poetsorg/poem/death-fugue, accessed November 12, 2012.

6. Mary Louise Pratt, "Arts of the Contact Zone," *Profession* (1991): 33–40, https:// serendip.brynmawr.edu/oneworld/system/files/PrattContactZone.pdf.

45

UNSCHOLARLY CONFESSIONS
ON READING

Katerina Teaiwa

They say to write well you should read well. I have to write regularly as an academic, but I'm currently struggling to identify good reading practices in my weekly or even monthly routine. But how do we define good practices? Is what influences us as academics primarily the "high-quality" sources—the peer-reviewed articles and books, the classical texts or novels, the rich ethnographic fieldwork or other reliable data—that we expect to find cited in our colleagues' work and that we regularly assign to our students? Or is it, or should it be, other forms of "writing"?

My colleagues often chat about the latest award-winning literature they've consumed, and when I read their work and reflect on their word choices and sentence structure, I can see clearly that regularly consuming good literature, nonfiction, or scholarly writing has helped shape their excellent choice of prose. Ideas are conveyed with just that right balance of substance, insight, and scholarly flourish. My late elder sister, Teresia Teaiwa, who was also an academic, a poet, and definitely a wordsmith, did this very well.[1]

The small library on my husband's bedside table displays titles such as *The Corporeal Image*, *Material Ecocriticism*, *The Island of the Colorblind*, *Musicophilia*, and others by Pramoedya Toer, Ursula Le Guin, Fyodor Dostoyevsky, Ray Bradbury, and Michael Pollan. His mother was an editor for Penguin, and their country home, before it was tragically destroyed in the

Black Saturday Victoria bushfires of 2009, held the most wonderful library of classics and more for readers of all ages. He didn't go to university for any kind of study until the age of thirty-two but was, and still is, a voracious and selective reader. Both he and Teresia read dictionaries as children. They read dictionaries like they were storybooks.

On my side of the bed are two novels by Johanna Lyndsey (*Tender Rebel* and *Heart of Thunder*), something by Nora Roberts, *25 Ways to Awaken Your Birth Power*, *What to Expect When You're Expecting*, *Nightmares and Dreamscapes*, and that trio of magazines I cannot pass at the checkout stand—*Woman's Day*, *New Idea*, and *Who*. I know a fair bit about what Kim Kardashian and Kanye West are purported to be up to, although I skip anything on Princess Kate, the Bachelor, and the Bachelorette. The best literature on my side of the bed is by Stephen King, and while *Tender Rebel* is now in the rubbish bin, I am still reading every other line of *Heart of Thunder*, featuring a male protagonist who is grossly just enough "savage" and just enough "civilized" to hold the attention of the feisty, redheaded female heroine.

How did I, a decolonizing, wannabe decarbonizing, armchair activist, university teacher, ethnographer, transdisciplinary Pacific Studies scholar, and actual book author, get to this place? Rather than automatically blaming the regular periods of academic burnout, the hormones flowing through my body in the third trimester of the second of what I'm calling "mechanically challenging pregnancies," or the current sleep deprivation associated with nighttime breast-feeding and cosleeping, I'd like to try to answer that question by looking back at my life as the product of an intensely cross-cultural Banaban-I-Kiribati-African American household.

I grew up in the Fiji Islands, in Savusavu, Levuka, Lautoka, and finally Suva, where we lived outside town in a new development called Tacirua Heights—inland, in a home with floor-to-ceiling books, magazines, encyclopedias, and dictionaries. The majority of our Pacific relatives, a community displaced by phosphate mining on Banaba in Kiribati, lived on Rabi Island in the far North, a place rather difficult to get to on any regular basis.[2] Unlike my husband's secular environment, our house also featured an abundance of Catholic objects, literature, and biblical texts. Our family of mum and dad, three girls, two dogs, and a short-lived cat occupied a modest, three-bedroom house on a street with no name, no telephone or television service (well, to be fair the whole of Fiji had no TV at the time), few neighbors, a 180-degree view of the Suva coast, and no rubbish collection. This last detail I mention because one of my clearest memories is of my

FIGURE 45.1. My father incinerating household waste in the backyard.
Photo by Katerina Teaiwa.

father suffering from the effects of a small explosion that happened during the routine household waste burn. It singed off all the hair from his legs and left many scars.

Around the fire pit we had an abundant and beautiful tropical flower and food garden producing bananas, coconuts, papaya, soursop, passion fruit, lemons, cassava, taro, bele, yams, chili peppers, curry leaf, vanilla, and star fruit among other produce (see figure 45.1). Inside the house was a veritable library and an old Betamax system and video screen on which we watched, on repeat, *Hello Dolly, Seven Brides for Seven Brothers, Fiddler on the Roof, Star Wars*, the *Faerie Tale Theater* series, and ballet tapes sent over from my grandmother in the United States, particularly *Coppelia, The Nutcracker, Swan Lake*, and Dance Theatre of Harlem.

These were complemented by cheap video rentals of taped American and Australian television shows such as *The Cosby Show, Facts of Life*, and *Young Talent Time*. When the video was off and my younger sister and I weren't holding our parents hostage as audience for our overchoreographed musical extravaganzas, there were my father's amazing stories of growing up on Tabiteuea in Kiribati, and on Rabi, of paying his way through primary and secondary school by working for Catholic priests, and of his many encounters with Fijian, Banaban, and I-Kiribati ghosts and spirits. We would join in Banaban community events, learn cultural dances, and attend masses held variously in the Kiribati, Fijian, and English languages while speaking just English at home. To add to the diversity, my sisters and I attended a Chinese primary school in Suva and spent many years doing rote-style reading and writing in Mandarin, taught with the bopomofo notation system. To say we were raised in Fiji with an eclectic mix of cultural content and influences would be putting it mildly.

My personal bookshelves were stacked with comics and books I had carefully collected and traded through my primary and secondary school years. They featured entire collections of Enid Blyton "classics," Nancy Drew, the Hardy Boys, dodgy Mills and Boon, Silhouette and Harlequin romance novels, and *Sweet Valley High*, along with *Archie*, *Asterix*, the fairly racist *Phantom* and *Tin Tin*, and other comics by Marvel and DC. My collections were formidable, and I would bury myself in these stories for hours at a time. This was not the norm for a young Pacific Islander. While a few of my friends were into reading, we were privileged in terms of our access to diverse forms of literature. This was a choice of my middle-class parents to spend their income in a certain way. A visible mark of status in Fiji is a new and large family car, preferably a four-wheel drive, and we always had the humblest car in town: a light-blue 1976 Honda Civic, then a banana-colored boat of a 1982 Hyundai Stellar, and at the end of high school a white 1984 Toyota Corolla (manual drive) that my mum still owns. Having an African American mother from a military family who was raised by a librarian and US Army colonel to value literature, dance, art, and music over all other material things certainly made a difference.

Although I wasn't always reading "the classics," and Enid Blyton has to be the worst-most-popular-British-author-of-all-time, all this was enough to foster an intense imagination and sense of creativity that has served me well in life and in academia. I became conscious of the ways in which different kinds of conspicuous consumption shaped and marked sociality and status in Fiji from a young age. I was perpetually embarrassed by our lack of visible affluence but less aware of the other forms of privilege we clearly had until I reached my PhD studies without ever taking a break from school. My sisters and I just constantly gulped down knowledge, and all three of us kept studying until two achieved PhDs and the other an MD. (See figure 45.2.)

One day in the early 1990s, while I was far from Fiji studying at Santa Clara University, my mother threw out or donated most of my hundreds

FIGURE 45.2.
Katerina, Teresia, and
Maria Teaiwa, 1977.
Photo courtesy of
Katerina Teaiwa.

of books, magazines, and comics. She'd actually secretly disapproved of my
reading choices and kept only the *Asterix* and *Tin Tin* collections, which I
maintain to this day. Aside from these and the large number of scholarly
books that I now keep in my office at work, I no longer have any books that
I particularly love or care for. I spend far more time on social media, especially Facebook and Twitter, and, when I can, consume a variety of television programs, including *The 100*, *Game of Thrones*, *Master Chef*, *The Biggest
Loser*, and *America's Next Top Model*. I still teach, write, research, present at
conferences, and publish academic articles and book chapters, but these are
now very clearly separate and discernible from the rest of my "literary" and
popular cultural consumption. Everything I read regularly is disposable or
accessible from a mobile device, and I gaze ambivalently at my excellent office collection, believing that I am an academic imposter.

So many influences shape us as academics, as anthropologists who study
others or, in my case, my own Pacific communities. Our approaches, methods, and words are shaped by a variety of factors beyond the scholarly

UNSCHOLARLY CONFESSIONS ON READING—243

FIGURE 45.3. Dusk at the base of Mount Majura near our home in Canberra. Photo by Katerina Teaiwa.

genealogies and lines of thought in which we visibly situate ourselves. Our scholarly writing often reflects just a fragment of our life histories or daily practices when we write in an effort to be more objective, more scientific, more authoritative, more scholarly in our work. I don't know why I cannot bring myself to read "good" books, but I am always reading in that sense of observing something carefully in order to make meaning and interpret the world. Reading popular culture matters.

In my book *Consuming Ocean Island*, I also share the late Epeli Hauʻofaʻs advice on "how to read our landscapes and seascapes."[3] I've been practicing such readings in a multiscalar fashion for decades. My husband reminded me of this during a phone call from the top of a mountain at Wee Jasper in the Yass Valley, just ninety minutes from where we now live in Canberra, two hours from the east Australian coastline. Our home is near the base of another mountain, Mount Majura, which I see every day from our bedroom window. My little family regularly walks its trails discussing ants, drop bears, kangaroo poo, and all the misspelling in the hastily produced nature signs that the housing developers of "the Fair," at the mountain's base, were required to erect. Canberra, which in the aboriginal Ngambri language is said to mean "cleavage," and for the Ngunnawal people, "meeting place," is, in all material ways, nothing like Suva. Nevertheless, of all the places I've lived, both these homes, one near the sea and one far from the sea, have provided security, nurturing, and the most inspiring grounds from which to read the world (see figure 45.3).

Notes

An earlier version of this essay appeared online in *Savage Minds: Notes and Queries in Anthropology*, November 2, 2015.

1. See some of Teresia's popular writing on her microwoman blog and at E-tangata, including "You Can't Paint the Pacific with Just One Brush Stroke," October 25, 2015, https://e-tangata.co.nz/korero/you-cant-paint-the-pacific-with-just-one-brush-stroke. See the many tributes to Teresia's life and untimely passing, including Olivier Jutel, "Vale Teresia Teaiwa," *Overland*, March 27, 2017, https://overland.org.au/2017/03/vale -teresia-teaiwa; Bess Manson, "A Life Story—Dr. Teresia Teaiwa 'Leading Light' of the Pacific, Dies, 48," Stuff.co.nz, April 22, 2017, https://www.stuff.co.nz/national/education /91548606/a-life-story—dr-teresia-teaiwa-leading-light-of-the-pacific-dies-48.

2. Katerina Teaiwa, *Consuming Ocean Island: Stories of People and Phosphate from Banaba* (Bloomington: Indiana University Press, 2015).

3. Epeli Hauʻofa, "Pasts to Remember," in Robert Borofsky, ed., *Remembrance of Pacific Pasts: An Invitation to Remake History* (Honolulu: University of Hawaiʻi Press, 2000), 466.

46

GUARD YOUR HEART AND YOUR PURPOSE

Faithfully Writing Anthropology

Bianca C. Williams

Above all else, guard your heart, for everything you do flows from it.
—Proverbs 4:23

Like many others, the blank page can terrify me. Simply starting a new blog post, an essay, or a book chapter can have me tumbling into hours, days, or weeks of shame-filled procrastination. These are the times that resistance and fear triumph, and I feel myself falling into a moody mixture of anger, frustration, sadness, and general feelings of incompetence. Oh, and sometimes there is crying. However, once I find successful methods for dragging the words that are in my head onto the page,[1] I then attempt to organize them in a way that makes sense, creates "new" knowledge, and contributes to multiple fields, ever aware that in some near future a committee will attempt to quantify my publication impact and decide whether they should grant me tenure.[2] Surprisingly, for the past three weeks writing and I have engaged in a truce—or, I should say, she has decided to get off my back, give me some room to breathe, and allow the words that infiltrate my dreams and my meditation sessions to flow a bit easier onto the page. What is interesting is that this period of writing peace has resulted in a new issue: I keep getting my best writing ideas while I'm in the shower.

You may be thinking: "How is this a problem? At least writing ideas are coming to you!" Yes, I agree. This shouldn't be a big issue, but have you ever tried to carefully record thoughts on your phone while you're covered in soap, trying not to get your phone wet, slip in the tub, or get water all over the bathroom floor? After a few days of repeatedly performing this balancing act, I began to reflect on what the connections between the shower and my writing might possibly be. What I learned were important lessons about vulnerability, purpose, faith, and how they influence my writing.

Vulnerability

It has become clear to me that the shower is one of the few places in my life where I feel that I can exercise vulnerability safely. Most of the time I am the only person in the shower, and unlike the rest of my hectic day, this occasion permits me a brief period to enjoy my body and consider my own thoughts. There are no mirrors, peer reviewers, blank screens, or cameras (that I know of) to judge me or remind me of the surveillance I am consistently under. I am naked, remarkably carefree, while prepping myself for the outside world. In the shower I can try arguments on for size, deciding whether that particular wording or theoretical concept will work, feeling free from critique (particularly my own, which can be the most vicious when it comes to my writing). For someone who is sometimes accused of overanalyzing, it is one of the few times in my day when I can just be.[3] My heart is open. Standing under the rushing water from the showerhead calms me as I wash off the condemnation, disappointment, and procrastination of yesterday to start anew. I press a reset button. I let go. And I talk to God.

Purpose

The way I see it, I was called to anthropology and to teaching because these are tools that allow me to learn truths about human experiences as people view them, experience them, and express them. This is anthropology's purpose. As I participate in research and teaching, anthropological approaches help me to learn about others while providing insight into myself. As a Black feminist cultural anthropologist, I constantly hear the call to engage in what my colleague Micah Gilmer describes as "heartwork": a form of "real teaching" that demands honesty, direct communication, vulnerability, and emotional investment. He argues that this labor is required to build communities and places that support those passionate about transforming the world. In

Gilmer's research, heartwork is embodied in Black male football coaches and teachers who lovingly invest in their student athletes despite their hearts being broken by the strain of this emotional labor, the lack of resources available to be successful in this work, and the various ways that educational institutions do not value or recognize the impact their commitment makes in students' lives or the community. Part of my difficulty with writing was that I did not feel comfortable being truly transparent about the connection between my heartwork and my writing. In fact, being honest and open about this connection can attract enormous pushback in academic circles, particularly in publication peer reviews or promotion-committee meetings. And because of the still very active role that racism plays within educational spaces, scholars of color may experience particular backlash against an explicit commitment to antiracist heartwork. But as I grow more comfortable with myself, my purpose, and my writing voice, I realize that trying to keep these passionate works—heartwork and writing—separate, in order to be validated or accepted by those in the academy, is simply killing my soul.

Faith

In Sienna Craig's essay in this volume, "On Unreliable Narrators," she writes that sometimes an anthropological truth is a knowing that many times goes beyond words. As you share your hypotheses, your analyses, your participant-observed "aha" moments with interviewees, a confidant, a colleague, or a student, there are moments when the knowing is deep down in your soul. And sometimes it can feel as if words are not enough. You may have this shared moment of knowing, but the best that you can do to acknowledge it is to share a look, an embrace, even a collective sigh. Even though it can feel limiting, in our writing we try our best to describe these soul-knowing truths; we attempt to describe, tell, teach, and explain. It takes vulnerability to attain this knowledge; and for me, it takes faith and Faith to write it.

From my perspective, writing is about purpose and faith. In my soul I have a deep desire to show the full humanity of Black women to ourselves and the world. I recognize that our liberation is connected to the liberation of everyone; therefore, in my research and my teaching, it is important to me to show how Black women pursue joy, happiness, love, and intimacy during our beautifully fierce struggles for equity and freedom.[4] This is my purpose. Engaging this mission and writing about it require faith. Faith that God has given me the skills, tools, and abilities to write the truths that I learn. Faith that He will protect me and guide me along this journey. Faith in myself to begin and complete this work. Faith that I can be disciplined enough to focus and not get distracted by things that can lead me to unbelief in myself, my mission, or Him. Faith that there is space to be a Christian academic who speaks and writes about her Faith.

My pastors over the years have taught me that everything we do requires belief and that I can choose to aim my believing energies in the direction of fear or faith. Furthermore, as the scripture above states, I understand that belief is not something you necessarily carry in your mind, but it is something you hold in your heart.

Words are powerful. The words we hear, transcribe, and create do things in the world and act on our hearts. It is possible that the difference in my writing over the past few weeks has been that my time in the shower—relaxing, thinking, praying, and just being—has helped me begin to truly believe that there is something in my writing worth telling. During these times, I have opened myself up to being vulnerable while decreasing the judgmental energy, have reconnected with my purpose, and have grown more faithful that I have the ability to successfully complete the writing required to do the heartwork.

Notes

An earlier version of this essay appeared online in *Savage Minds: Notes and Queries in Anthropology*, February 17, 2014.

1. Thanks to Kerry Ann Rockquemore and the National Center for Faculty Development & Diversity's Faculty Success Program, Naomi Greyser's amazing writing coaching, and the helpful tips of Wendy Laura Belcher's *Writing Your Journal Article in 12 Weeks*, I have a tool kit of strategies to help pull me out of the painful territory of writer's block.

2. Since writing this essay in 2014, I have successfully earned tenure. However, the trepidation and fear that I describe here about pretenure writing as "heartwork" accurately predicted the difficulties that I encountered during the tenure review process. In Manya Whitaker and Eric Anthony Grollman's *Counternarratives from Women of Color Academics: Bravery, Vulnerability, and Resistance* (New York: Routledge, 2018), I talk about the victory of earning tenure nonetheless and being dedicated to continually speaking and writing with "radical honesty," which I view as my disciplinary and pedagogical practice.

3. I am aware that for many people who may feel the weight of society's oppressive standards and expectations around beauty (particularly trans and cis women), the bathroom and the shower may not be a peaceful place and may in fact be a site for battle. Please know that I do not mean to minimize these struggles but am only writing of my most recent experiences in this space.

4. In fact, I argue that pursuing happiness is a political project for Black women. See Bianca C. Williams, *The Pursuit of Happiness: Black Women, Diasporic Dreams, and the Politics of Emotional Transnationalism* (Durham, NC: Duke University Press, 2018), as an example of this. My book examines a group of African American tourists who use international travel to Jamaica and the internet as tools for pursuing happiness, while briefly escaping US-based racism and sexism.

47

WRITING ANTHROPOLOGY AND SUCH, OR "ONCE MORE, WITH FEELING"

Gina Athena Ulysse

When I write, there's a slight lag: a whatever space-between when words strung together into phrases or sentences are transmitted onto the page with fingers trained as intermediaries. A right-hand injury made me identify this pause as I became more conscious of various aspects and levels in my writing. Not being able to type gave me a new relationship to interludes in my process.

After my injury I started to learn a dictation program that made me grouchy. It insisted I follow its rules, stripping off the last vestiges of an old accent and making me pronounce certain words the Anglo way so it recognized them. Fortunately, it also decidedly made me very happy and even freer: in some ways this limitation helped open me to just what it is that I want to write at this particular point in my life and, most importantly, for what reason.

The basics matter, so here they are: I am a tenured faculty member at Wesleyan University, a black woman from Haiti who speaks her mind and used to describe herself as a performance artist masquerading as an academic or an accidental academic. I have never been conventional (not as a grad student or as pretenure faculty) and am certainly not about to make a U-turn now. More often than not, I choose to honor the verve that drives my quest to confront the visceral. All of that to say, I take risks. My writing has always occurred within intersections from theory to form. As I have yet to meet a human subject who lives life along disciplinary lines, I don't usually fret about it.

(*Fair warning: Unless you consider yourself something of a misfit trying to navigate this terrain, this may not be for you. To be direct, it is imperative that you sincerely explore the various potential professional implications of your intentions. In other words, consider what it will mean if you decide to "write against the grain," as the inimitable Faye V. Harrison[1] puts it, to also engage in decolonizing anthropology. By this she means to intentionally disrupt archaic notions of anthropology as normative and in the process consider the array of interventions that have broadened and that continue to broaden concepts of this discipline.*)

What I have found over the years is that the more aware I am of both the broader professional and personal contexts within which I write, the easier it is for me to write. Looking back, I recall those moments when I was a dissertating grad student battling the paralysis that came with the all-too-common fear of being a first-generation everything working to make space for herself as an expert in a discipline where decades later minorities are still underrepresented. I made it through and faced said fears again when writing the book. At one point I was truly stuck, spending hours at the office unable to write anything new. I got over this block and owe the deluge that followed in part to the senior white male colleague who once bellowed, "You can't give a fuck! You will never write if you are worried about your critics. You will never write!"

His brazen privilege reminded me of previous conversations with my advisor and mentors about professional paths, theoretical lineages, and decisions concerning what it means to do reflexive anthropology. Be prepared for the navel-gazing backlash (check!), the silencing (check!), the charge that such work is soft or illegitimate (check! check!) and too political (check!). I embraced the reflexive turn precisely to consider both what I had learned and how I came to acquire that knowledge. Moreover, I deploy reflexivity to expose what I like to call the "social luxury of whiteness" because as a black woman, I certainly do not benefit from the convenience of being "unmarked," as the late Michel-Rolph Trouillot has written.[2] (Through ethnography and theory, these concerns were all meticulously addressed in my first book.) I remain especially bent on pursuing strategic impulses that are explicitly and simultaneously artistic, decolonial, and feminist in praxis. I call myself a post-Zora interventionist, and this approach continues to suit my projects and my chosen interlocutors. Yet the old fears and issues still come up (there are more evaluations and even more gatekeepers), although I confront them much quicker as I get older. Once they are out of the way, other impediments to my writing tend to be rather practical, such as career plans, enough time, the right conditions, and a healthy body and hand.

When I was a junior faculty member, muddling through the unfair extra burden of a joint position in African-American studies and anthropology, there was a little more protection and also sabbaticals that allowed me to carve spaces needed to get the first book done. However, nothing had been enough preparation for the gendered, racialized, and classed divisions of affective labor after tenure. The achievement of job security in many instances throws everyone into a fictive equal category that disregards differential treatment by others based on positionality or what history has written on our bodies. This absence of boundaries ultimately determines who is allowed to receive and actually receives material and symbolic support to pursue a future as an intellectual and who is expected to be faithfully committed to institution building. Although so much of our work is invisible, we also have to remind our peers that Black women are not genetically coded for service. We are not in institutions to fill the Black academic mammy slot. Often, we are also inundated with affective work, especially if we are politically committed to certain issues that plague historically white institutions that will inevitably and unevenly affect underrepresented faculty, staff, and students, so we end up with less time left to think critically and process, let alone write. That's the primary reason that fewer women and minorities are full professors. Indeed, in more ways than one, I almost became a casualty of the ivory ceiling.

Luckily, the performer had been slowly removing her mask over the years while a devastating earthquake forced a detour from my second project and lured me into new and welcoming directions. Listening to my muses and responding to the call of 1/12/2010 (the date of the earthquake) inspired experimentation with different forms of writing and expression. The situation in Haiti—the reason I became an anthropologist—rendered the stakes the highest they have ever been during my academic career. I embarked on an urgent public anthropology spree, penning opinion pieces, blogging and performing both for sanity and because I could offer another perspective. In the end I produced distinctive works that were not part of the "original" "plan" (as if there was one) but that now constitute an "unconventional" book of short-form essays and blogs.[3]

These days, I am no longer professionally split between a program and a department. The structural conditions that once impeded me, and practically required a survival guide, no longer exist. For the very first time in my entire career as faculty, I can create unencumbered time to be contemplative, thus ready to engage a work that has been on the back burner as I develop installments of a large-scale performance project. I find it useful and fun to think about my writing time as studio time.

Conditions need to be optimal yet flexible. Now that I have to rely on the disciplining microphone to capture my thoughts, I try to accommodate my very specific habits. I opt for regular, longer slots of time when the outside world cannot intrude. I turn off all electronics except iTunes. I need music, especially when starting something new. I have been listening to the same Mozart boxed set for over twenty-five years. Thank god for the invention of the compact disc. Yet I prefer the atmosphere of a noisy café when revising. I have playlists for different phases of writing, with everything from Bookman Eksperyans to Awolnation. Decades ago, I realized that I am not a linear writer but more of a quilt maker. I am content when I produce chunks. I have also learned to not berate myself if I can't come up with anything. There are works by certain poets and art books near my desk (or in the movable studio bag) that I need and reach for when words are not whirling out of my head as I face the screen. As long as I am present in the space and in conversation with artists or even in silence, I now consider myself writing.

Viewing writing as a practice that requires my full attention has helped me cultivate a healthier and more integrated relationship to my discursive and expressive meditations. It's not a chore; I look forward to the process. As I have to manually (and painfully) scroll pages, my injured hand reminds me why the work I do must be of deeper significance, why it must truly matter to me and also be full of inspiration.

Postscript: eight months after publication of this piece, I decided to go up for promotion to a full professor with the aforementioned "unconventional" book and my other creative public anthropology works. I had spent well over a decade building a career of a particular kind. Indeed, I took what some thought was a risky step, knowing that anthropology is changing, certainly not fast enough for those among us on different paths, but the fact is that this is what I do now.

Post-postscript: I got promoted to full. These days, my ethnographic work exists in the realm of the artistic. My writing begins with a commitment to creativity and goes on from there.

Notes

An earlier version of this essay appeared online in *Savage Minds: Notes and Queries in Anthropology*, January 27, 2014. This was written in 2014 on the anniversary of Zora Neale Hurston's 123rd birthday. The title is a riff on both Hurston's controversial 1938 essay, "Art and Such," and the only musical episode of *Buffy the Vampire Slayer* in the series' sixth season. Thanks to Carole McGranahan and Regina Langhout for their critical comments.

1. Faye V. Harrison, Carole McGranahan, Kaifa Roland, and Bianca Williams, "Decolonizing Anthropology: A Conversation," *Savage Minds: Notes and Queries in Anthropology*, 2016, https://savageminds.org/2016/05/03/decolonizing-anthropology-a -conversation-with-faye-v-harrison-part-ii.

2. Michel-Rolph Trouillot, *Global Transformations: Anthropology and the Modern World* (New York: Palgrave, 2003), 72.

3. Gina Athena Ulysse, *Why Haiti Needs New Narratives: A Post Quake Chronicle* (Middletown, CT: Wesleyan University Press, 2015).

48

THE ANTHROPOLOGY OF BEING (ME)

Paul Tapsell

The greatest challenge of being an anthropologist is being me. From one decade to the next I have been a cross-cultural island of self-consciousness, framed by the cross-generational memories of wider kin. Wisdom comes in many forms, but as I tell my students (at least those who turn up to class), it cannot be found on the internet. Somewhere between my father's Māori generation of desperately trying to be English and my children's reality of being overtly Māori, you find . . . me.[1]

Raised in the tribally alienated rural heartlands of Waikato naïveté (built on nineteenth-century confiscations at gunpoint), I had a view of the world that was one of barefoot summers by the ocean, while the rest of the year was underpinned by frosts, fog, rugby, and ducking for cover in a rurally serviced school surrounded by affluent dairy farms and horse studs. Right from the start, teachers placed me neither at the front nor at the back of the classroom. Kids in the front were mostly fourth-generation descendants of English settlers, while at the back were the ever-sniffling Māori who had no shoes and walked five miles to school across farmlands, one steaming cowpat to the next. And there I was, from age five, placed right in the middle, on the boundary between a white-is-right future and an uncivilized dark-skinned past.

Weekends provided respite, often spent with my grandmother while Dad mowed an acre of lawn on our tribal property back in Rotorua. She used taonga (treasured ancestral belongings) to instill a deeper understanding of the proud history to which Māori belonged, decades before these stories found their way into mainstream classrooms. Taonga, either at her museum or off the mantelpiece, made history all the more real to me, especially when performed during death rituals on my ancestral marae (community village courtyards) of Maketu and Ohinemutu.

Life in the 1960s and 1970s seemed so simple, so straightforward. You were either Māori (dark like Dad) or English (lily-white like Mum). If you were Māori, society deemed you dirty, lazy, and good only for fixing roads or driving buses. If you chose to be English, no matter your skin color, you could participate in a national ideology of being "one people," but only as long as you played by the rules. I did not play by the rules. My very left-wing Irish grandmother filled my head with a whole different way of seeing the world. For her, colonial New Zealand was extremely unjust, and Māori had been royally screwed by the English. She kept the home fires of a proud ancestry alight, becoming the most feared "Māori" in our village. In 1915 her husband and twenty-five other kinsmen had fought for God and Empire on foreign soil, killing indigenous people of another land in the name of an English king, but for what? To return home as second-rate citizens, shot to pieces, and told to dig ditches on lands now owned by wealthy farmers? She fought for their recognition, banging on prime ministers' doors until finally these veterans also qualified for war pensions.

Given this background, my gravitation toward anthropology and later specialization in museum ethnography (Pitt Rivers Museum, Oxford University) was always going to happen. I grew up as a member of a tribe famous for producing, protecting, and prestating taonga across tens of generations, many of which are now found in museums throughout the world. My earliest formal memories were shaped by whakapapa (genealogically layered narratives) from elders who animated surrounding landscapes with great deeds of my ancestors. I was raised to be proud of my whakapapa. But when my grandmother died, my world was tipped upside down. My parents shifted us away from perceived negative influences of tribalism to let the cities shape their children into more urbane citizens of modern integrated New Zealand. By the age of eighteen I had dropped out of education and fled to Australia on a one-way ticket. Like so many other Māori, I wanted to be anywhere but here, anywhere but living in 1970s white conservative backwater colonial New Zealand.

Over the next decade I found solace through professional sport and writing, providing me a useful vehicle by which to travel the world and experience a multitude of cultures as an outsider looking in. The more I engaged with others, the more I began to reflect on my own cultural self and childhood experiences of being Māori in a still racially divided nation. And then overnight England joined the EU (then known as the EEC), and New Zealand was forced to radically reinvent itself to survive economically. Leveraging Māori identity became a horizon of new opportunity: a point of difference on which the government sought to market national uniqueness. Its flagship was an international touring exhibition of taonga, named Te Māori (1984–1887), representing a new Aotearoa New Zealand: an island nation that dared to imagine a bicultural future built on the 1840 Treaty of Waitangi. In the wake of Te Māori was born the Museum of New Zealand Project, better known today as Te Papa: two cultures, one nation.

Beneath today's flagging bicultural ideology still exists the unaddressed premise of being Māori: kin accountability to source marae communities. It represents tribally ordered rights and responsibilities according to ancestral context. But where does such a philosophy of knowledge fit in a bicultural nation based on urban Māori ethnic identity beyond the horizon of New Zealand's 780 tribal marae? The treaty promised the protection of such communities, but it now stands for the delivery of globalized tribal (Iwi) organizations based on laws of exclusive ownership at the expense of kin belonging and inclusion. It was the genesis of these fascinating bicultural tensions that drew me back to university and into anthropology.

My academic training was initially underpinned by post-structuralism with a healthy injection of ethnicity, but it was when I stepped outside the Western paradigm of grid-ordered Cartesian epistemology that my engagement with the "field at home" became real. Some might refer to my approach as reflexive ethnography, bordering on neotraditionalism. But closer inspection of my writings might also reveal a reorientation of knowledge according to a genealogical accountability to source, beyond any currently practiced indigenous methodology. Let's call it being "preindigenous": a counterpoint to current globalized Māori organizations (Iwi) or "iwification." I remain my late grandmother's work in progress, continuing to challenge the status quo as I explore cross-generational consciousness through museums and taonga.

My ongoing challenge is to find effective ways to communicate to the field what it really means to be the Other when described from the position of my anthropological Self. Two decades on, the boundaries of misunderstanding in wider New Zealand are growing even wider. Who is doing useful anthropology of our cultural crisis when needed most? Māori urban dysfunctionality and tribal depopulation dominate our headlines.[2] I threw myself into this fray a decade ago, and today it has evolved into www.māorimaps.com, a digitally born cross-generational reconnection gateway.

So with last thoughts of elders, grandmother, and mentors Sir Hugh Kawharu and Greg Dening, here I am again, at the boundary of difference negotiating being (me) with the rest of the universe.

Notes

An earlier version of this essay appeared online in *Savage Minds: Notes and Queries in Anthropology*, October 12, 2015.

1. Māori literally translates as "normal." It was applied as a self-ascription by the original inhabitants of New Zealand in counterdistinction to the British, European, and American visitors who began crossing our shores in 1770.

2. See this Native Affairs Maori Television news clip for a recent example: http://www.maoritelevision.com/news/latest-news/native-affairs—lonely-paepae, accessed June 1, 2017.

WRITING AND KNOWING

49

WRITING AS COGNITION

Barak Kalir

I will know what I precisely want to say in this piece only when I finish writing it.

This enigmatic sentence is not meant as an alluring opening statement, nor is it a sign for an experimental literary method that I will be employing in this essay. For what it's worth, this sentence captures my principal insight into the process of writing. It is an insight that I gained after years of experiencing much frustration with writing, after producing endless drafts of the same text, after nights and days spent on trying "to get it right," after struggling not to lose my focus, not to get lost in the texts I tried so hard to write.

Luckily, I do not feel like that anymore. But it has been a long ride.

Initially, facing my frustration with writing—when I was struggling with chapters in my doctoral dissertation or with my first attempt at publishing an article in a peer-reviewed journal—I was inclined, and even determined, to attribute my pains to the fact that the ideas in my head were not sharp enough at the point of writing. I repeatedly told myself as a beaten mantra: "You need to be very clear about what you want to say *before* you sit down and start writing." I felt angrily vindicated after every article or book that I read, thinking it was so obvious that the authors knew exactly what they wanted to argue and illustrate.

I started to draw my arguments on a blank sheet in preparation for writing. I made tentative tables of content before I had written even one chapter. I sketched road maps for the order of sections in an article; I decided on the data to be included and on the theories to be used. Notwithstanding my best efforts at having clarity in my head and being well prepared for the writing phase, it always ended up pretty much the same. Once the words began to accumulate on the screen in front of me, the text seemed to take on its own direction, leaving me halfway, confused about my main argument, about the debates in which I intervene, about the subtleties that I try to get across. Why can I not control my text? Why does it take on a different form from the one I had in mind? After all the preparation I invested in having a clear focus, why can I not stick to it?

Sharing my writing frustrations with peers at the department and in meetings with colleagues at conferences, I quickly discovered that my predicament was nothing special. It seemed that everyone was suffering to some degree from the excruciating process of writing. I must admit that it made me feel better. It was a relief to realize that it wasn't only my shortcomings as a writer that turned this endeavor into a permanent struggle. There appeared to be something about the essence of writing that challenged anyone who attempted it.

My breakthrough came one day while talking with the late Gerd Baumann, a wonderful anthropologist and a gifted writer. For many years, Gerd Baumann thought me various "tricks of the trade" for good writing. Helpful as these tricks were, they never really succeeded to elevate, not even to decently mitigate, my writing struggles. One day, complaining to him for the nth time about my latest struggle with an unyielding text, Gerd grinned at me and emitted a rhetorical question that would change my idea about writing forever: "When will you realize that writing is a second cognitive process?"

I'm sure that for many people this sentence is an obvious one, perhaps even banal or clichéd. For me, however, it served as a crucial eye-opener. Not because I could never before think or feel that this was the case about writing but because there are things that you need to hear from someone in order for their full meaning to dawn on you.

Writing is not about putting into words the mental ideas you have in your head. Writing is a process in which you digest, make sense, and form your mental ideas in ways that are inevitably different from toying with ideas in your head or talking them over with colleagues or presenting them at a conference. There is something about the externalization of ideas in a textual form that activates and brings with it a particular cognitive process. This is why writing is by definition a puzzling and creative process. It is not about transforming thoughts into words; it is about transforming thoughts. Period.

It is after we have written about something that we should do our best to make sure that the text we produce captures the thoughts that evolved out of the very writing process.

I hope I managed that much in this short piece. If not, I will give it another go and produce some more text. Text that brings to light thoughts I didn't even know I had.

Note

An earlier version of this essay appeared online in *Savage Minds: Notes and Queries in Anthropology*, December 7, 2015.

50

THINKING THROUGH THE UNTRANSLATABLE

Kevin Carrico

I recently finished translating a book, Tsering Woeser's *Tibet on Fire* (*Immolation au Tibet, la honte du monde*),[1] in a project that combines the two main components of my career path thus far: translation and anthropology. Prior to entering academia, I worked as a translator in Shanghai. And now as a political anthropologist, I still engage in the occasional translation of texts that I consider uniquely insightful. This brief essay is an attempt to think through the relationship between these two activities via my recent work on self-immolation in Tibet.

Prior to entering the translation industry, the distant and thus romanticized notion of translation conjured images of simultaneous interpreters at the United Nations, talking frantically into earpieces or banging away at keyboards to enable communication for a global community. Soon after entering the industry, however, I found that professional translators spend a considerable amount of time sitting at their desks and staring at screens as they translate one inane document after another. Now that I have finished this washing-machine manual, should I get started on this blueprint for the annual city carnival layout or just save that for tomorrow? I often found myself leaning towards the latter option.

I thus eventually made the transition to anthropology, a discipline that draws upon many of the same skills employed in translation, such as linguistic competence, familiarity with the sociocultural and political context, and the ability to read (or listen) between the lines . . . albeit in considerably more stimulating settings. Despite my own admitted hesitation to draw a simple parallel between the two activities, there is much that they share in common: each takes difference and makes it comprehensible, finding commonality. The main difference is that anthropology should ideally employ these skills towards more contemplative ends than translation, an ideal that does not, however, always match the everyday reality of academic life.

Nowhere have I encountered greater challenges for my translation skills and analytical capabilities than in the study of self-immolation in Tibet. Since 2009, more than 150 Tibetans have chosen to set their bodies on fire in protest against the current situation in Tibet. As these events have unfolded, I have attempted to write on this topic,[2] as well as to translate some of Tibetan scholar Tsering Woeser's reflections on this phenomenon.[3] Whether writing or translating, this is a topic that has brought me far away from the mundane world of washing-machine manuals and blueprints, challenging me to think through and make sense of a most extreme experience.

Self-immolation would seem to be an absolute, even untranslatable form of difference: as I sit here before a computer screen on a November day in Central Oklahoma, there are few phenomena in life that could seem more remote than someone's conscious decision to set their body alight and the unthinkable bodily experience that follows. This remoteness would seem to highlight the promise of both translation and anthropology, which can begin to bring us closer to other people's worlds, whether through the translation of self-immolators' final statements or through the analytical attempt to answer the most pressing questions of why, and where to go from here. Yet alongside this seeming promise, I have found in the process of translating and writing that self-immolation creates seemingly irresolvable challenges for the articulation of these events in words, which reliably fail in relation to the act under description. Someone sets their body alight, gradually being engulfed in flames. We call this act "self-immolation" and attempt to put together coherent sentences to explain why this is happening.

This unique challenge of putting words to this act has, however, been uniquely productive for recalibrating my perspective on the relationship between writing and thinking. In contrast to the founding assumptions of both translation and anthropology, I have begun to think that what the world needs is not always more words. After all, how many words have been spoken or written about Tibet over the years? The discussion is far too often expressed through such abstract and even fundamentally alienated notions as historical sovereignty, economic development, territorial control, or even conspiratorial narratives about the "Dalai Lama clique." Such concepts provide solace that we know what we are talking about, and, one after another, these phrases are comfortingly very easy for me to translate back and forth between languages without much thought at all.

Parallel to the distance between my lived experience and the act of self-immolation, however, we must also note the fundamental distance between largely hollow and self-reproducing modes of communication and the concrete experience on the ground in Tibet producing the act of self-immolation. Self-immolation is an act that is impossible to translate because it requires no translation, taking us beyond words, so many of which have already been exhausted on the topic of Tibet. Writings on Tibet often exist in a cycle of polarized and self-reinforcing opinions and accompanying identifications. Instead, self-immolation gives us a very visible and visceral experience of human suffering without vengeance against others, an extreme and unthinkable experience nevertheless providing an inerasable image of fundamental common humanity beyond language.

What self-immolation and other such extreme experiences require of us, then, is not necessarily more writing and certainly not more talking, but rather more thinking. Actual thinking, usually the source of initial interest in an academic career, can easily be lost in the realities of this career, with its daily deluge of emails, class preparation, job applications, revisions, and the rush to publish. Leaving the translation industry in search of more room for contemplation, I have ironically found that sometimes in academia there is even less time for thinking. The challenge of self-immolation and the discovery that anything that one says or writes seems to never fully live up to this act have produced a unique pause in this flurry of activity that has been strangely liberating, highlighting contemplation not only as an essential part of the writing process but also as a productive end in and of itself.

In his *Psychoanalysis of Fire*, Gaston Bachelard proposes that contemplation and even the pursuit of knowledge itself originate from the human relationship to fire.[4] This relationship between fire and thought, he argues, can be seen in the hypnotic and contemplative gaze directed towards the relatively mundane embers of a fireplace. The flames that have been ignited across Tibet have provoked and will continue to provoke observation, contemplation, and commentary from scholars and other concerned individuals around the world, in hopes of better understanding the realities of Tibet today. But the challenge of thinking through these flames has taught me an equally important lesson: as scholars in a cutthroat academic industry wherein communication never rests, in the hurry to write or lecture or argue for our viewpoint, sometimes we lose sight of the importance of the fundamental act of contemplation. These remote and untranslatable events on the Tibetan plateau, then, have also helped me to rediscover, in and beyond the act of writing, the place of silent contemplation.

Notes

An earlier version of this essay appeared online in *Savage Minds: Notes and Queries in Anthropology*, November 17, 2014.

1. Tsering Woeser, *Tibet on Fire: Self-Immolations against Chinese Rule* (London: Verso, 2016).

2. Kevin Carrico, "Chinese State Media Representations," *Hot Spots*, April 8, 2012, https://culanth.org/fieldsights/chinese-state-media-representations.

3. Tsering Woeser, "Self-Immolation and Slander," *Hot Spots*, April 8, 2012, https://culanth.org/fieldsights/self-immolation-and-slander-woeser.

4. Gaston Bachelard, *The Psychoanalysis of Fire* (Boston: Beacon, 1964).

51

FREEZE-DRIED MEMORY CRUMBS

Field Notes from North Korea

Lisa Sang-Mi Min

I.

If writing field notes is a method of preservation for later writing, then writing field notes in north Korea is like freeze-drying, a particular technique of preservation.[1] Freeze-drying transforms raw material into lightweight, more portable entities with a prolonged shelf life. Like all forms of preservation, it is an energy- and labor-intensive process, one distinguished by its capacity to retain much of the color, aroma, and form of the original raw state. Freeze-drying heightens the sensuous dimensions, the essences become more intense, but the material itself becomes so delicate and fragile that it is dangerously subject to deterioration. It can crumble, break into pieces, or if its porous membrane is exposed to even the slightest amount of moisture, it can get soggy, presenting certain challenges in the transfer, storage, and reconstitution of the raw material. When the usual modes of writing field notes are not at one's disposal, freeze-drying presents another possibility with which to work.

II.

The smell of the metro
dirt, human, warm damp stone, faint scent of paint
no perfumes, no products, nothing to mask what is

This is the memory of socialist industry. A nostalgic scene of scents and sounds, of metal and discipline, of the underground and a rhythm of the everyday.[2] I am both a part of the scene and not: part of the scene because I am in the dream of north Korean utopia and not because I know it is already falling.[3] It is a sensuous flashback, like Alexander Samokhalov's watercolors of female metro builders in Moscow, a memory felt in a body.

Handwritten into notebooks, sometimes quickly scribbled between bus rides to glorious monuments, and at other times carefully composed, my notes from north Korea are preserved atmospheres, encounters, and questions. They are from a fieldwork reimagined in an impossible encounter with the "other" Korea, what the cold war legacy does much to prevent. Unlike journalistic accounts that continually return north Korea to a totalitarian paradigm or that aim to uncover the truth of things by going undercover, my approach sought new ways of engaging with what was readily observable by anyone traveling there. These were moments that "might be barely sensed and yet are compelling," events that connected my writing to the aesthetically heady, complex experience of socialism.[4]

Not knowing what kind of note taking would be a good or bad or risky kind of note taking, for whom, when, and how, I did not write freely or thickly. Instead, I assembled phrases, weighted words, gathered together bits and pieces of raw material that could lead me back to a scene, an image, a color, to certain rooms and exchanges that suggested openings to other ways of imagining, thinking, and writing north Korea.

> 5 days without
>   screens
>   internet
>   advertisements
>   hot water
>   enough sleep
>   the state this produces

When fieldwork takes place over a number of short visits rather than unfolding over a long stretch of months, the observations take on another kind of intensity. My notes are crumbs taken from this world, condensed, potent, amplified in their poignancy like haikus in the way Andrey Tarkovsky describes them: the poetic form "cultivates its images in such a way that they mean nothing beyond themselves, and at the same time express so much that it is not possible to catch their final meaning."[5]

Edelweiss
karaoke
Has she seen Sound of Music?

As compelling as it is, the possibility of transforming perishable matter into conserved entities is also shot through with risk and volatility. In transporting and storing these fragile bits, they are bound to crumble here and there, parts of them lost, others becoming damp and mushy, a variable jumble of debris as they move through space and time.[6]

Karl Marx's birthday

Resuscitated into a vignette, this note would take me back to the steps of the Juche Tower in north Korea's capital city, Pyongyang. The Juche Tower with its eternally glowing flame, the beating heart of the country. I met a tour guide there who told me that his birthday was the same day as Karl Marx's and was surprised I didn't know it. In what sense should I have known it? It was summer. I didn't know at the time that this could be my last visit. Instead of staying with the group, we would soon sneak away for a beer at the Taedonggang brewery just across the street, tucked behind an alley. Like so many other encounters that unfolded in the margins, in peripheral view. This moment raised questions about socialist subjectivity, Great Leaders, ideology, political power, liminality, some of the central themes in my work, but also left them in the midst of gaps and broken bridges.

III.

Writing, then, is the reconstitution of the freeze-dried into an entity of expanded essences and affects, however fleeting. Writing is the water restored to the crumb that returns weight and texture, however fraught.

Toni Morrison uses a metaphor of flooding to render the workings of memory. All water has "perfect memory" of the terrain traversed, and it can always find its way back whence it came.[7] Revisiting my field notes, I follow in the wake of their rush but also wallow in the soaking, steeping, saturating.

Knowledge comes when field notes as crumbs turned writing can place us in a scene, catch us in the pull of a raw state that makes itself manifest. This wouldn't be a knowledge that confirms the truth of things or that proves the goodness or badness of things. This is knowledge as perfect memories formed from imperfect crumbs.

Notes

1. Democratic People's Republic of Korea (DPRK), North Korea, north Korea, 조선민주주의인민공화국, 북조선, 북한. The term used is structured by what Shine Choi (2014) calls a "contest" between whose story of the country should be believed and holds legitimacy. With this in mind, I use "north" Korea instead of "North" Korea. See Shine Choi, *Re-Imagining North Korea in International Politics: Problems and Alternatives* (London: Routledge, 2014), and also Richard Roy Grinker, *Korea and Its Futures: Unification and the Unfinished War* (New York: Palgrave Macmillan, 2000).

2. See Svetlana Boym, *The Future of Nostalgia* (New York: Basic, 2001), 258, where she describes nostalgia as a "remembered sensation."

3. Susan Buck-Morss, *Dreamworld and Catastrophe: The Passing of Mass Utopia East and West* (Cambridge, MA: MIT Press, 2002).

4. Kathleen Stewart, "Atmospheric Attunements," *Environment and Planning D: Society and Space* 29 (2011): 445.

5. Andrey Tarkovsky, *Sculpting in Time*, trans. Kitty Hunter-Blair (New York: Alfred A. Knopf, 1987), 106.

6. The crumb of memory is thus charged. "Memories come at you like space junk," as Lauren Berlant and Kathleen Stewart write in *The Hundreds*. "Thought is an afterthought." See Lauren Berlant and Kathleen Stewart, *The Hundreds* (Durham, NC: Duke University Press, 2019), 6.

7. Toni Morrison, "The Site of Memory," in *Inventing the Truth: The Art and Craft of Memoir*, ed. William Zinsser (New York: Houghton Mifflin, 1995), 99. I thank Trinh T. Minh-ha for introducing me to this text.

52

WRITING THE DISQUIETS OF A COLONIAL FIELD

Ann Laura Stoler

Writing (and what is not written) is my field of work. Not writing "field-work" as we know it in ethnography when we "go to the field," but in some ways not so different from what we might find in Marilyn Strathern's sense of "immersion" or in Vincent Crapanzano's parse of fieldwork as the "subsuming intersubjective relations in the engagements themselves."[1] Mine offers a different inflection where writing itself—what people write and what they don't, their circumlocutions and habits of writing, the constant explanation and interpretation attributed to misleading properties of actual behavior, the performance of writing (the harsh scribble across a neatly penned page), the weight and quality of the paper, and who reads what—is the engagement and my labor. The terrain is the colonial field and an effort for more than forty years to discern, craft, and redraw an historical field of colonial and imperial governance, one that makes space for what is not already readily conceived as imperial or as a decidedly colonial matter.[2] My reflection has been on the conceptual and tactile methodologies we might need to think the scope and scale of colonial effects in ways that are neither policed by nor confined to the jurisdictions and censorships of colonial archives themselves. I understand it as an effort to register both the opacities and consuming violences of imperial durabilities, their tangible and intangible qualities.

Pressure points in the unstable flux between the self-assured and anxious writing of colonialisms' agents, architects, and ardent commentators seemed to ricochet, producing a visceral reactive, dissonant writing of my own. There is nothing seamless and smooth about it: a grim reminder of how Foucault described Georges Canguilhem's writing as an erratic exercise of irruptive gestures.[3] How to respond to repetitive officialese and neither be stupefied by its lull nor caught in its net? Being subsumed "by the relations in the engagement," as Crapanzano puts it, is there as well, but the "immersion" is of a very different sort, in the unstable logics which colonial agents prescribed and in those moments when those logics failed them, in the selective paper trails they left for each other, or in the often abrupt inquisitional demands that might disrupt the calm archival protocol in a slice across a page.[4]

What feels insistent is an effort to capture in tone and sensibility the subjacent imperial duress in seemingly benign sites, to glean a vocabulary that makes sense and uncommon sense of colonial dispositions, and to retain sympathy, fear, pity, violence, and security in a concurrent field with the connective tissue that binds them—that of the political rationalities and the unreason threaded through them. Writing the disquiets of a colonial field is to be willing to yield to the force and fragility of both dominant and displaced histories, to not be blinded by the glare of assertive writing, or to be seduced by the uncertain declarations that hover in the shadows. If the epistemic anxieties that I tracked in *Along the Archival Grain* were of those about whom I've sought to write, they are undoubtedly mine as well, in working through the arrogances of and distrust in colonial reason and its affective registers. Thus, perhaps the "emotive entanglements" of fieldwork, as Crapanzano describes them, are of another register, but not so very different after all.[5]

Colonial fields provoke political and writerly disquiets and demands on both content and form. Some are those we know well: how close to the bone one describes colonial violences without verging on pornography (or perhaps, less obviously, how to render the unequal damages on colonial subjects and agents without flattening their starkly different effects) and how to render the pressure on a pen and the feel of onion-skin paper with analytic and affective precision that does not reduce to the precious. Other emotive entanglements emerge at another scale: how to retain the singularity of particular colonial pasts and their durabilities in the present without assuming repetition, without either severing that past from the present or assuming they are the same. How to retain not the clean cut of colonial pasts distinct from postcolonial conditions but the quixotic movement between sporadic eruption of colonial effects and enduring damages, suspended in soils and psychic distress with new permutations. Rather than rupture or continuity, I've sought to think about what I call the "recursive" quality of colonial histories marked by the uneven, unsettled, contingent quality of histories that fold back upon themselves and in that refolding reveal new surfaces, unexposed fissures, undisclosed planes.[6]

This work shares with contemporary ethnography an abiding sense that there is no defined field prior to the questions we ask. These questions sometimes take form in response to moments of disquiet, in which choices of content and form remained provisionally adequate at best. One such disquiet came repeatedly in grappling with how to think about the dour despair of the relatively well-placed Dutch civil servant Frans Carl Valck, with whom I had spent so many years and whose sometimes contorted writing practices fill the final chapters of *Along the Archival Grain*. Valck was a well-connected civil servant first in Bali and then in Sumatra and Java who upon learning about the murder of a European planter's family tried to argue to his superiors that the atrocities were those committed by Europeans themselves, rather than by Javanese who worked on the estates. He paid a dear price, being relocated and then resigning from the civil service. Valck wrote and wrote and seemed to do nothing else, so much so that he hardly could get to the scenes of crimes on which he was required to report. His writing was of rumors, canned scripts of planters that didn't match what else he heard, from hearsay that was more accurate than the accounts of those who he had imagined should be reliable, those of the whites themselves. Details in the writing held me fast as epistemic things otherwise difficult to grasp—and perhaps naively as the shock of the "real"—only years later realizing that it was not unlike Gaston Bachelard's insistence that he sought to write a history of epistemological detail, something I thought I had been doing all along, tracking the minutiae mobilized to access and assess which differences were converted into colonial distastes and credible stories, fashioned to mark racial distinctions, and which were not.[7] It's not just that details matter, but rather their placement and timing as evidentiary claims. Carlo Ginzburg reduces them to "clues," but their force lies elsewhere—colonial taxonomies depended on indexes to mark differences made to matter, to mark an anomalous being in the world of a different human kind—thus the feverish search for tangible "indices" of those intangibles that couldn't be seen or measured.

Frans Carl Valck was not someone easy to like. He appears in the archival records in the 1870s in a succession of failed projects in which his credibility as an effective civil servant deserving promotion is on the line and with respect to his own self-image as an able, caring, credible father. I knew in fragments how he sat when he wrote his missives, of his dog under his legs, and of his increasingly cumbersome weight, but not what brandy he drank, or who washed and starched his clothes, or the smell of his anxious midnight sweat. I knew something of his punctilious concern for proper decorum and his ravaged pride. Setting out to convey something of someone I found I disliked perhaps as much as he disliked himself, the bar was set at an impossible limit to imagine an interiority of his lived place and time as nuanced as our own. I was struck by his capacity to know and to not know what colonialism did on the ground, to know with some of his senses and then to partially look back and then away, a disposition that seemed eminently his and yet also of our time.

I disliked his grown daughter even more. When I found myself one gray morning in a Hague archive confronted with the exquisitely embossed red leather diary she had bought for her trip, with barely one thing she could find to write about (all but two pages were empty) upon her arrival in Java where she had not been since she was a small girl, my own writing seized up. The font seemed too small, the distant gaze of academic writing too measured for my disdain at her empty page. So there, just five pages from the end of the book, I blurted out my impatience in an eruptive gesture, a shout in the dark against her fussy, sullen stance. Her desultory despair was neither exemplary of colonial relations nor significant in its own right, but somehow a punctum of the sort of flattened sensibility that such an enclosed colonial milieu could create, the trained habits that insist on foreclosures among its dulled and most devotional supporters.

Even harder was how to deal with the silent wail in the multiple drafts of an unsent letter, of the complaint of her father who after he was honorably discharged and humiliated by what he saw as an unjust dismissal, wrote and rewrote and wrote again, a defense of his honor. Pressing hard to write about someone whose allegiances I could not share, still his "politics of disregard"—that capacity to look and look away—seemed to broach a more intractable space of living inside imperial formations both like and unlike our own. But why imagine that their disregard for what was around them was so deeply a part of our current moment?

I lectured on the chapter before the book came out, and a former Israeli soldier, a young woman, came up to me breathless at the lecture's end, for she found Valck's unstable stance, his capacity to know and to look away, disturbingly a mirror of her own. As anthropologists whose signature trope is to make familiarities seem strange, to estrange the familiar and relish that tension, there's nothing particularly significant about this, but here the stakes felt as though they were raised to a different political pitch, for she and I both offered our own challenge to George Orwell's powerful claim in "Shooting an Elephant" that colonialism's underlings grew faces to fit their masks.[8] It was this almost imperceptible gap between face and mask that I tried to leave open, moving as Valck moved in the intricacies of his everyday between what he knew of the "barbarisms" of Europeans that he named, the betrayals that he anticipated, and the loyalty that he professed to a system whose archive only made room for his incompetencies as functionary and father. Perhaps I should have included the carefully penned plea on the thick foolscap paper. But that too would have been inadequate to muster what it must have been like to have been dismissed in the prime of his life, sentenced to a still life, with the unsent copies carefully preserved, the only testimony that he thought might be heard and that he knew would not.

Foucault's defining of critique as "the art of reflective insolence" is one turned not against others but against the norms and investments on which one's own position and posture depend.[9] Bourdieu's "fieldwork in philosophy" is similarly a call for attentiveness, both epistemological and personal, as he puts it, "an instrument of vigilance" as a "a weapon against yourself": a writing on the "dark side of comfort."[10] Slicing through that iconic compound field and work opens new configurations, like the writing, neither fixed nor formulaic, and subject to the making. The political spaces/possibilities are potential, awaiting how field, work, and writing are jointly conceived and perhaps, despite our intentions otherwise, refract the risks we are willing to take and how we choose to account for ourselves.

Notes

1. Marilyn Strathern, "The Ethnographic Effect I," in *Property, Substance and Effect: Anthropological Essays on Persons and Things* (London: Athlone, 1999); Vincent Crapanzano, "At the Heart of the Discipline," in *Ethnographic Fieldwork: An Anthropological Reader*, ed. Antonius C. G. M. Robben and Jeffrey A. Sluka (Malden, MA: Wiley-Blackwell, 2012), 547–62.

2. "Ann Laura Stoler: Interviewed by E. Valentine Daniel," *Public Culture* 24, no. 3 (2012): 487–508.

3. Michel Foucault on Canguilhem.

4. Crapanzano, "At the Heart of the Discipline," 553.

5. Crapanzano, 553.

6. Ann Laura Stoler, *Duress: Imperial Durabilities in Our Times* (Durham, NC: Duke University Press, 2016), 1–36.

7. Gaston Bachelard, *La philosophie du non: Essai d'une philosophe du nouvel esprit scientifique* (Paris: Presses Universitaires de France, 1940), 12.

8. George Orwell, "Shooting an Elephant," in *Collected Essays* (London: Secker and Warburg, 1961).

9. Michel Foucault, "What Is Critique?" in *The Politics of Truth*, ed. Sylvère Lotringer (Los Angeles: Semiotext(e), 1997).

10. Pierre Bourdieu, *In Other Words: Essays towards a Reflexive Sociology* (Stanford, CA: Stanford University Press, 1990), 27.

53

ON ETHNOGRAPHIC UNKNOWABILITY

Catherine Besteman

What if I told you to write what you don't know?

I ask this because I find the oft-offered advice to "write what you know" both alarming and silencing. Isn't ethnography at least partially about unknowability? If we acknowledge that textual recording is a form of fixing knowledge, how does one write what one doesn't know? How can our writing play on the edge between knowing and not knowing, refusing to fix the unknown by writing it into existence? Exploring this playful and vexing tension in ethnographic writing is my current preoccupation.

A STORY MIGHT help illuminate my query.

A few years ago, some friends in the refugee community in Maine with whom I do ethnographic work rekindled an old dispute. Tensions over leadership and representation plagued their relationship, and in the latest eruption people with knives broke through the apartment wall of my good friend Khalar. Khalar and his family fled the apartment and filed charges with the police. He and another man took out protection orders against each other. A defamation lawsuit filed by one against the other began making its way through the court system. A few days later, another friend, Ahmed, told me that this newest fighting was generated by Khalar's first wife's rage against his new second wife. The problems between the two women were radiating out through their respective kin groups, provoking small but violent eruptions between family members.

"WAIT," I SAID to Ahmed. "Khalar has a second wife?"

I was spending countless hours every week with Khalar on community projects. I understood the tensions over leadership and representation between Khalar and the other men as emanating from things that happened back in their country of origin, things that happened in the refugee camp, personality clashes, and the particular contextual politics of diasporic community building. My understanding did not extend to include marital disputes. How did I not know that Khalar had married again? A few months previously, Romana had begun attending social events with Khalar. Reading their interaction as marital, I had then asked if they were recently married, but Khalar insisted they were siblings. I recalled him telling me a few weeks prior that Zeynab, a local community leader, was negotiating a payment from him to his wife, which is what usually happens when a man marries a second wife. Stunned by my conversation with Ahmed, I phoned Khalar and asked, testily, "You're married to Romana?" I was hurt that he had felt the need for obscurity with me. How had I managed to miss this?

"No!" He retorted. "She's my cousin [cousin and sibling are often used interchangeably]. She was married but never had any children. My mother [who still lived in Khalar's natal village in Africa] arranged the marriage. She insisted on it. How could I say no? So Romana and I will have children, and I will register myself with DHHS as their father."

Despite Khalar's attempts to define the relationship as a sort of extra-wedlock favor and filial duty, and although there was no community ceremony, and although Khalar cannot have a legal polygynous marriage to Romana in the United States, it is clear that to others in the refugee community Romana is his second wife and not just a duty to Khalar's mother. The rancor between her and Khalar's first wife continued to animate community divides, reaching a climax when each woman took out a restraining order against the other.

I know that because polygyny is illegal in the United States, it is usually not announced outside the community. I know that Khalar wants to be viewed as an American-style community leader and (rightly) suspects non-Somalis are judgmental against polygyny. I know that Khalar is trying to find ways to assuage the anger of his first wife by minimizing the emotional significance of his second marriage. Is his translation of his marriage as filial duty an attempt to maintain an unknowability about his marital life not only to me but to others in the community as well?

This incident reminded me to question what I have a right to know and what "knowing" actually means. When I write about internal tensions within the refugee community, which knowledges do I include and which do I leave unrecorded? How do I claim to "know" the relevance of Khalar's marriage to intercommunity tensions if he insists otherwise? At moments like these, I feel the enormity of what I don't know, of what my interlocutors (quite reasonably) don't want me to know, and, sometimes, of the things I don't actually want to know. Decades ago, James Clifford wrote about ethnography's partial truths, reminding anthropologists that ethnographies, as crafted texts, are inherently incomplete efforts to impose tidy boundaries on untidy subjects. But recognizing the partiality of our accounts is something different from recognizing unknowability: those things that are never fully understood, feelings that remain untranslatable, the incommensurabilities encountered in fieldwork. How should our writing reflect respect for the things we do not know and do not have the right to know? How do we do this without domesticating the unknown?

Note

An earlier version of this essay appeared online in *Savage Minds: Notes and Queries in Anthropology*, November 10, 2014.

"AAA Guidelines for Tenure and Promotion Review: Communicating Public Scholarship in Anthropology." Accessed November 8, 2018. https://www.americananthro.org/AdvanceYourCareer/Content.aspx?ItemNumber=21713.

Ahmed, Sara. *Queer Phenomenology: Orientations, Objects, Others.* Durham, NC: Duke University Press, 2006.

Akbar, Kaveh. "Orchids Are Sprouting from the Floorboards." *Linebreak* 40, no. 2 (spring 2016). http://thejournalmag.org/archives/11342.

"Ann Laura Stoler: Interviewed by E. Valentine Daniel." *Public Culture* 24, no. 3 (2012): 487–508.

"Archaeology, Sexism and Scandal/Reviews." Rowman and Littlefield. Accessed April 28, 2017. https://rowman.com/ISBN/9781442230033.

Bachelard, Gaston. *La philosophie du non: Essai d'une philosophe du nouvel esprit scientifique.* Paris: Presses Universitaires de France, 1940.

Bachelard, Gaston. *The Psychoanalysis of Fire.* Boston: Beacon, 1964.

Bandelier, Adolph F. *The Delight Makers.* New York: Dodd, Mead, 1890.

Barad, Karen. *Meeting the Universe Halfway: Quantum Physics and the Entanglement of Matter and Meaning.* Durham, NC: Duke University Press, 2007.

Bateson, Gregory. *Steps to an Ecology of Mind.* Chicago: University of Chicago Press, 1972.

Bay Area Open Space Council. "Here and Now: Kashia Coastal Reserve." June 1, 2015. Video, 4:25. https://vimeo.com/144147365.

Behar, Ruth. *Translated Woman: Crossing the Border with Esperanza's Story.* Boston: Beacon, 1993.

Behar, Ruth. *The Vulnerable Observer: Anthropology That Breaks Your Heart.* Boston: Beacon, 1997.

Belcher, Wendy Laura. *Writing Your Journal Article in Twelve Weeks.* Thousand Oaks, CA: SAGE, 2009.

Benedict, Ruth. *Patterns of Culture*. New York: Houghton Mifflin, 1934.

Benjamin, Walter. "The Storyteller: Reflections on the Works of Nikolai Leskov." In *Illuminations: Essays and Reflections*, edited by Hannah Arendt and translated by Harry Zohn. New York: Schocken, 1969.

Bennett, Jane. *Vibrant Matter: A Political Ecology of Things*. Durham, NC: Duke University Press, 2010.

Ben-Oni, Rosebud. "Orchids We Have Been: On the Transformative Power of Longing." *Kenyon Review Online*, August 19, 2016, http://www.kenyonreview.org/2016/08/orchids-transformative-power-longing.

Berggen, Asa, and Ian Hodder. "Social Practice Methods and Some Problems for Field Archaeology." *American Antiquity* 68 (2003): 421–34.

Bolender, Karen. "R.A.W. Assmilk Soap." In *The Multispecies Salon*, edited by Eben Kirksey, 64–86. Durham, NC: Duke University Press, 2014.

Bonilla, Yarimar. "Guadeloupe on Strike: A New Political Chapter in the French Antilles." NACLA *Report on the Americas* 42 (2009): 6–10.

Bonilla, Yarimar, and Rafael Boglio Martinez. "Puerto Rico in Crisis: Government Workers Battle Neoliberal Reform." NACLA *Report on the Americas* 43 (2010): 6–8.

Bonilla, Yarimar, and Jonathan Rosas. "#Ferguson: Digital Activism, Hashtag Ethnography, and the Racial Politics of Social Media." *American Ethnologist* 42 (2015): 4–17.

Borges, Jorge Luis. "The Analytical Language of John Wilkins." In *Other Inquisitions, 1937–1952*, translated by Ruth L. C. Simms, 101–5. Austin: University of Texas Press, 1964.

Bourdieu, Pierre. *In Other Words: Essays towards a Reflexive Sociology*. Stanford, CA: Stanford University Press, 1990.

Bourgois, Philippe. *In Search of Respect: Selling Crack in El Barrio*. Cambridge: Cambridge University Press, 2003.

Boyle, James. *The Public Domain: Enclosing the Commons of the Mind*. New Haven, CT: Yale University Press, 2008.

Boym, Svetlana. *The Future of Nostalgia*. New York: Basic, 2001.

Buck-Morss, Susan. *Dreamworld and Catastrophe: The Passing of Mass Utopia in East and West*. Cambridge, MA: MIT Press, 2002.

Butler, Judith. *Giving an Account of Oneself*. New York: Fordham University Press, 2005.

Call, Wendy, and Sasha Su-Ling Welland. "Living Elsewhere in 16 Steps." *Chain* 9 (2002): 59–69.

Carrico, Kevin. "Chinese State Media Representations." *Hot Spots*, April 8, 2012. https://culanth.org/fieldsights/109-chinese-state-media-representations.

Celan, Paul. "Death Fugue." Poets.org. 1948. http://www.poets.org/poetsorg/poem/deathfugue.

Cep, Casey N. "A Thousand Words: Writing from Photographs." *New Yorker*, February 26, 2014. http://www.newyorker.com/books/page-turner/a-thousand-words-writing-from-photographs.

Clifford, James. "Introduction: Partial Truths." In *Writing Culture: The Poetics and Politics of Ethnography*, edited by James Clifford and George E. Marcus, 1–26. Berkeley: University of California Press, 1986.

"The Colorado Coalfield War Archaeological Project." Accessed August 24, 2018. https://www.du.edu/ludlow/project_000.html.

Colwell-Chanthaphonh, Chip. "History, Justice, and Reconciliation." In *Archaeology as a Tool of Civic Engagement*, edited by Barbara J. Little and Paul A. Shackel, 23–46. Lanham, MD: AltaMira, 2007.

Cram, Shannon. "Becoming Jane: The Making and Unmaking of Hanford's Nuclear Body." *Environment and Planning D: Society and Space* 33, no. 5 (2015): 796–812. doi: 10.1177/0263775815599317.

Crapanzano, Vincent. "At the Heart of the Discipline." In *Ethnographic Fieldwork: An Anthropological Reader*, 2nd ed., edited by Antonius C. G. M. Robben and Jeffrey A. Sluka, 547–62. Malden, MA: Wiley-Blackwell, 2012.

Cruikshank, Julie. *Do Glaciers Listen? Local Knowledge, Colonial Encounters, and Social Imagination*. Vancouver: UBC, 2005.

Das, Veena. *Life and Words: Violence and the Descent into the Ordinary*. Berkeley: University of California Press, 2007.

Deeb, Lara, and Jessica Winegar. *Anthropology's Politics: Disciplining the Middle East*. Stanford, CA: Stanford University Press, 2016.

De León, Jason. *The Land of Open Graves: Living and Dying on the Migrant Trail*. Berkeley: University of California Press, 2015.

Deleuze, Gilles. *Desert Islands and Other Texts, 1953–1974*. New York: Semiotext(e), 2004.

Demastes, William W. *The Cambridge Introduction to Tom Stoppard*. Cambridge: Cambridge University Press, 2013.

Derrida, Jacques. *Of Grammatology*. Baltimore: Johns Hopkins University Press, 1998.

Dhompa, Tsering Wangmo. *In the Absent Everyday*. Berkeley: Apogee, 2005.

Didion, Joan. "On Keeping a Notebook." In *Slouching towards Bethlehem*, 131–41. London: Andre Deutch, 1969.

Dillard, Annie. *The Writing Life*. New York: Harper Perennial, 1989.

Duranti, Alessandro. *Linguistic Anthropology*. Cambridge: Cambridge University Press, 1997.

Dusek, Val. "An Inquiry Into Modes of Existence: An Anthropology of the Moderns." *Notre Dame Philosophical Journal* (2014). https://ndpr.nd.edu/news/an-inquiry -into-modes-of existence-an-anthropology-of-the-moderns.

Dyson, Stephen. *Ancient Marbles to American Shores*. Philadelphia: University of Pennsylvania Press, 1998.

Edmonds, Mark Roland, and Rose Ferraby. *Stonework*. Orkney, Scotland: Group VI, 2012.

Evans-Pritchard, E. E. *Witchcraft, Oracles and Magic among the Azande*. Oxford: Oxford University Press, 1937.

Falcone, Jessica. "Maitreya, or the Love of Buddhism: The Non-event of Bodh Gaya's Giant Statue." In *Cross-Disciplinary Perspectives on a Contested Buddhist Site: Bodh Gaya Jataka*, edited by David Geary, Matthew R. Sayers, and Abhishek Singh Amar, 153–71. New York: Routledge, 2012.

Fassin, Didier. *Enforcing Order: An Ethnography of Urban Policing*. Translated by Rachel Gomme. Cambridge: Polity, 2013.

Fassin, Didier. "Why Ethnography Matters: On Anthropology and Its Publics." *Cultural Anthropology* 28, no. 4 (2013): 621–46.

Fordham, Signithia. "Write-ous Indignation: Black Girls, Dilemmas of Cultural Domination and the Struggle to Speak the Skin We Are In." In *Anthropology off the Shelf: Anthropologists on Writing*, edited by Alisse Waterston and Maria D. Vesperi, 79–92. Malden, MA: Wiley-Blackwell, 2011.

Fortun, Kim. "Ethnography in Late Industrialism." *Cultural Anthropology* 27, no. 3 (2012): 446–64. http://www.culanth.org/articles/135-ethnography-in-late-industrialism.

Foucault, Michel. *The Order of Things: An Archaeology of the Human Sciences*. New York: Vintage, 1994.

Foucault, Michel. "What Is Critique?" In *The Politics of Truth*, edited by Sylvère Lotringer. Los Angeles: Semiotext(e), 1997.

Geertz, Clifford. *Works and Lives: The Anthropologist as Author*. Stanford, CA: Stanford University Press, 1988.

Gero, Joan. "Archaeological Practice and Gendered Encounters with Field Data." In *Gender in Archaeology*, edited by R. Wright, 251–80. Philadelphia: University of Pennsylvania Press, 1996.

Ghodsee, Kristen R. *From Notes to Narrative: Writing Ethnographies That Everyone Can Read*. Chicago: University of Chicago Press, 2016.

Ghosh, Amitav. *The Glass Palace*. New Delhi: Ravi Dayal, 2000.

Ghosh, Amitav. *The Hungry Tide*. London: HarperCollins, 2005.

Gilmer, Micah. "'You Got to Have a Heart of Stone to Work Here': Coaching, Teaching, and 'Building Men' at Eastside High." PhD diss., Duke University, 2009.

Goldstein, Donna M. "'*Experimentalité*': Pharmaceutical Insights into Anthropology's Epistemologically Fractured Self." In *Medicine and the Politics of Knowledge*, edited by Susan Levine, 118–51. Cape Town: HSRC, 2012.

Goldstein, Donna M. *Laughter out of Place: Race, Class, Violence, and Sexuality in a Rio Shantytown*. Berkeley: University of California Press, 2003.

Goldstein, Donna M., and Kira Hall. "Post-election Surrealism and the Hands of Donald Trump." *HAU: Journal of Ethnographic Theory* 7 (2017): 397–406.

Goldstein, Donna M., and Magdalena E. Stawkowski. "James V. Neel and Yuri E. Dubrova: Cold War Debates and the Genetic Effects of Low-Dose Radiation." *Journal of the History of Biology* 48 (2015): 67–98.

Gottleib, Alma. "The Anthropologist as Storyteller." In *The Anthropologist as Writer: Genres and Contexts in the Twenty-First Century*, edited by Helena Wulff, 93–117. New York: Berghahn, 2016.

Gottleib, Alma, and Philip Graham. *Parallel Worlds: An Anthropologist and a Writer Encounter Africa*. Chicago: University of Chicago Press, 1994.

Haas, Bridget M. "Citizens-in-Waiting, Deportees-in-Waiting: Power, Temporality, and Suffering in the U.S. Asylum System." *Ethos* 45 (2017): 75–97.

Hall, Kira, Donna M. Goldstein, and Matthew Bruce Ingram. "The Hands of Donald Trump: Entertainment, Gesture, Spectacle." *HAU: Journal of Ethnographic Theory* 6, no. 2 (2016): 433–47.

Harrison, Faye V., Carole McGranahan, Kaifa Roland, and Bianca Williams. "Decolonizing Anthropology: A Conversation." *Savage Minds: Notes and Queries in Anthropology.* May 3, 2016. https://savageminds.org/2016/05/03/decolonizing-anthropology-a-conversation-with-faye-v-harrison-part-ii.

Hau'ofa, Epeli. "Pasts to Remember." In *Remembrance of Pacific Pasts: An Invitation to Remake History*, edited by Robert Borofsky. Honolulu: University of Hawai'i Press, 2000.

Heaney, Seamus. *Opened Ground: Selected Poems, 1966–1996.* London: Macmillan, 1999.

Hejinian, Lyn. "The Rejection of Closure." Poetry Foundation. Accessed October 1, 2018. http://www.poetryfoundation.org/learning/essay/237870.

Horgan, John. "Stream of Thought Description of Teaching James's 'Stream of Thought': A Work of Faction." *Scientific American* Blog. December 7, 2013. https://blogs.scientificamerican.com/cross-check/stream-of-thought-description-of-teaching-jamese28099s-e2809cstream-of-thoughte2809d-a-work-of-faction.

Horst, Zander. *Fact, Fiction, "Faction": A Study of Black South African Literature in English.* Tübingen, Germany: Narr, 1999.

Hurston, Zora Neale. *Mules and Men.* Philadelphia: Lippincott, 1935.

Ingold, Tim. "Anthropology Is *Not* Ethnography." *Proceedings of the British Academy* 154 (2008): 69–92.

Ingold, Tim. "That's Enough about Ethnography!" *HAU: Journal of Ethnographic Theory* 4, no. 1 (2014): 383–95. doi: https://doi.org/10.14318/hau4.1.021.

Iyer, Pico. *The Global Soul: Jetlag, Shopping Malls, and the Search for Home.* New York: Knopf Doubleday, 2000.

Jackson, Michael. *At Home in the World.* Durham, NC: Duke University Press, 1995.

Joseph, May. *Nomadic Identities: The Performance of Citizenship.* Minneapolis: University of Minnesota Press, 1999.

Joyce, Rosemary A. *The Languages of Archaeology: Dialogue, Narrative, and Writing.* Oxford: Blackwell, 2002.

Kaiser, Alan. *Archaeology, Sexism and Scandal: The Long-Suppressed Story of One Woman's Discoveries and the Man Who Stole Credit for Them.* Lanham, MD: Rowman and Littlefield, 2015.

Kincaid, Jamaica. *A Small Place.* New York: Farrar, Straus and Giroux, 1988.

King, Lily. *Euphoria.* New York: Grove, 2014.

Klinkenborg, Verlyn. *Several Short Sentences about Writing.* New York: Vintage, 2012.

Kolshus, Thorgeir. "The Power of Ethnography in the Public Sphere." *HAU: Journal of Ethnographic Theory* 7, no. 1 (2017): 61–69.

Kroeber, Alfred L. "Introduction." In *American Indian Life*, edited by Elsie Clews Parsons, 5–16. New York: B. W. Huebsch, 1922.

Langness, L. L., and Gelya Frank. "Fact, Fiction and the Ethnographic Novel." *Anthropology and Humanism Quarterly* 3 (1978): 18–22.

Latour, Bruno. *Aramis, or the Love of Technology.* Cambridge, MA: Harvard University Press, 1996.

Latour, Bruno. *An Inquiry into Modes of Existence: An Anthropology of the Moderns.* Translated by Catherine Porter. Cambridge, MA: Harvard University Press, 2013.

Latour, Bruno, and Steve Woolgar. *Laboratory Life: The Construction of Scientific Facts.* Princeton, NJ: Princeton University Press, 1986.

Lefevre, Henri. *Everyday Life in the Modern World.* New York: Harper and Row, 1971.

Le Guin, Ursula K. *The Left Hand of Darkness.* New York: Walker, 1969.

Le Guin, Ursula K. *The Wave in the Mind: Talks and Essays on the Writer, the Reader, and the Imagination.* Boston: Shambhala, 2004.

Lévi-Strauss, Claude. *Tristes Tropiques.* Translated by John Russell. New York: Criterion, 1961.

Lévy-Bruhl, Lucien. *How Natives Think.* Princeton, NJ: Princeton University Press, 1985.

Limón, José. *Dancing with the Devil: Society and Poetics in Mexican-American South Texas.* Madison: University of Wisconsin Press, 1994.

Loynaz, Dulce Maria. *Poemas sin nombre.* Madrid: Aguilar, 1953.

Malinowski, Bronislaw. *Argonauts of the Western Pacific.* Long Grove, IL: Waveland, 1922.

Mauss, Marcel. *The Gift: The Form and Reason for Exchange in Archaic Societies.* London: Routledge, 1990.

McCarthy Brown, Karen. *Mama Lola: A Vodou Priestess in Brooklyn,* rev. ed. Berkeley: University of California Press, 2001.

McGranahan, Carole. "Ethnography beyond Method: The Importance of an Ethnographic Sensibility." *Sites: A Journal of Social Anthropology and Cultural Studies* 15, no. 1 (2018): 1–10.

McGranahan, Carole. "*Sa spang 'mda gnam spang 'mda*: Murder, History, and Social Politics in 1920s Lhasa." In *Khams pa Local Histories: Visions of People, Place, and Authority,* edited by Lawrence Epstein, 103–26, Leiden: Brill Academic Press, 2002.

McGranahan, Carole. "What Is Ethnography? Teaching Ethnographic Sensibilities without Fieldwork." *Teaching Anthropology* 4 (2014): 22–36.

McLean, Stuart. "SEA." In *Crumpled Paper Boat: Experiments in Ethnographic Writing,* edited by Anand Pandian and Stuart McLean, 148–76. Durham, NC: Duke University Press, 2017.

McPhee, John. "The Encircled River." *New Yorker,* May 2, 1977.

Morrison, Toni. "The Site of Memory." In *Inventing the Truth: The Art and Craft of Memoir,* edited by William Zinsser, 83–102. New York: Houghton Mifflin, 1995.

Nading, Alex. *Mosquito Trails: Ecology, Health, and the Politics of Entanglement.* Oakland: University of California Press, 2014.

Naipaul, V. S. *An Area of Darkness: A Discovery of India.* London: Picador, 1995.

Narayan, Kirin. *Alive in the Writing: Crafting Ethnography in the Shadow of Chekhov.* Chicago: University of Chicago Press, 2012.

Narayan, Kirin. "Ethnography and Fiction: Where Is the Border?" *Anthropology and Humanism* 24, no. 2 (1999): 134–47.

Narayan, Kirin. *Storytellers, Saints, and Scoundrels: Folk Narrative in Hindu Religious Teachings.* Philadelphia: University of Pennsylvania Press, 1989.

O'Brien, Tim. *The Things They Carried.* Boston: Houghton Mifflin, 1990.

Ogden, Laura. *Swamplife: People, Gators, and Mangroves Entangled in the Everglades.* Minneapolis: University of Minnesota Press, 2011.

Olson, Greta. "Reconsidering Unreliability: Fallible and Untrustworthy Narrators." *Narrative* 11 (2003): 93–109.

Ong, Aihwa. *Flexible Citizenship: The Cultural Logics of Transnationality*. Durham, NC: Duke University Press, 1999.

Ortner, Sherry. *Anthropology and Social Theory: Culture, Power, and the Acting Subject*. Durham, NC: Duke University Press, 2006.

Ortner, Sherry B. "Generation X: Anthropology in a Media-Saturated World." In *Anthropology and Social Theory: Culture, Power, and the Acting Subject*, edited by Sherry B. Ortner. Durham, NC: Duke University Press, 2006.

Orwell, George. *Nineteen Eighty-Four*. New York: Penguin, 1949.

Orwell, George. "Politics and the English Language." *Horizon* 13, no. 76 (1946): 252–65.

Orwell, George. "Shooting an Elephant." In *Collected Essays*. London: Secker and Warburg, 1961.

Packer, Martin. *The Science of Qualitative Research*. Cambridge: Cambridge University Press, 2011.

Pamuk, Orhan. *The Innocence of Objects: The Museum of Innocence, Istanbul*. New York: Abrams, 2012.

Pamuk, Orhan. *The Museum of Innocence*. Toronto: Knopf Canada, 2010.

Pandian, Anand. *Reel World: An Anthropology of Creation*. Durham, NC: Duke University Press, 2015.

Pandian, Anand, and Stuart McLean, eds. *Crumpled Paper Boat: Experiments in Ethnographic Writing*. Durham, NC: Duke University Press, 2017.

Parikka, Jussi. *A Geology of Media*. Minneapolis: University of Minnesota Press, 2015.

Pound, Ezra. *ABC of Reading*. London: Faber and Faber, 1936.

Pratt, Mary Louise. "Arts of the Contact Zone." *Profession* (1991): 33–40. https://serendip.brynmawr.edu/oneworld/system/files/PrattContactZone.pdf.

Quimby, George I., and Alexander Spoehr. "Acculturation and Material Culture." *Fieldiana—Anthropology* 36, no. 6 (1951): 107–47. http://www.biodiversitylibrary.org/item/25060#page/4/mode/1up.

Raffles, Hugh. *In Amazonia: A Natural History*. Princeton, NJ: Princeton University Press, 2002.

Riley, Peter, *Excavations*. Hastings, UK: Reality Street, 2004.

Rizvi, Uzma Z. "Accounting for Multiple Desires: Decolonizing Methodologies, Archaeology and the Public Interest." *India Review* 5, nos. 3–4 (2006): 394–416.

Rizvi, Uzma Z. "Checkpoints as Gendered Spaces: An Autoarchaeology of War, Heritage and the City." In *The Oxford Handbook of the Archaeology of the Contemporary World*, edited by Paul Graves-Brown, Rodney Harrison, and Angela Piccini, 494–506. Oxford: Oxford University Press, 2013.

Rizvi, Uzma Z. "Decolonizing Archaeology: On the Global Heritage of Epistemic Laziness." In *Two Days after Forever: A Reader on the Choreography of Time*, edited by Omar Kholeif, 154–63. Berlin: Sternberg, 2015.

Rizwan, Sahil. "13 Animals Who Are Way More Gangster Than You." *BuzzFeed*, September 22, 2015. https://www.buzzfeed.com/sahilrizwan/gangstanimal.

Roberts, Victoria. "Where There's Smoke, There's Mirrors." *New Yorker*, February 9, 1998.

Robinson, David. *Excavations at Olynthus VII: The Terra-Cottas of Olynthus Found in 1931*. Baltimore: Johns Hopkins University Press, 1933.

Robinson, David. *Excavations at Olynthus XIV: Terracottas, Lamps, and Coins Found in 1934 and 1938*. Baltimore: Johns Hopkins University Press, 1952.

Robinson, Marilynne. *Gilead*. New York: Farrar, Straus and Giroux, 2004.

Robinson, Marilynne. *Housekeeping*. New York: Farrar, Straus and Giroux, 1980.

Robinson, Marilynne. *When I Was a Child I Read Books*. New York: Farrar, Straus and Giroux, 2012.

Rosaldo, Renato. *Culture and Truth: The Remaking of Social Analysis*. Boston: Beacon, 1989.

Rosaldo, Renato. *The Day of Shelly's Death: The Poetry and Ethnography of Grief*. Durham, NC: Duke University Press, 2014.

Roveland, Blythe. "Reflecting upon Archaeological Practice: Multiple Visions of a Late Paleolithic Site in Germany." In *Ethnographies of Archaeological Practice: Cultural Encounters, Material Transformations*, edited by M. Edgeworth, 56–67. Lanham, MD: AltaMira, 2006.

Rowell, Andrew. "Preface." In *Green Backlash*, xiv–xv. New York: Routledge, 1996. https://content.taylorfrancis.com/books/download?dac=C2004–0-209904&isbn=9781351565004&format=googlePreviewPdf.

Royal, Te Ahukaramû Charles. *Te Ara: The Encyclopedia of New Zealand*. Government of New Zealand. September 24, 2007. http://www.teara.govt.nz/en/papatuanuku-the-land/page-5.

Sahlins, Marshall. *What Kinship Is—and Is Not*. Chicago: University of Chicago Press, 2013.

Samuelson, Pamela. "Academic Author Objections to the Google Book Search Settlement." *Journal on Telecommunications and High Technology Law* 8 (2010): 491–522.

Sanford, Victoria. *Buried Secrets: Truth and Human Rights in Guatemala*. New York: Palgrave Macmillan US, 2003.

Schmidt, Nancy. "The Nature of Ethnographic Fiction: A Further Inquiry." *Anthropology and Humanism Quarterly* 6 (1981): 8–18.

Schrire, Carmel. *Digging through Darkness: Chronicles of an Archaeologist*. New Brunswick, NJ: Rutgers University Press, 1995.

Schumacher, Julie. *Dear Committee Members: A Novel*. New York: Random House, 2014.

Schwerner, Armand. *The Tablets*, vol. 1. Orono, ME: National Poetry Foundation, 1999.

Sebald, W. G. *The Emigrants*. London: Harvill, 1996.

Shankman, Paul. "The Public Anthropology of Margaret Mead: *Redbook*, Women's Issues, and the 1960s." *Current Anthropology* 59, no. 1 (2018): 55–73.

Singh, Bhrigupati. *Poverty and the Quest for Life: Spiritual and Material Striving in Rural India*. Chicago: University of Chicago Press, 2015.

Somers, James. "Torching the Modern-Day Library of Alexandria." *Atlantic*, April 20, 2017. https://www.theatlantic.com/technology/archive/2017/04/the-tragedy-of-google-books/523320.

Spector, Janet D. "What This Awl Means: Toward a Feminist Archaeology." In *Engendering Archaeology: Women and Prehistory*, edited by Joan M. Gero and Margaret W. Conkey, 388–406. Cambridge, MA: Basil Blackwell, 1991.

Spencer, Jonathan. "Anthropology as a Kind of Writing." *Man* 24, no. 1 (1989): 145–64.

Stewart, Kathleen. *Ordinary Affects*. Durham, NC: Duke University Press, 2007.

Stewart, Kathleen. "Atmospheric Attunements." *Environment and Planning D: Society and Space* 29 (2011): 445–53.

Stoler, Ann Laura. *Duress: Imperial Durabilities in Our Times*. Durham, NC: Duke University Press, 2016.

Stoller, Paul. "Ethnography/Memoir/Imagination/Story." *Anthropology and Humanism* 32, no. 2 (2007): 178–91.

Stone, Nomi. "Drones: An Exercise in Awe-Terror." PoetryNet. Accessed October 1, 2018. http://www.poetrynet.org/month/archive2/stone/poem2.html.

Strathern, Marilyn. "The Ethnographic Effect I." In *Property, Substance and Effect: Anthropological Essays on Persons and Things*. London: Athlone, 1999.

Sullivan, Shannon, and Nancy Tuana, eds. *Race and Epistemologies of Ignorance*. Albany: SUNY Press, 2007.

Tamisari, Franca. "'Personal Acquaintance': Essential Individuality and the Possibilities of Encounters." In *Moving Anthropology: Critical Indigenous Studies*, edited by Tess Lea, Emma Kowal, and Gillian Cowlishaw, 17–36. Darwin, Australia: Darwin University Press, 2006.

Tarkovsky, Andrey. *Sculpting in Time*. Translated by Kitty Hunter-Blair. New York: Knopf, 1987.

Taussig, Michael. *Law in a Lawless Land: Diary of a* Limpieza *in Colombia*. Chicago: University of Chicago Press, 2005.

Taussig, Michael. *Walter Benjamin's Grave*. Chicago: University of Chicago Press, 2006.

Teaiwa, Katerina. *Consuming Ocean Island: Stories of People and Phosphate from Banaba*. Bloomington: Indiana University Press, 2015.

Theidon, Kimberly. "'How Was Your Trip?' Self-Care for Researchers Working and Writing on Violence." Drugs Security and Democracy Program, DSD Working Papers in Research Security, New York. Social Science Research Council, 2014. https://kimberlytheidon.files.wordpress.com/2014/04/dsd_researchsecurity_02_theidon.pdf.

Thomson, Marnie Jane. "Mud, Dust, and *Marougé*: Precarious Construction in a Congolese Refugee Camp." *Architectural Theory Review* 19, no. 3 (2015): 376–92.

Trouillot, Michel-Rolph. *Global Transformations: Anthropology and the Modern World*. New York: Palgrave, 2003.

Tsing, Anna. *In the Realm of the Diamond Queen*. Princeton, NJ: Princeton University Press, 1993.

Tuck, Eve, Marcia McKenzie, and Kate McCoy. "Land Education: Indigenous, Postcolonial, and Decolonizing Perspectives on Place and Environmental Education Research." *Environmental Education Research* 20, no. 1 (2014): 1–23.

Ulysse, Gina Athena. *Why Haiti Needs New Narratives: A Post Quake Chronicle*. Middletown, CT: Wesleyan University Press, 2015.

Van Dyke, Ruth M., and Reinhard Bernbeck. *Subjects and Narratives in Archaeology*. Boulder: University Press of Colorado, 2015.

Vesperi, Maria D. "Attend to the Differences First: Conflict and Collaboration in Anthropology and Journalism." *Anthropology News* 51, no. 4 (2010): 7–9.

Vesperi, Maria D., and Alisse Waterston. "Introduction: The Writer in the Anthropologist." In *Anthropology off the Shelf: Anthropologists on Writing*, edited by Alisse Waterston and Maria D. Vesperi, 1–11. Malden, MA: Wiley-Blackwell, 2011.

Viveiros de Castro, Eduardo. *Cannibal Metaphysics: For a Post-structural Anthropology*. Minneapolis: Univocal, 2014.

Waterston, Alisse, and Maria D. Vesperi, eds. *Anthropology off the Shelf: Anthropologists on Writing*. Malden, MA: Wiley-Blackwell, 2011.

"The Way Home." *Time*, August 7, 1944. http://content.time.com/time/subscriber /article/0,33009,886154,00.html.

Weidemann, Anders, dir. *30 Degrees in February*. SVT, 2012.

"What's the Best Way?" SNL Transcripts. Accessed April 22, 2017. http://snltranscripts .jt.org/92/92ibestway.phtml.

Whitaker, Manya, and Eric Anthony Grollman. *Counternarratives from Women of Color Academics: Bravery, Vulnerability, and Resistance*. New York: Routledge, 2018.

White, E. B. *Stuart Little*, special read-aloud ed. New York: HarperCollins, 1999.

White, Hayden. "Storytelling: Historical and Ideological." In *Centuries' Ends, Narrative Means*, edited by Robert Newman. Stanford, CA: Stanford University Press, 1996.

White, Hayden. "The Value of Narrativity in the Representation of Reality." *Critical Inquiry* 7, no. 1 (1980): 5-27.

Whitehead, Alfred North. *Process and Reality*. New York: Free Press, 1978.

Williams, Bianca C. *The Pursuit of Happiness: Black Women, Diasporic Dreams, and the Politics of Emotional Transnationalism*. Durham, NC: Duke University Press, 2018.

Williams, Raymond. *People of the Black Mountains*. Vol. 1, *The Beginning*. London: Chatto and Windus, 1989.

Woeser, Tsering. "Self-Immolation and Slander." *Hot Spots*, April 8, 2012. https:// culanth.org/fieldsights/105-self-immolation-and-slander-woeser.

Woeser, Tsering. *Tibet on Fire: Self-Immolations against Chinese Rule*. London: Verso, 2016.

Wulff, Helena. "Introducing the Anthropologist as Writer: Across and within Genres." In *The Anthropologist as Writer: Genres and Contexts in the Twenty-First Century*, edited by Helena Wulff, 1–18. New York: Berghahn, 2016.

Young, Donna. "'The Empty Tomb' as Metaphor." *Religion and Society* 5, no. 1 (2014).

CONTRIBUTORS

WHITNEY BATTLE-BAPTISTE, a native of the Bronx, New York, is a scholar-activist who views the classroom and the campus as a space to engage contemporary issues with a sensibility of the past. Her primary research is in interpreting how the intersection of race, gender, class, and sexuality look through an archaeological lens. She has excavated sites in Virginia, Tennessee, Boston, Great Barrington, and her current project, a community-based heritage site at Millars Plantation on Eleuthera, Bahamas. She is professor in the Department of Anthropology and director of the W. E. B. Du Bois Center at UMass Amherst.

JANE EVA BAXTER is associate professor of anthropology at DePaul University. She is a teaching professor with research interests in the archaeology of labor, gender, identity, and childhood, and conducts fieldwork in the United States and the Bahamas.

RUTH BEHAR was born in Havana, Cuba, and grew up in New York City. She is the Victor Haim Perera Collegiate Professor of Anthropology at the University of Michigan and the recipient of a MacArthur Fellows "Genius" Award and a Guggenheim Fellowship. A storyteller, poet, educator, and public speaker, Behar is the author of *The Presence of the Past in a Spanish Village*, *Translated Woman: Crossing the Border with Esperanza's Story*, and *The Vulnerable Observer: Anthropology That Breaks Your Heart*. She coedited *Women Writing Culture*, one of the first books to call attention to the creative ethnographic writing of women in anthropology. Behar frequently visits and writes about her native Cuba and explores her return journeys in *An Island Called Home: Returning to Jewish Cuba* and *Traveling Heavy: A Memoir in between Journeys*. Also a creative writer, Behar's coming-of-age novel, *Lucky Broken Girl*, won the Pura Belpré Author Award. Her bilingual book of poems, *Everything I Kept/Todo lo que guardé*, is her most recent publication.

ADIA BENTON is associate professor of anthropology and African studies at Northwestern University. She writes about inequality in the distribution of care in settings "socialized" for scarcity. This means understanding the political, economic, and historical factors shaping how care is provided in complex humanitarian emergencies and in longer-term development projects. She has also written about race in medical humanitarian images, nongovernmental organizations, and security paradigms in infectious-disease outbreaks. Her first book, *HIV Exceptionalism: Development through Disease in Sierra Leone*, won the 2017 Rachel Carson book prize, which is awarded by the Society for Social Studies of Science (4S).

LAUREN BERLANT teaches English at the University of Chicago. Her recent work includes *Cruel·Optimism* (2011), *Sex, or the Unbearable* (with Lee Edelman, 2014), *Desire/Love* (2012), and *The Hundreds* with Kathleen Stewart (2019).

ROBIN M. BERNSTEIN is associate professor of anthropology, a faculty associate in the Health and Society Program (CU Institute of Behavioral Science), and faculty affiliate of the Center for Global Health (Colorado School of Public Health). She received her BA in anthropology from Rutgers in 1997 and her PhD from the University of Illinois, Urbana-Champaign, in 2004. Her research focuses on growth and development, life history evolution, and maternal and infant health.

SARAH BESKY is assistant professor of anthropology and international and public affairs at Brown University. She specializes in the study of nature, capitalism, and labor in South Asia and the Himalayas. She is the author of *The Darjeeling Distinction: Labor and Justice on Fair-Trade Tea Plantations in Darjeeling India* (2014) and *Tasting Qualities: The Past and Future of Tea* (2020) as well as several articles on agriculture and social justice. She coedited (with Alex Blanchette) *How Nature Works: Rethinking Labor on a Troubled Planet* (2019).

CATHERINE BESTEMAN teaches anthropology at Colby College. Her research focuses on mobility, militarism, sovereignty/citizenship, and racism, topics she has studied in South Africa, Somalia, and the United States. Her books include *Making Refuge: Somali Bantu Refugees and Lewiston, Maine* (2016), *Transforming Cape Town* (2008), *Unraveling Somalia* (1999), and the edited volumes *Life by Algorithms* (2019), *The Insecure American* (2009), *Why America's Top Pundits Are Wrong* (2005), and *Violence: A Reader* (2002). A 2012 Guggenheim Fellow, her recent work has also been supported by the Rockefeller Foundation, the American Council of Learned Societies, the Wenner Gren Foundation, and the National Endowment for the Arts.

YARIMAR BONILLA is professor in the Department of Africana, Puerto Rican, and Latino Studies at Hunter College and the PhD Program in Anthropology at the Graduate Center of the City University of New York. She is the author of *Non-sovereign Futures: French Caribbean Politics in the Wake of Disenchantment* (2012) and editor of *Aftershocks of Disaster: Puerto Rico Before and After the Storm* (2019). Her latest book project focuses on the political and social aftermath of Hurricane Maria in Puerto Rico.

KEVIN CARRICO is senior lecturer in Chinese studies at Monash University. His research examines nationalism and ethnic tensions in China, Tibet, and Hong Kong. He is the author of *The Great Han: Race, Nationalism, and Tradition in China Today* and the translator of Tsering Woeser's *Tibet on Fire: Self-Immolations against Chinese Rule.*

C. ANNE CLAUS is a cultural anthropologist researching environmental issues in contemporary Japan. Her research focuses on transnational conservation and sustainable seafood consumption. She has also published work on the socioeconomic impacts of conservation policies on coastal communities, the political ecology of disasters, and conservation social science. Since 2014 she has been an assistant professor in the Anthropology Department at American University in Washington, DC.

SIENNA R. CRAIG is associate professor of anthropology at Dartmouth University. A cultural anthropologist whose work focuses on health and illness in cross-cultural perspective and on migration and social change, she is the author of *Horses like Lightning: A Story of Passage through the Himalayas* (2008) and *Healing Elements: Efficacy and the Social Ecologies of Tibetan Medicine* (2012), and the coeditor of *Medicine between Science and Religion: Explorations on Tibetan Grounds* (2010). From 2012 to 2017, she served as the coeditor of *HIMALAYA, Journal of the Association for Nepal and Himalayan Studies.* A 2018 Guggenheim Fellow, Craig enjoys writing across genres, from poetry and memoir to children's literature, fiction, and narrative ethnography.

ZOË CROSSLAND is associate professor in the Department of Anthropology and director of the Center for Archaeology at Columbia University. Her research draws upon semiotic approaches to explore the problems of archaeological and forensic evidence and to investigate archaeology's relationship to the past and to the dead body. Recent publications include *Ancestral Encounters in Highland Madagascar: Material Signs and Traces of the Dead* (2014) and, coedited with Rosemary Joyce, *Disturbing Bodies: Perspectives on Forensic Archaeology* (2015). She is currently working on a book titled *The Speaking Corpse,* which explores forensic anthropology and popular empiricism.

LARA DEEB is professor of anthropology at Scripps College. She is the author of *An Enchanted Modern: Gender and Public Piety in Shi'i Lebanon* (2006), coauthor with Mona Harb of *Leisurely Islam: Negotiating Geography and Morality in Shi'i South Beirut* (2013), and coauthor with Jessica Winegar of *Anthropology's Politics: Disciplining the Middle East* (2016). Deeb has published widely on gender, Islam, morality, transnational feminism, Lebanon, and the politics of knowledge production. She currently serves on the editorial boards of the *Journal of Middle East Women's Studies* and *Comparative Studies of South Asia, Africa, and the Middle East.*

K. DRYBREAD is an anthropologist who currently teaches at the University of Colorado, Boulder. Her research examines relationships between citizenship and violence in Brazil. She has written on prison rapes and murders, political corruption, and the meanings of mundane mass graves.

JESSICA MARIE FALCONE is associate professor of cultural anthropology at Kansas State University. She has conducted wide-ranging research on transnational Asian religions and culture in the age of globalization, and she has done anthropological projects with competitive collegiate Gujarati-American folk dancers, Tibetan refugees in India, Buddhists practicing online in a virtual world, Sikh and Hindu Americans just after 9/11, grass-roots farmer activists in India, nonheritage Tibetan Buddhist practitioners, and Soto Zen Buddhists in Hawai'i, among others. Her first book, *Battling the Buddha of Love: A Cultural Biography of the Greatest Statue Never Built*, about the controversial Maitreya Project in India, was published in 2018.

KIM FORTUN is professor and chair of the Department of Anthropology at the University of California, Irvine. She is the author of *Advocacy after Bhopal: Environmentalism, Disaster, New Global Orders* (2001), former coeditor of *Cultural Anthropology*, and is now playing a lead role in the development of the Platform for Experimental, Collaborative Ethnography (http://worldpece.org).

KRISTEN R. GHODSEE is professor of Russian and East European studies at the University of Pennsylvania. She has authored nine books, including *The Left Side of History: World War Two and the Unfulfilled Promise of Communism in Eastern Europe* (Duke University Press, 2015), *From Notes to Narrative: Writing Ethnographies That Everyone Can Read* (2016), and *Red Hangover: Legacies of 20th Century Communism* (Duke University Press, 2017). Ghodsee has held visiting fellowships at Harvard, at the Institute for Advanced Study in Princeton, at the Freiburg Institute for Advanced Studies (FRIAS) in Germany, and at the Aleksanteri Institute at the University of Helsinki, Finland.

DANIEL M. GOLDSTEIN is professor emeritus in the Department of Anthropology at Rutgers University. He is the author of three monographs: *The Spectacular City: Violence and Performance in Urban Bolivia* (Duke University Press, 2004), *Outlawed: Between Security and Rights in a Bolivian City* (Duke University Press, 2012), and *Owners of the Sidewalk: Security and Survival in the Informal City* (Duke University Press, 2016); and coauthor of *Decolonizing Ethnography: Undocumented Immigrants and New Directions in Social Science* (Duke University Press, 2019). He is the coeditor (with Enrique D. Arias) of the collection *Violent Democracies in Latin America* and (with D. Asher Ghertner and Hudson McFann) the forthcoming *Futureproof: Security Aesthetics and the Management of Life*. A political and legal anthropologist, Goldstein specializes in the anthropology of security, immigration, and social violence.

DONNA M. GOLDSTEIN is professor of anthropology at the University of Colorado, Boulder. She is the author of *Laughter out of Place: Race, Class, Violence, and Sexuality in a Rio Shantytown* (2003, 2013) and recipient of the 2004 Margaret Mead award. She writes within the fields of medical anthropology, anthropology of the environment, and science and technology studies (STS), and has written about pharmaceutical politics and about the election and racial politics of Donald Trump. She is currently working on a project that examines the history of cold war science and nuclear energy in Brazil.

SARA L. GONZALEZ is assistant professor of anthropology at the University of Washington, Seattle. She works at the intersection of tribal historic preservation, colonial studies, and public history, examining how community-based participatory approaches to research improve the empirical and interpretive quality of archaeological narratives, while also situating archaeology within a more respectful and engaged practice. This research evaluates how indigenous values and methods can be integrated into archaeological field practice, as well as into archaeology undergraduate education and field-based training. Her research has been published in *Anthropocene, American Indian Quarterly, American Antiquity,* and *Archaeologies: Journal of the World Archaeological Congress.*

GHASSAN HAGE is professor of anthropology and social theory at the University of Melbourne. He works in the comparative anthropology of nationalism, multiculturalism, and racism. He has held many visiting professorships around the world, including at the Ecole des Hautes Etudes en Sciences Sociales, Paris; the University of Copenhagen; the American University of Beirut; and Harvard University. He is the author of *White Nation* (2000), *Against Paranoid Nationalism* (2003), and *Alter-Politics: Critical Anthropology and the Radical Imagination* (2015). His latest work is *Is Racism an Environmental Threat?* (2017).

CARLA JONES is associate professor of anthropology at the University of Colorado, Boulder. Her research analyzes the cultural politics of appearance in urban Indonesia, with particular focus on femininity, aesthetics, and Islam. She has written extensively on manners, self-improvement, and middle-class respectability during the Suharto and post-Suharto periods in Jogjakarta and Jakarta, and is the coeditor, with Ann Marie Leshkowich and Sandra Niessen, of *Re-orienting Fashion: The Globalization of Asian Dress* (2003). Her current work situates anxieties about Islamic style in the context of broader debates about exposure and corruption.

IEVA JUSIONYTE is assistant professor of anthropology and social studies at Harvard University. Her research focuses on borders, statecraft, security, crime, and the media. Jusionyte's first book, *Savage Frontier: Making News and Security on the Argentine Border* (2015), is based on her fieldwork with journalists in the tri-border area of Argentina, Brazil, and Paraguay. Her second book, *Threshold: Emergency Responders on the U.S.-Mexico Border* (2018), won the California Series in Public Anthropology International Publishing Competition.

ALAN KAISER is professor of archaeology at the University of Evansville. He has published on issues of Roman culture in Spain, urbanism across the Roman empire, and streets as an organizing principle in Roman cities. He is the author of three books, including *The Urban Dialogue: An Analysis of the Use of Space in the Roman City of Empúries, Spain* (2000), *Roman Urban Street Networks* (2009), and *Archaeology, Sexism and Scandal: The Long-Suppressed Story of One Woman's Discoveries and the Man Who Took Credit for Them* (2014).

BARAK KALIR is associate professor at the Department of Anthropology, University of Amsterdam. He is the codirector of the Institute for Migration and Ethnic Studies and currently leads a five-year ERC-funded project, "The Social Life of State Deportation Regimes," in which the implementation of deportation policies is ethnographically examined in six countries: Greece, Spain, France, Romania, Israel, and Ecuador. His recent publications include a special issue on "Nonrecording States between Legibility and Looking Away" (*Focaal: Journal of Global and Historical Anthropology,* 2017), and "Afterword: On Transitive Concepts and Local Imaginations—Studying Mobilities from a Translocal Perspective" (*Mobilities, Boundaries, and Travelling Ideas: Rethinking Translocality beyond Central Asia and the Caucasus,* 2018).

MICHAEL LAMBEK holds a Canada Research Chair at the University of Toronto, Scarborough, where he is professor of anthropology. Among his books are *Human Spirits* (1981), *Knowledge and Practice in Mayotte* (1993), *The Weight of the Past* (2002), *The Ethical Condition* (2015), and *Island in the Stream: An Ethnographic History of Mayotte* (2018), as well as edited collections on religion, irony, memory, bodies and persons, and ethical life. He has taught at the London School of Economics and delivered the Tanner Lecture titled "Concepts and Persons" at the University of Michigan in 2019. His current writing project is titled *People Who Live in Glass Houses*.

CAROLE MCGRANAHAN is professor of anthropology at the University of Colorado. She is the author of *Arrested Histories: Tibet, the CIA, and Memories of a Forgotten War* (Duke University Press, 2010) and coeditor with Ann Laura Stoler and Peter Perdue of *Imperial Formations* (2007) and with John F. Collins of *Ethnographies of U.S. Empire* (Duke University Press, 2018). From 2015 to 2016, she edited the "Writers' Workshop" series on the anthropology blog *Savage Minds: Notes and Queries in Anthropology*.

STUART MCLEAN studied English literature at the University of Oxford and obtained his PhD in sociocultural anthropology from Columbia University. He is currently professor of anthropology and global studies at the University of Minnesota. He has carried out fieldwork in Ireland and the Orkney Islands. He has also attempted to explore the possibilities of that latterly much neglected genre of anthropological writing, the comparative essay. His recent publications include *Crumpled Paper Boat: Experiments in Ethnographic Writing* (coedited with Anand Pandian) and *Fictionalizing Anthropology: Encounters and Fabulations at the Edges of the Human*.

LISA SANG-MI MIN is a PhD candidate in sociocultural anthropology at the University of California, Berkeley. Her work examines the North Korean political through the prism of postcommunism, sovereignty, theories of the image and imagination, and border sites. As part of this endeavor, she is exploring the limits and possibilities of anthropological writing and knowledge in a place seen as impossible for fieldwork, in a state deemed "totalitarian" and thereby foreclosed to ethnographic methods.

MARY MURRELL is an honorary fellow in the University of Wisconsin-Madison Department of Anthropology. She is currently completing a book manuscript titled *The Open Book: An Anthropologist in the Digital Library*. Before becoming an anthropologist, she served for thirteen years as the acquisitions editor for anthropology at Princeton University Press.

KIRIN NARAYAN is professor of anthropology and South Asian studies at Australian National University. Her interest in narrative and ethnography has yielded books in several different genres: *Storytellers, Saints and Scoundrels: Folk Narrative in Hindu Religious Teaching* (1989), a novel, *Love, Stars and All That* (1994), *Mondays on the Dark Night of the Moon: Himalayan Foothill Folktales*, in collaboration with storyteller Urmila Devi Sood (1997), a family memoir, *My Family and Other Saints* (2007), *Alive in the Writing: Crafting Ethnography in the Company of Chekhov* (2012), and *Everyday Creativity: Singing Goddesses in the Himalayan Foothills* (2016). Her current research with Ken George has been supported by an ARC Discovery Project Award and explores the intersections of religion, artisanship, narrative, creativity, and technology in India.

CHELSI WEST OHUERI is a sociocultural anthropologist and assistant professor in the Department of Slavic and Eurasian studies at the University of Texas, Austin. Her scholarship and teaching focus on race and racialization, belonging, marginalization, and health disparities. She has conducted extensive ethnographic research in Southeastern Europe and Central Texas. Her book manuscript in process is based on research with Romani, Egyptian, and Albanian communities in Albania.

ANAND PANDIAN teaches anthropology at Johns Hopkins University. His most recent books with Duke University Press are *A Possible Anthropology: Methods for Uneasy Times* (2019) and *Crumpled Paper Boat: Experiments in Ethnographic Writing* (2017), coedited with Stuart McLean.

UZMA Z. RIZVI is associate professor of anthropology and urban studies at the Pratt Institute, Brooklyn, and visiting research scholar at the American University of Sharjah, UAE. Rizvi's research interests include decolonizing archaeology, ancient urbanism, critical heritage studies, new materialism, and the postcolonial critique. A primary focus of her work contends with archaeological epistemologies and methodologies, and changed praxis based on decolonized principles and participatory ethics. Rizvi has intentionally interwoven archaeology with cultural criticism, philosophy, critical theory, art, and design. Her new monograph, *The Affect of Crafting: Third Millennium BCE Copper Arrowheads from Rajasthan, India* (2018), follows other publications, including volumes such as *Archaeology and the Postcolonial Critique* (2008), *Handbook on*

Postcolonial Archaeology (2010), and *Connections and Complexity: New Approaches to the Archaeology of South Asia* (2013). Most recently, her article "Archaeological Encounters: The Role of the Speculative in Decolonial Archaeology" (2019) was published in a special issue on archaeology and futurity in the *Journal of Contemporary Archaeology*. She is a member of the *Anthro[dendum]* blog collective (previously *Savage Minds*). She has written for *E-Flux, The New Inquiry, The Con, TANK,* and *LEAP,* among other online art/culture/politics magazines. Rizvi specializes in studying third-millennium BCE communities in the MENESA region, as well as being a critical voice for global issues related to issues around equity and justice.

NOEL B. SALAZAR is research professor in anthropology at the University of Leuven, Belgium. He is editor of the *Worlds in Motion* book series, coeditor of various edited volumes and special issues, and author of numerous peer-reviewed articles, books, and book chapters on mobility and travel. He is secretary-general of the International Union of Anthropological and Ethnological Sciences, past president of the European Association of Social Anthropologists, and founder of AnthroMob, the EASA Anthropology and Mobility Network. In 2013 Salazar was elected as member of the Young Academy of Belgium.

BHRIGUPATI SINGH is currently assistant professor of anthropology at Brown University. His first book, *Poverty and the Quest for Life: Spiritual and Material Striving in Rural India* (2015), was awarded the Joseph Elder Prize in the Indian Social Sciences and an Award for Excellence in the Study of Religion from the American Academy of Religion. He is the coeditor of *The Ground Between: Anthropological Engagements with Philosophy* (2014) and has published numerous articles on religion, politics, and media. He is currently working on an ethnography of mental health issues in "resettlement" colonies in Delhi and a book of essays titled *Waxing and Waning Life: Investigations at the Threshold of Mental Illness and Health.*

MATT SPONHEIMER does research on the ecology of early hominins and associated fauna in Africa. He has also directed and codirected several multidisciplinary projects on the ecology of living mammals, both large and small, in South Africa. Much of his work is focused on nutritional and isotopic ecology. He is the director of the Nutritional and Isotopic Ecology Lab (NIEL) at the University of Colorado at Boulder.

KATHLEEN STEWART teaches ethnographic writing in workshops at the University of Texas, Austin. Her books include *A Space on the Side of the Road: Cultural Poetics in an "Other" America* (1996), *Ordinary Affects* (2007), *The Hundreds* with Lauren Berlant (2019), and *Worlding* (in preparation).

ANN LAURA STOLER is Willy Brandt Distinguished University Professor of Anthropology and Historical Studies at the New School for Social Research. She has worked for some thirty years on the politics of knowledge, colonial governance, racial epistemologies, the sexual politics of empire, and ethnography of the archives. Her books include

Capitalism and Confrontation in Sumatra's Plantation Belt, 1870–1979 (1985, 1995), *Race and the Education of Desire: Foucault's History of Sexuality and the Colonial Order of Things* (1995), *Carnal Knowledge and Imperial Power: Race and the Intimate in Colonial Rule* (2002, 2010), *Along the Archival Grain: Epistemic Anxieties and Colonial Common Sense* (2009), *Duress: Imperial Durabilities in Our Times* (2016), and the volumes *Tensions of Empire: Colonial Cultures in a Bourgeois World* (with Frederick Cooper, 1997), *Haunted by Empire: Geographies of Intimacy in North American History* (2006), *Imperial Formations* (with Carole McGranahan and Peter Perdue, 2007), and *Imperial Debris: On Ruins and Ruination* (2013).

PAUL STOLLER is professor of anthropology at West Chester University. He is the author of articles and books ranging from ethnography to memoir to biography, and is a regular *Huffington Post* blogger on anthropology, Africa, higher education, and politics. In 2013 he received the Anders Retzius Gold Medal in Anthropology from the king of Sweden. His most recent book is *Adventures in Blogging: Public Anthropology and Popular Media* (2018).

NOMI STONE is assistant professor of poetry at the University of Texas, Dallas. Her academic book, *Pinelandia: Human Technology and American Empire* (forthcoming), is a political phenomenology of American empire, and recent articles appear in *Cultural Anthropology* and *American Ethnologist*. Her first collection of poems, *Stranger's Notebook* (2008), is inspired by her fieldwork in North Africa, and her second collection of poems, *Kill Class* (2019), is based on fieldwork within war trainings in mock Middle Eastern villages constructed by the US military across America. Winner of a Pushcart Prize, Stone has poems recently appearing in *The New Republic, The Best American Poetry, Poetry,* and widely elsewhere.

PAUL TAPSELL descends from the central north island tribes of New Zealand. He became the first Maori curator at Rotorua Museum (1990–94); gained his doctorate in museum ethnography at Oxford (1998); completed a postdoc at the Australia National University (1999–2000); became first Maori director of the Auckland Museum (2000–2008); was dean of Te Tumu School and professor and chair of Maori Studies at the University of Otago (2009–17); and served as director of Research and Collections at Museums Victoria (2017–18). He has curated eleven exhibitions in six countries, is a past New Zealand book award winner (History and Biography, 2001), an Eisenhower Fellow (2005), and founding director of Maorimaps.com (2009). In mid-2018 Tapsell was appointed professor of Australian indigenous studies at the University of Melbourne, where he continues to teach, research, and assist kin communities recover well-being.

KATERINA TEAIWA is associate professor in Pacific studies and gender, media, and cultural studies, School of Culture, History and Language at the Australia National University, as well as vice-president of the Australian Association for Pacific Studies. Her book *Consuming Ocean Island: Stories of People and Phosphate from Banaba* (2015) focuses on histories of phosphate mining, imperialism, and environmental displacement in the central Pacific. In 2017 Teaiwa transformed her research into a solo multimedia exhibition, *Project Banaba*, for the Carriageworks arts precinct in Sydney. In 2019 it toured to MTG Hawkes Bay Tai Ahuriri in New Zealand.

MARNIE JANE THOMSON holds a PhD in anthropology from the University of Colorado. Her research focuses on Congolese refugee experiences of violence and dislocation to reveal the politics of humanitarian intervention in both Tanzania and the Democratic Republic of Congo. Funded by the Wenner-Gren Foundation and the Social Science Research Council, Thomson has conducted multisited ethnographic research in Tanzania, Congo, and UNHCR hubs in Nairobi, Kenya, and Geneva, Switzerland. She has published in anthropology and architecture journals, refugee studies volumes, and several public anthropology forums; she was the first recipient of the Society for Applied Anthropology Human Rights Defender Award.

GINA ATHENA ULYSSE is a feminist artist, anthropologist, and poet. She is the author of *Downtown Ladies: Informal Commercial Importers, A Haitian Anthropologist and Self-Making in Jamaica* (2008), *Why Haiti Needs New Narratives: A Post-Quake Chronicle* (2015), and the award-winning *Because When God Is Too Busy: Haiti, Me and THE WORLD* (2017), a collection of performance texts, photographs, and poetry. She was the invited editor of *e-misférica's Caribbean Rasanblaj*. Her other works have appeared in *Gastronomica, Liminalities, Souls,* and *Transition*.

ROXANNE VARZI is professor of anthropology and film and media studies at UC Irvine. She has a PhD in social cultural anthropology from Columbia University and was the recipient of the first Fulbright for doctoral dissertation fieldwork in Iran since the Iranian Revolution. Her first ethnography, *Warring Souls: Media, Martyrdom and Youth in Post Revolution Iran,* was published by Duke University Press in 2006. Her short stories have appeared in two anthologies of Iranian American writing as well as in the *New York Press* and in *Anthropology and Humanism Quarterly,* for which she won a short story award for fiction. She is also a filmmaker (*Plastic Flowers Never Die,* 2009) and a sound artist ("Whole World Blind," at Publicbooks.org). Her book *Last Scene Underground: An Ethnographic Novel of Iran* won a 2016 Independent Publishers Gold Medal award for fiction.

SITA VENKATESWAR is programme coordinator and associate professor in the social anthropology programme at Massey University. She is also associate director of the New Zealand India Research Institute. Her current research interests include regenerative and multispecies approaches to farming and food futures. She applies intersectional and decolonizing research methodologies within contemporary contexts of South Asia.

MARIA D. VESPERI is professor of anthropology at the New College of Florida, where she earned the American Anthropological Association/Oxford University Press Award for Excellence in Undergraduate Teaching of Anthropology in 2009. She is executive coordinating editor of *Anthropology Now,* a cofounder of the Society for the Anthropology of North America, and founder of its major publication, *North American Dialogue*. She was a *Tampa Bay Times* staffer from 1981 to 1993 and served as a trustee of the Poynter Institute from 1995 to 2015. Her publications include *Anthropology off the Shelf: Anthropologists on Writing*, coedited with Alisse Waterston (2009); *City of Green Benches: Growing Old in a New Downtown* (1998); and *The Culture of Long Term Care: Nursing Home Care* (1995), a coedited volume of ethnographic research. In 2017 she received the American Anthropological Association's Anthropology in Media Award, and in 2018 she was selected by the Society of Anthropology of North America for its SANA Prize for Distinguished Achievement for the Critical Study of North America. Her current project compares ethnography and narrative journalism.

SASHA SU-LING WELLAND is associate professor of gender, women, and sexuality studies and an affiliated faculty member in anthropology, China studies, and comparative history of ideas at the University of Washington. She is the author of *A Thousand Miles of Dreams: The Journeys of Two Chinese Sisters* (2006) and *Experimental Beijing: Gender and Globalization in Chinese Contemporary Art* (Duke University Press, 2018). She has published articles in *Journal of Visual Culture, Signs: Journal of Women in Culture and Society*, and *Yishu: Journal of Contemporary Chinese Art*, and she curated the exhibit *Cruel/Loving Bodies* (Beijing and Shanghai, 2004; Hong Kong, 2006).

BIANCA C. WILLIAMS is associate professor of anthropology at the Graduate Center, CUNY. She earned her PhD in cultural anthropology, and a graduate certificate in African and African American studies, from Duke University. Williams is a recipient of the American Anthropological Association and Oxford University Press Award for Excellence in Undergraduate Teaching of Anthropology. Her research interests include Black women and happiness; race, gender, and equity in higher education; and emotional labor in Black feminist organizing and leadership. In her book *The Pursuit of Happiness: Black Women, Diasporic Dreams, and the Politics of Emotional Transnationalism* (Duke University Press, 2018), Williams examines how African American women use travel to Jamaica and the internet as tools for pursuing happiness and critiquing American racism and sexism. Additionally, she has written about "radical honesty" as feminist pedagogy in the collection *Race, Equity, and the Learning Environment* and has published on #BlackLivesMatter, plantation politics and campus activism, and tourism in the journals *Souls, Cultural Anthropology, Teachers College Record*, and on the blogs *Savage Minds* and *Anthropoliteia*.

JESSICA WINEGAR is professor of anthropology at Northwestern University. She is the author of *Creative Reckonings: The Politics of Art and Culture in Contemporary Egypt* (2006), which won the Albert Hourani Book Award, for the best book in Middle East studies, and the Arnold Rubin Outstanding Book Award, for the best book on African arts. She is also a coauthor, with Lara Deeb, of *Anthropology's Politics: Discipline and Region through the Lens of the Middle East* (2016). She has published numerous articles on the arts and cultural production, the state, Islam, revolutionary movements, aesthetics, and knowledge production.